SANYA

SANYA

My Life with
Aleksandr Solzhenitsyn

by

Natalya A. Reshetovskaya

Translated from the Russian by Elena Ivanoff

The Bobbs-Merrill Company, Inc.
Indianapolis/New York

Contents

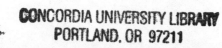

Translator's Note

～～～～

All quotations from Aleksandr Solzhenitsyn's works appearing in this translation are based on the original Russian provided by Natalya Reshetovskaya. Although the differences are slight, I thought it best to follow the author's citations on the supposition that they may have been taken from earlier versions. As for Solzhenitsyn's poems, I believe they are appearing in English translation here for the first time.

It was my intention to have no accompanying glossary of Soviet acronyms and terms to this translation. Thus, wherever possible, I have avoided acronyms by spelling out the institution, agency or project involved. As for slang expressions or colloquialisms, I have tried to use the closest English counterparts. The two exceptions are the terms *sharashka* (explained in detail in the book itself) and *zek* (an abbreviation for prisoner), which have been retained because by now they have become universally familiar to readers of Solzhenitsyn's works.

Finally, it should be pointed out that the book *Sanya* has become much more than a simple translation of the original Russian text. During the process of translation and subsequent to that time, the author made extensive revisions and substantive changes, frequently deleting material and adding a considerable amount of material that is wholly new. Hence this authorized English language edition is substantially different from earlier versions. Since it is the most recent edition available, I think it safely can be assumed that *Sanya* most accurately reflects the author's feelings and opinions at this time, incorporating a great deal of material that has not been published before.

E. I.

SANYA

1
The Five of Us

Aleksandr Solzhenitsyn and I met in 1936, near the beginning of our first year at the University of Rostov-on-Don.

During lunch hour Koka, Kira, and I were standing around talking animatedly. I was wolfing down the sandwiches I had brought from home.

Suddenly the kids looked up and exclaimed, "The Walrus!"

A tall, lean youth with thick, light hair was bounding up the stairs two steps at a time. He explained that he was attending some lectures in our Chemistry Department. He had a rapid-fire speech. But then everything about him seemed rapid, headlong. Sanya Solzhenitsyn had very mobile features.

SANYA

His eyes either darted from one person to the other or focused on me with interest. Later on, he recalled that at the first moment he did not see all of my face. An enormous apple, which I was munching between bites of my sandwich, covered the lower part.

The boys talked a lot about their school days, referring to themselves as the Three Musketeers. Sanya was Athos, Koka was Porthos and Kira was Aramis. Their conversation was studded with references to heroic figures from the most varied literary sources imaginable; there were ancient gods, of course, and historical personages galore. They knew everything under the sun, all three of them: that was the way I saw them.

My new friend Koka—Nikolai Vitkevich—had gone to school with Sanya, Lida Ezherets, and Kirill Simonian in Rostov. In 1936, when Sanya enrolled in the Department of Physics and Mathematics, Lida entered the Pedagogical Institute; Koka and Kira went into chemistry at the same university. And the Chemistry Department is where I also enrolled.

While I was in high school I had begun to study piano at the Rostov Music Academy. I was lucky to get Evgeny Fedorovich Girovsky, an excellent teacher. A fellow student of mine, with whom I played two piano duets, was the talented Gayan Chebotarian, who later became a composer.

At that time I intended to devote myself totally to music when I finished school. But I also loved science very much, and I often spent my free time trying to solve mathematical problems that had not even been assigned to us. Chemistry took second place after math. Later, I grew to love this science too, especially after I found the solution to that mysterious table with signs for the familiar and the as yet unknown chemical elements which hung in our chemistry hall. It turned out that the table of the genius Mendeleyev contained all the tiny blocks out of which our universe was built, and, what is more, it left space for those to be discovered in the future. On the assumption that mathematics was after all not something for a woman's head, even if she did possess good reasoning powers, I chose chemistry. That is how I met and immediately became friends with Koka and Kira, before I met Sanya.

Kirill transferred to medical school the next year, but Koka and I stuck to chemistry until we graduated in 1941. For the entire five years we sat next to each other, managing to combine listening to the lectures or conducting experiments with running discussions of "various ideas" (Koka's expression): what we had heard at lectures, what had happened to us or what each of us had read, then or earlier; or, simply, each day as it was lived.

As a result, we became the "heroes" of gibes and comments in the department's wall newspaper aimed at those who jibber-jabber during lectures. However, the teacher forgave us our infractions because we were good students. And had it not been for Koka's uncompromising character, both of us would have been graduated from the university with honors. At the state examination on the fundamentals of Marxism-Leninism, Koka refused on principle to reply to one of those supplementary, "iffy" questions such as "What would have happened if . . ." He cited Lenin's negative attitude to such conjectural formulations. The members of the examination board angrily lowered his mark. This was so unfair that we all went as a group to the rector to ask that Koka be permitted to take the examination over. Professor Shenker, the board chairman, proposed that he write a statement requesting a reexamination on the grounds of being ill during the examination.

"You know perfectly well that's not the reason," Koka answered him.

To me, the diploma incident showed Koka's character in its entirety.

Sanya and Koka were good school friends. A particular bond between them was their love of travel.

In the summer of 1936 they both acquired bicycles. The following summer they took a bicycle tour along the Georgian Military Highway, and in the summer of 1938 they pedaled through the Ukraine and the Crimea.

At the beginning of 1939 Koka readily accepted Sanya's suggestion that they enroll as correspondence students at the Moscow Institute of Philosophy, Literature, and History, the famous MIFLI. Henceforth they would proceed shoulder to shoulder. Along with their university courses, they would study the "Oldsters"—their nickname for the celebrated philosophers of the past—and then they would work along parallel lines: Koka in the field of pure thought, and Sanya in art criticism.

In the summer of that year, after registering at MIFLI, the two friends exchanged their bicycles for a boat trip along the Volga. Buying a boat in Kazan for 225 rubles, they took serious books with them instead of fishing rods, and sailed down the Volga, accumulating impressions and studying their MIFLI subjects. They arrived in Kuibyshev after a three-week trip. Here they had the good fortune of selling their boat for 200 rubles. Thus the trip had cost them only twenty-five rubles.

Later, there were more trips together, with Kirill joining them. Twice a year, during the university holidays, they went to Moscow for the summer and winter examinations at MIFLI.

At home, that fall of 1936, I carried on so much about my

new acquaintances, and with such exuberance, that finally my mother suggested I invite the trio to visit us.

They came to call on the evening of November 7—Sanya, Koka, and Kirill, plus three girl students from our university. We played forfeits and it fell to my lot to perform at the piano. I played Chopin's Fourteenth Etude.

We all had to wash up in our little room before sitting down at the table for tea with some of Mother's special treats. Sanya poured water on my hands out of a pitcher. Then and there he said, "I must tell you that you play the piano beautifully."

Mother liked the whole group, but most of all she liked Kirill, who captivated her with his sad, expressive eyes. And, indeed, his life was anything but gay and carefree. His mother was suffering from a long, serious illness, and all the responsibility for her, as well as for his younger sister, Nadya—today a well-known composer—lay on his youthful shoulders.

Ten days later, on November 17, there was another party, this time organized by the biology students for Liulya Oster's birthday. Liulya had been a high-school classmate of our Three Musketeers. That night I was introduced to Lida Ezherets. As Kirill led her up to me he said in a very meaningful tone: "Natasha, this is—Lida." We had already heard much about each other. Kirill had once told Lida almost disbelievingly, "Do you know that Natasha is just like us?" This, naturally, was the highest praise.

Of course I could not possibly have imagined that twenty years later, in 1956, I would receive a letter from Solzhenitsyn reading: "Today is exactly twenty years from the day when I considered myself utterly and irrevocably in love with you: the party at Liulya's; you in a white silk dress and I (playing games, joking, but taking it all quite seriously) on my knees before you. The next day was a holiday—I wandered along Pushkin Boulevard and was out of my mind with love for you."

That very same evening Sanya Solzhenitsyn decided to write a historical novel. And the following day, when he was mulling over his project, I appeared to him as one of the heroines, to bear the lilting name of Lucy Olkhovskaya.

That year I was more Koka's friend than anyone else's. During the winter holidays he taught me how to play chess, and that summer how to ride a bicycle. When he and Sanya were on their Georgian Highway tour, Koka even wrote me a letter—which failed to arrive thanks to the vagaries of the mails. At that time Sanya told me nothing about his feelings. Whatever they were, they certainly inspired him to flights of poetry. He confessed to them only in his diary.

When we were in our second year at the university, a series of dancing classes was begun. Curiously enough, Sanya and I were the only ones of our group to sign up. Hence it was no surprise to anyone that we became a dancing couple.

We also started going out together to university parties, and we danced only with each other. Sanya would pick me up at home, and usually I played the piano for him before we left. Apart from the pieces I was learning, I remember often playing Braga's "Serenade" for him.

I was happy with things as they were, and I did not want any changes at all.

Then suddenly, on July 2, 1938, as we sat together in Rostov's Theatrical Park, Sanya declared his love for me. He spoke of how he visualized me always at his side in his future life. And he was expecting an answer.

What did I feel toward Sanya? Was it love—that love for whose sake one is ready to forget everything and everyone and plunge headlong into its abyss? At that time this was the only way I could understand the meaning of true love (I got it out of books, of course). Today, with a lifetime of experience behind me, it is still the only way I know how to understand true love.

My life was so varied in those days that it seemed Sanya could not take the place of everything, even though he already meant a great deal to me. For me the world did not consist of him alone. Nevertheless, it seemed that something had to be decided, something had to be said at once. I turned away, laid my head on the back of the park bench, and began to cry . . .

Then came July 5. Tamara Tseretelli, a well-known singer, was giving a concert in the May First Gardens. Sanya was reserved, overpolite, taciturn.

Did that mean everything was over? Suddenly my full life lost its attractiveness. If only what used to be could have remained that way forever! I could not bear to give up the way things were before. I wanted everything to stay just as it was. Could this be what love was all about?

A few days later I, hitherto always reserved in word and deed, wrote Sanya a note to say I loved him.

And everything did remain as I wanted it to—though not altogether the way it was before. Gradually a great tenderness and affection flowed into our relationship. It was becoming more and more difficult to separate after an evening together, more and more painful not to give in to our desires.

To merge our beings or to part—that was how I began to see our situation. In the next letter I wrote to Sanya, I suggested that we part. In reply, he handed me a missive which, it turned out, he had prepared some time before for just such an eventuality.

SANYA

He wrote that he could not conceive of me in the future in any other role save that of his wife. On the other hand, he feared this might interfere with his main goal in life. To achieve the success he wanted, and which he counted on, he had to finish MIFLI as quickly as possible after graduating from the university. Meanwhile I was to complete my studies at the conservatory. This in itself would make rigorous demands on our time. But "time could be placed in jeopardy" by the myriad and inevitable trivia of family life. These trivia, he declared, might ruin us before we had a chance to "spread our wings." Time! This one word summed up the basic obstacle to our immediate marriage. Sanya could not see a way out of this dilemma, and that was why he too was suffering.

After listing everything that could possibly rob us of "the time to spread our wings," Sanya named yet another potentially "pleasant-unpleasant consequence"—a child.

Solzhenitsyn's views on this matter were to change more than once. Years later, while he was in prison, he regretted that we had no children; then, when he was free again, he decided that people who faced "big tasks" needed "spiritual," not physical, progeny. Later still, Solzhenitsyn's views and practice in this area of being were to change once again.

In early 1939 we agreed that we would marry in the spring of 1940, toward the end of our fourth university year.

Now Sanya could not afford to lose a single minute. Even while waiting for a trolley he would flip through a set of small homemade cards on one side of which he had inscribed some historical event or personage and on the other the corresponding dates. Often, before a concert or a movie began, I would test his memory using the same endless cards: When did Marcus Aurelius reign? When was the Edict of Karakol promulgated? And many other questions along the same lines. Latin words and expressions were neatly recorded on other little cards.

If we were not planning to go to a movie or a concert, we would make a date to meet at ten o'clock at night, which was the closing time for the reading room. Sanya was more willing to sacrifice sleep than study time for the sake of his beloved.

❧

The spring of 1940 arrived. We chose April 27 as the date for registering our marriage. Even then my future husband loved numbers divisible by nine. When we left the marriage registry office, on this warm but windy day, Sanya made me a present of his photograph, which bore the following inscription: "Will you under all circumstances love the man with whom you once united your life?"

These memoirs are an attempt to answer this question, posed to me by my husband and by fate . . .

We did not tell anybody about the registration, and a few days later I left for Moscow to do my field work.

It was my first time in Moscow. There I made the acquaintance of my uncle, Valentin Konstantinovich Turkin, a film writer and a professor at the State Film Institute, and of my uncle's first family: the older Veronica, his former wife, and the younger Veronica, his daughter. I stayed with Veronica Nikolaevna and went through my practical training at The Institute for Science and Research, which was conveniently located near my aunt's residence on Patriarch Ponds.

On June 18 my husband arrived for the summer session at MIFLI. I rushed to meet him.

On that happy day Sanya and I strolled through the Park of Rest and Culture and wandered into the Neskuchny Gardens. Of course we could not suspect that we would be here again, five years later, and under quite different circumstances. Then we would be separated by barbed wire and would be communicating by sign language, he perched on the third-story window sill of a house in Kaluzhskaya Plaza, where he was laying parquet floors, and I gazing up at him from these very same Neskuchny Gardens.

At the end of July, on my uncle's advice, we rented a cottage in Tarusa, not far from Moscow, and spent our "honeymoon" there. Our little hut was at the very edge of the forest. We did not do a lot of roaming; instead, we preferred to stretch out comfortably in the shade of the birch trees, while my husband read aloud to me from Sergei Esenin's poems or Tolstoy's *War and Peace,* often enough finding a resemblance between the two Natashas.

Both of us read and studied, together and separately. Sanya was preparing ahead of time for the next term's work at MIFLI, and I was filling up the gaps in my education.

From Tarusa, finally, we both wrote our respective mothers and friends that we had gotten married, and we received their congratulations. The congratulations from friends were not very sincere for a number of reasons. As I learned later from Kirill, Koka was upset by my marriage to Sanya, although he did not give the slightest indication of this to me. After all, Sanya was his friend. Kirill grieved for me: he feared that Sanya's despotism—which even then was becoming apparent to his friends—would crush my independence and would not permit my personality to develop.

Life has proven my friends right. But it required thirty long years for me to admit this to myself.

❧❧

Something new in the way of a wedding present awaited us back in Rostov. My husband began receiving a higher student allowance. He got the increase that fall because he was not only an honor student but an activist as well. This involved amateur talent activities, publication of a wall newspaper, and, in general, active participation in social and public affairs.

Sanya and I were thus able to take up residence on our own, away from our families. The room we found on Chekhov Lane was small but comfortable, even though we had to put up with a cantankerous landlady. It was convenient because we lived quite close to my mother and her sister's family, and to Sanya's mother. Also, my husband's two favorite reading rooms were nearby. In the first year of our marriage—and it was also the last before a long separation—we were both busy beyond measure. After an early breakfast we would run to the university; or, if there were no classes, Sanya would leave for the library while I stayed at home to prepare for the last remaining special subjects or to write reports for my course work.

On weekdays we would meet later, at my relatives' home, where at three o'clock we would have lunch. For Sanya's sake, lunch was supposed to be exactly on time. But if it happened to be delayed, Sanya would take the familiar little cards out of his pocket and have me test him.

After lunch my husband would again run off to the library, and he would continue studying even at home—very often until two in the morning, to the point of giving himself a headache. Although he understood that one should not drive oneself so hard, he could not stop himself. After all, he had to be first, first! Come what may! Whatever the price!

On Sundays we permitted ourselves to begin the day a little later than usual. Sundays were also different from other days because we lunched at the home of Sanya's mother. This was always a festive occasion for her. She put all her talents, all her love into serving us the most delicious meals possible.

SANYA

The energy, the deftness, the speed with which she did everything, despite her illness (she had active tuberculosis), were amazing. Her speech was rapid-fire, just like her son's, only interrupted by brief coughing spells; and she had the same mobile features.

Solzhenitsyn's apprehensions that marriage would interfere with his plans for the future faded away. He realized that by marrying he had not only lost nothing in the way of precious time, but actually had gained more. No longer did he have to make appointments with her; take her frequently to concerts, theaters, films; or stroll with her at night along streets and boulevards. When he was particularly desirous of her, she was always right there, at his side. True, sometimes the wife whined and deplored the fact that there were fewer amusements in their life, that the notions of "being guests" and "entertaining guests" had almost ceased to exist.

That year it seemed to me at times that my husband was a machine wound up for all eternity. It became a little frightening. But Sanya drew alluring pictures of how things would be for his wife: we would work the next year in a village school (he would study village mores while he was at it) and then we would try to move to Moscow, where he would finish at MIFLI and I would study at the Moscow Conservatory. It was worth being patient for the sake of all these prospects.

In spite of our crowded schedule, in the spring of 1941 Sanya and I took part in amateur talent reviews at colleges and technical schools in the Rostov Region: he recited poetry and I played music.

Our group seldom got together that year. The last time was on Lida's name day, April 20. Lida by then was a postgraduate student at the Pedagogical Institute. In a month Koka, Sanya, and I were going to take the state board examinations.

Sitting on Lida's balcony, we couldn't help admiring the gay-colored, milling crowd on brightly lit Engels Street. This was Rostov's main street, as Nevsky is Leningrad's. It was just as straight, and the young people loved to stroll along it in the same way. None of us could have foreseen that in two months this street would be plunged into nightly darkness, while most of the carefree, strolling young people would be donning military uniforms.

2

War

O n Sunday morning, June 22, 1941, a young man stepped off the train from Rostov onto the platform of Moscow's Kazan Station. With this three-hour trip to Moscow, Aleksandr Solzhenitsyn, twenty-two years of age, was embarking upon a new life. Having passed his last examination in the Department of Physics and Mathematics of Rostov University, he had decided to abandon the exact sciences and dedicate himself totally to literature.

Sanya had come to Moscow to take the second-year examination at MIFLI, the Moscow Institute of Philosophy, Literature, and History. Mathematics would now serve him as a way to earn his daily bread. For his soul, for his long-cherished aim in life, he required a full and well-rounded education in the humanities. From his earliest years Sanya Solzhenitsyn had dreamed of becoming a writer.

> Young Gleb was growing up in the city. Success was showered upon him from the cornucopia of science. He noticed that he was agile of mind, but that there were others with minds even more agile than his and whose vast store of knowledge was overpowering. He reasoned that the only people of any consequence were those who carried in their heads the legacy of world culture: encyclopedists, scholars versed in antiquity, devotees of the fine arts; versatile men with a multifaceted education. These were the elect and one must belong to them.*

Off to suburban Sokolniki by trolley, to the Institute. In the entrance hall, course lists and examination schedules.

MIFLI—this was the road to the top! The most renowned professors in the country could be found here. Even the students of the Institute had an elusive air that distinguished them not only from assorted medics and engineers but also from literary scholars at other great institutions. Only the year before, Aleksandr Tvardovsky, a recent student of MIFLI, had been awarded the Order of Lenin for one of his poems.

Sanya's fervor did not subside even when he learned that correspondence students would not be housed in a traditional school building nearby, but in a hostel in the Stromynka district, where they would be thrown together with other outside students from Moscow University.

---

* From *The First Circle*

But finally, it seemed, his affairs were more or less settled. His books, his course outlines were all stacked in the
drawers of the night table, and the radio in his room was
turned on.

Suddenly an announcer's voice asked listeners to stand by
for an important government message. What's this? A vague
but disquieting premonition of something momentous in the
offing swept over him.

It was war! War with Germany.

Many MIFLI students volunteered on the spot. Sanya,
however, had left his draft card in Rostov. He would have to
be mobilized there. He must leave at once! He wanted to apply
for service in the artillery, but would his "limited fitness" status
make that difficult?

It was Sanya's nervous system that was responsible for the
classification of "limited fitness." Anyone who has seen por-
traits of Solzhenitsyn has noticed the scar running across the
right side of his forehead. As it happened, everyone took it for
granted that this must be a souvenir of the war or of prison.
Even I, who remembered this scar from our very first meeting,
never questioned my husband about it. Somehow it would
have been an awkward thing to do.

It was only in 1973, a good third of a century after we met,
that I learned the origin of this scar from Kirill Simonian, my
husband's old friend, now a distinguished surgeon. Kirill and I
had not seen each other for twenty years. We eyed each other
with curiosity.

"You know, Kira," I said, "I am trying to make new sense
out of so many things. I am trying to understand the past
better—so that I can understand the present—understand
what happened. It seems to me that the sources of all this lie
somewhere far in the distant past."

And just as I had made up my mind to have a very serious conversation, for some odd reason I started off with the subject of—the scar.

Kirill did not seem surprised. "You surely must know," he said, "that Sanya was very sensitive as a child. He couldn't bear it when anyone in class received a higher mark than he did. If Sanya sensed that his answer to the teacher's question was not headed for an A, his expression changed; his face would become white as chalk, as if he were about to faint. For this reason his teachers would hasten to say, 'Sit down, Sanya. I'll ask you another time.' And they would postpone giving him a grade.

"Sanya's overreaction to the slightest irritant kept even us, his closest friends, from ever criticizing him. Even when he was class monitor and would enter our names—mine, Lida's, his closest friends'—into the disciplinary book with a peculiar air of satisfaction, we kept silent.

"Keeping a wary eye on Sanya's nervousness, the teachers conducted themselves in the same way. In the long run, this bred in him a sense of infallibility, of privilege, as though he were always exceptional.

"On one occasion, however, the history teacher, Bershadsky, began to give Sanya a dressing-down, and Sanya actually fell to the floor in a faint, striking his head against a desk and suffering a deep gash on his forehead. Everyone was very frightened. After this incident the teachers became even more cautious in their behavior toward Sanya."

Kirill told me more about those early years. "It seems to me that the person who instilled in us a love of literature and the arts was Anastasia Sergeyevna Griunau," he continued. "She taught us from the seventh year on. She approached her subjects literally with rapture, and this rubbed off on us. We did not feel like children with her, because she treated us as adults.

"We wrote essays on Shakespeare, Byron, Pushkin. We surrounded ourselves with extracurricular material, and each one of us tried to outdo the other. Gradually it became clear that Lida Ezherets, Sanya Solzhenitsyn, and I outshone the others.

"At first we wrote very bad, very imitative poetry. Then Anastasia Sergeyevna suggested that we get together and write novels. At the same time we began to publish a satirical magazine in which we wrote poems and epigrams about each other, or even about the teachers, and received from them evaluations such as 'witty,' 'not very witty,' 'witty but tactless,' and so on.

"Infatuation with the theater was added to all this in the ninth and tenth years. We organized drama groups and rehearsed plays by Aleksandr Ostrovsky, Chekhov, Rostand. We had ready-made characters for any role in our class. Sanya, of course, had to be first even here and he was always given the romantic leads. In fact he even tried to enroll in the Zavadsky Studio in 1936. But his vocal cords nipped his theatrical career in the bud. His voice was always on the hollow side.

"After finishing school, when all three of us ended up in different specializations, our meetings were much more infrequent, but our infatuation with literature remained. Lida turned out to be the most consistent one of all. After graduating from the Pedagogical Institute and after completing her postgraduate studies at Moscow University, she became a literary critic. The two of us were in a literary circle at the House of Medical Workers."

During the conversation I am describing, a second, more profound theme was being covertly struck. After all, people do not speak only with words. It seemed to me that from time to time a "counterpoint" arose between us. All of us had been very enamored of the Huxley novel in our youth.

As often happens in life, several days after that meeting with Simonian, leafing through my husband's letters, I stumbled upon a curious pronouncement of his, connected with *Point Counter Point*. Solzhenitsyn was struck by Huxley's remark that "everything that happens is intrinsically like the man it happens to." He started to test this against his own life and was astonished by the accuracy of the observation. Most "incidents," he wrote, if one takes the trouble to analyze them, turn out to be the product, the imprint, of the character of the person to whom they happen.

It would be interesting to know what Solzhenitsyn himself would say about this now. I have heard him discuss the thought that every people deserves its fate. But what about every individual?

❧

When the war broke out, our marriage was a little more than a year old.

Sanya returned to Rostov, where I was, and rushed to the military registration and enlistment office. There it was suggested to him that he wait until he was called up.

Meantime, almost all the other graduating students of the university were called up. Among them was our best friend, Koka Vitkevich, who was sent to the Military Chemistry Academy for officers' training courses.

As for Sanya, in September of 1941 he and I began to teach in the little town of Morozovsk. He was teaching mathematics and astronomy and I chemistry and the foundations of Darwinism.

In the evenings we often sat around the porch of the house
we were staying in, having long discussions with the neighbors
—a married couple, the Bronevitskys. They lived in an odd
little world of their own and interpreted all the events that
occurred at the front in their own way. When there was talk
in the news summaries of our units having "withdrawn" from
some town of ours, Bronevitsky would inform us which town
had been taken by the Germans.

Gradually the conversations became more and more frank,
and we learned that behind Bronevitsky lay the same grievous
ordeal that awaited my husband in the future: prison. At that
time, however, Bronevitsky's admission did not help us understand or justify his bitterness.

Despite the fact that war news dominated our lives, and we
were heartsick over the setbacks at the front—not to speak of
having to watch the endless lines of evacuees trudging through
our railway station—we were still capable of becoming infatuated with teaching. We loved to exchange opinions about the
successes and failures of our students. The ardent, knowledge-
hungry eyes of the children when they first learned from us
something completely new to them, something they had never
heard of before, gave us a sense of importance. For this reason
we tried to conduct our classes in as interesting and creative
a way as possible.

In the middle of October, Sanya was called up. Many years
later he was to write: "How difficult it was to leave home that
day of October 18, 1941, but it was only from that day on that
my life began. We never know at the time what is happening
to us!"

After a month in the army Sanya wrote me that his unit
was being formed into a horse-drawn transport battalion. Instead of the artillery he had longed for, Solzhenitsyn the math-

ematician, with his university diploma, found himself in a transport unit.

> The war began, and Nerzhin's first assignment was as a driver in a horse-drawn transport unit. Choking with shame, awkwardly, he rounded up horses in the pasture to bridle them and leap on their backs. But he knew neither how to ride a horse nor how to harness one. He did not even know how to pitch hay with a fork. And every nail he drove would invariably bend under his hammer as though doubling up with laughter at the incompetence of the master.*

Time seemed to have stopped for Solzhenitsyn.

To harness horses, while still being in the deep rear, was excruciating. And this—at a time when Kerch fell. At a time when the fiercest battles were raging for the capture of Rostov. He became despondent. His perennial optimism and *joie de vivre* were replaced by apathy, indifference to everything. All he wanted was the end of the war, so he could return to his loved ones and to his old pursuits.

In the November 27 issue of *Pravda* I read: "The enemy must be stopped everywhere. The critical situation demands it."

And here was I, alone in Morozovsk, alarmed and tense.

I shortened the days by trying to educate myself. History, geography, the German language, even astronomy: at night I would hasten outdoors to study the starry firmament. I would knit. I even made short entries in a diary. I waited for letters, and I waited for an improbable miracle.

And, in fact, the miracle occurred: on November 29, in a

---

* From *The First Circle*

voice that thundered all across the country, Levitan the announcer* said that Rostov—our Rostov—had been recaptured!

During those days my diary began to sparkle with exclamation marks: "Victory at the gates of Moscow! Marching toward Orel! We are advancing! Tarusa! (Our Tarusa!) Naro-Fominsk! Novosil! Kerch and Feodosiya! Maloyarslavets!"

But there were still no changes in Sanya's situation. "Today I was cleaning up the manure and remembered that it was my name day—which was as inappropriate as anything could be," he wrote me on December 25.

The life of a transport driver was depressing. In moments of duress, there were dreams about the end of the war. And yet: "One cannot become a great Russian writer, living in the Russia of 1941-43, without having been at the front."

Waiting for my husband's letters became a way of life. When there were no letters for a long time, I reread the earlier ones. And every morning I waited with hope that the postman might bring me a small, three-cornered wartime envelope.

On March 23, after breakfast, I was sitting by the window reading *Molot*, the Red Army paper. A smiling Red Army man in a greatcoat and a fur hat came up to the window. I could not believe my eyes! Like a madwoman I dashed into the yard, feeling as if I might faint on the spot. My thoughts were racing: Where is he going? Is he on his way to the front? How soon will he have to leave me? . . . No, he had been sent on a mission and had stopped off to see me. He did not have to leave until late that night. What happiness! The entire day was one big celebration.

---

* Yuri Levitan was the most popular announcer on Radio Moscow during World War II—Ed.

SANYA

I gave Sanya my photograph with the inscription: "After half a year's separation, I bravely meet the new and even longer separation. It will not be a final one."

He left a few minutes after three the next morning.

I was very proud of my husband. Who had ever heard of a rank-and-file soldier being sent on a military mission? Everybody took him for a staff worker, and he was in no hurry to disabuse them of their belief.

This mission, to the Headquarters Staff of the Stalingrad Military Command, was to decide my husband's fate.

His diploma worked like magic. He was at once assigned to artillery training.

✌∾✌

In February and March there was a relative lull at the front, but our lives—my husband's and mine—saw some important changes. Sanya bade farewell to his "horse company," and I returned to Rostov.

Keeping pace with the cart carrying my luggage, drawn by a little boy, I could not stop smiling to myself. Nothing frightened me: the broken windows, the mounds of ruins, the burned-out buildings.

A few days later I was already employed as a laboratory worker in the Department of Physics and Mathematics at Rostov University. We were working on important things—manufacturing artillery fuses. We made them ourselves, out of glass test tubes; we calibrated them, filled them up, and sealed them.

I had every right to boast to my husband, "I am working under the slogan DEATH TO THE GERMAN INVADERS. So don't give yourself airs, and be proud of your wife!"

At this time Rostov was still very near the front. The Germans, after all, had been pushed only thirty-five miles away from us. Taganrog was still in their hands.

Every fourth day, everyone in our department set out for the highway to dig antitank ditches. Trolleys were not running in Rostov. One had to go on foot across town to Selmash (through all of Nakhichevan), and then across the steppes. It took five hours to get there and back; add to that seven hours of shovel work.

I had never been noted for robust health, and at the beginning it was not easy to perform what was considered the duty of everybody who happened to be in the vicinity of the front lines. I caught a cold after the first workout on the highway; after the second the cold turned into a bad case of flu. But soon I was drawn into the routine of the highway work. I got used to it—especially when spring finally asserted itself. Young blades of grass appeared everywhere; the trees began greening. The air was clean and healthy, and physical labor no longer seemed arduous.

Something else was disturbing me: there was no word from Sanya.

And then, on May 2, Taisia Zakharovna, Sanya's mother, who was as expansive as I was by nature, came flying into the lab. I could tell by her face that she was a bearer of glad tidings. Smiling mysteriously, she opened her little purse and handed me the long-awaited three-cornered envelope.

"From where?" I could barely contain myself.

"From Kostroma."

"How did he get there?"

Oh, how happy I was! Sanya was in an officers' training school; he was already enrolled. And he would remain not a month or two, but until August 1.

All my fears evaporated in an instant. I felt lighthearted—
life had been so kind to me.

Two weeks had hardly gone by after Sanya's arrival at the
military school before he began to complain about the new life
there, to which he could not resign himself. Even the fact that
he carried a special briefcase for books annoyed the command-
ing officer, who called it "student self-indulgence" and ordered
him to put it away. Particular attention was paid to the way the
bed was made, how the blanket was folded and the pillow arranged; how the forage cap sat on his head; how the mug was
washed and rinsed; and a thousand other minuscule duties that
had to be performed before one could carve a miserly hour of
"free" time out of a day.

Sanya had to wash and polish his boots three or four times
a day; no sooner was there a spot than a bawling-out or a
work detail ensued. His basic complaint was that he was surrounded by adolescents.

I was growing perplexed by my husband's complaints about
the lack of free time. After all, this was a military college and
the courses were greatly accelerated by the war. One should
adjust oneself. The war would end and the time would come
when everyone, including my husband, could occupy himself
with whatever pleased him most. In the meantime, it wouldn't
hurt him to restrain his passion for self-education.

Come to think of it, war is indeed a strange thing. Sanya
had left for the front, but he was living in the deep rear. He
was studying, he was planning a novel, *The Sixth Course*,
about students in wartime. Whereas we, who were left behind
at home, learned about war before he did. The front was here,
right next to us, thirty-five miles away. And we were beginning
to feel this more and more. At night we would be awakened

by the horrible rattle of our ack-ack guns, we heard the wailing of German planes, the strikes of falling bombs.

The bombings were stepped up. They came not only at night but during the day. During one of these bombardments the laboratory wing of the Physics and Mathematics Building was destroyed. All that remained were two little keys dangling helplessly from the fingers of Vera, our senior lab technician. Gone was our splendid auditorium, our library, and all our papers, which we had carelessly left behind in our desk drawers when we went down to the bomb shelter.

The house on Chekhov Lane where my husband and I had lived was destroyed. The school building and the conservatory where I had studied were no more.

And yet this did not seem the most terrible thing of all. The little piece of paper—EVACUATION LIST—which we clutched in our hands meant that our town was again to be abandoned to the enemy.

We left at night in a terrible thunderstorm. No sooner had we crossed the railway bridge than the sirens warned us that the German planes were coming. Our train slowed down and stopped. The ack-ack guns were firing right next to us, and soon we saw a column of smoke and fire rise over Rostov, in the Budennovsky district as before. It was eleven o'clock when we reached Kushchevska Junction. We heard bombs exploding. The Germans were destroying the roadbed behind us. At Krylovskaya we saw a gigantic crater and the crippled cars of a hospital train.

It was said that a bomb hit the Rostov railway bridge right after we had passed over it.

The farther southeast we traveled from our doomed city, the less we felt the impact of the war. Taisia Zakharovna had left Rostov with us, but she decided to head for Georgievsk to rejoin her older sister. We worried about her. But what would happen to those who remained behind?

It was amazingly quiet in Kislovodsk. What a beautiful park this resort town had; what a lovely fragrance suffused all the streets! It was impossible to believe that somewhere there were bombs, shells, conflagrations.

In Kislovodsk my mother and I were to stay with Mother's elder sister, Evgeniya Konstantinovna Vladimirova, my aunt Zhenya. Her husband was in the army. Her older daughter, Tanya, who was my age, was a doctor in the hospital. Nadya, the younger one, was still in school.

Gradually, Mother and I revived. Everything that had happened began to seem imaginary, like a delirium.

The Novocherkassky Theater ensemble gave a play in the Kursaal. Mother and I went to see *The Lady of the Camellias* and shed some tears over the sorrowful fate of Marguerite.

In the middle of the night of August 4 we were awakened by Tanya, who had run home from the hospital where she was on duty. We could barely make out what she was trying to tell us: the railroad link with Minsk had been severed. We were cut off. In the morning the hospital was to be evacuated. Everyone had to leave on foot. We could all be evacuated with Tanya.

My aunt Zhenya had no doubts. She and Nadya would go with us.

What should Mother and I do? I wavered for an instant. We had known where we were going when we left Rostov. But now? Where to? Into the unknown? And with no money? . . . The Germans might not even come to Kislovodsk. After all, they were expected to be brought to a halt at any moment.

"But if you stay behind, won't you be parting with Sanya?"

my mother said indignantly, raising her voice. Her words had a sobering effect on me; if we were caught behind the German lines, Sanya and I would be totally separated. I jumped up and began to collect everything I had started out with in Rostov: photographs that were dear to me, Sanya's letters and poems, short stories of his that I especially liked, my diaries. I was never to regret my actions.

As we traveled southward once more, I somehow managed to make brief entries in my diary. This was my first journey on foot through the Caucasus, along the Piatigorsk-Nalchik Highway. It was a wide road, rather straight, without steep climbs. There were no mountains nearby, but when the morning dawned, the distant snow-capped peaks rose in all their splendor.

August 6. We left Piatigorsk on foot, following the supply carts. All told, we covered eight miles this day. Dragging our belongings along was maddeningly difficult. Then we had an accident. A wheel broke on the supply wagon. We began to unload things from the two other wagons so we could put our provisions on them. We barely squeezed our possessions in. After the first ordeal, Nadya and I were suddenly seized with inordinate energy. Things lost weight. Cold nights; hot days. Pauses at creeks. We drink water, we bathe, we even wash our hair. We feel romantic, notwithstanding the situation.

August 7. Gradually we stuff our things, one after the other, into the carts; even our precious knapsacks.

Twenty miles for the day. We left early, about 5:00 A.M. Rest in the afternoon.

August 8. To avoid lagging behind, we hung on to

the cart. If we dropped back one step, it was only with the most agonizing effort that we could catch up again.

I walk, and I remember Anderson's tale, "The Mermaid." Late in the evening we reach Nalchik. We spend the night on the street . . .

As I later learned, Kirill Simonian arrived in Nalchik from Piatigorsk at about the same time. He .came directly from Kislovodsk over the Iutsa mountain range.

Trains were running out of Nalchik to Baku, and steamers were leaving from Baku—but very seldom. And it was not easy to get on one of them. But our food was running out.

We ate the bread so economically that nothing was lost. We collected the crumbs and dried them out in a bowl. Then we ground them, mixed them with sugar—of which we still had a little left—poured some water into the bowl—and the "sugar kasha" was ready. The only bad thing was that the two spoonfuls allotted to each one of us could not fill even our shrinking stomachs.

Once, as another portion of bread crumbs was being dried in the sun, an imposing military man approached our group at Baku harbor. Never in all my life had I seen Aunt Zhenya's eyes sparkle so!

This was Pavel, her adopted son.

It turned out that the military unit in which Pavel was serving had rolled all the way back to Baku in its retreat.

Of course, we were overjoyed. But Pavel also turned out to be a "good genie" for us. We no longer starved.

At the same harbor of Baku I once came face to face with Emil Mazin, one of Sanya's university classmates.

Like Sanya, Emil had been classified by the military as fit for limited duty only. He had married at just about the same time we did, and at the beginning of the war he had also taught mathematics in a village. Now here he was, being evacuated with his wife and their year-old daughter.

We got on a boat before they did, and for a long time thereafter I knew nothing more about Emil.

Throughout our long, excruciating journey eastward into Soviet Asia, thoughts of Sanya's whereabouts gave me no peace. I wrote him with almost no hope of the letters ever reaching him. From Tashkent I sent my husband a few lines. There was no paper so I jotted them down on a telegraphic money order form:

> My dearest!
> Where are you?
> We will probably stop for a while in Alma-Ata. What happens next no one knows. I live in the hope that you will eventually find me . . .

We arrived in Alma-Ata the night of September 6 and slept in the rain in a little garden by the railroad station. The next day we found an apartment and tackled the problem of looking for work.

> *September 19.* Went alone for bread and in my mind drew such a vivid picture of meeting Sanya that I had a little cry over it, realizing how utterly unrealistic this all was. We must leave Alma-Ata on the twenty-third.
> Novorossisk has been abandoned long ago. Battles on the outskirts of Stalingrad.
> *September 21.* A letter from Sanya! He will be in Kostroma until September 15.

Hurray! This meant he was still safe, and that he had received the letters I was sending "into the void"! We had not lost track of each other! But the fifteenth had already passed. Now there was nowhere I could write to him. I continued to make brief entries in my diary:

September 23. We left for Taldy-Kurgan.

September 30. I almost have a job at the technical school.

October 2. Delivered my first lecture on inorganic chemistry. Battles in Stalingrad, Mozdok, and Novorossisk.

Took a chance and wrote Sanya in Kostroma. If he has already left, perhaps they will forward my letter . . .

October 13. A telegram from Sanya from Kostroma! I replied by telegram.

That's the thirteenth for you! It turns out to be a lucky date!

"My dearest!" I responded. "Must I describe to you my joy, my astonishment, when Mother brought me your telegram? This after a three-and-a-half-months' lapse! How happy I am that you are still in Kostroma," said my message. "Now I must run to work at the technical school, where I lecture on inorganic chemistry. Every day, for four to six hours, I substitute for absent instructors. Write, write."

And he answered with a long letter from which I learned about all the worries that had plagued him during the summer. He wrote about the black void of July and August when he was beside himself with anxiety over me. After this, my safety, even in faraway Kazakhstan, seemed a boundless happiness to him—"for you are alive, you have remained for me, I have something to live for, to fight for." My husband recalled that there had been moments in July when he felt he had nothing more to live for. He had wanted to consign his studies to hell and request assignment to the Caucasus. The morning news summaries hit him like an electric shock.

Sanya asked whether I had managed to save at least one of his photographs. "In general," he wrote, "I am even afraid to ask what you have managed to preserve. Just what could you have managed to salvage when you had to travel on foot all the way to Nalchik?"

But some time later Sanya nevertheless still asked what remained of his notebooks and sundry writings left in Rostov. "And one other question: Where are my MIFLI records?"

Funny? Perhaps. But understandable. MIFLI was one of the paths to literature.

As these letters were coming in, I became firmly established in the technical school. At the end of October studies were temporarily interrupted for harvesting the sugar beet. I worked in the fields with the students. During the smoke break we gnawed with gusto on the large heads of sugar cane. Then I returned to my classroom again. Once more my conviction was confirmed: "How interesting, alive, and fascinating it is to teach!"

The November holidays were approaching.

"The summer-and-autumn campaign is coming to a close. What are the results?" Sanya asked himself this question and continued:

Stalin will summarize them one of these days in a speech. But it can already be said: Russian fortitude is immense! For two summers Hitler has been trying to tilt this boulder with the hands of all of Europe. But he did not push it over. Nor will he push it over in another two summers!

What will this winter bring us? If the army finds it possible to repeat last year's advance—and this in the direction of Stalingrad-Rostov—the results could be colossal. The recapture of Rostov would be a sufficient result in itself for the whole winter campaign—for the Fritzes on the Don, for the Fritzes in the Caucasus, for the Fritzes in Berlin.

Sanya's graduation was drawing close: "Our certifications have already been written, all our records have been summed up—now the documents are being sent to Moscow."

And then, finally:

My dear Natashenka!

Am writing in terrible haste from the Kostroma Station. The graduation order was just read out to us. Half of me is dressed in uniform, the rest of the outfitting comes tomorrow. All accounts are squared with Kostroma.

Your Lieutenant

3

The Front

*I*n the spring of 1943 Sanya's whereabouts were a mystery to me. As for Koka, I received a postcard from him one day which, instead of an army post-office number, carried the most ordinary return address: Orel Region, Novosil District, Village of Chernyshino.

Koka invariably ended his postcards with the same question: "What do you hear from Xander?" But this time he was to receive the answer before I received his card.

On July 7, two absolutely identical military letters arrived: they were stamped the same way, depicting the same soldier hurling a grenade.

SANYA

Only one letter was addressed in Sanya's handwriting; the other was in Koka's. *They had met!*

Fate had decided to play endless tricks on them. It turned out that the two friends had been living side by side, walking along the very same dirt roads and crossing one and the same bridge.

And now Koka was with Sanya, and it was just as though they were living at a health spa. They lay around in the shade of trees, listened to the chirping of birds, sipped tea, and smoked cigarettes. "During this time," my husband wrote, "we talked everything out, we argued things out to the end, and we got everything off our chests."

Soon I received a photograph of the two of them together. Sanya still wore the tiny cubes in his lapels, but Koka's epaulets featured little stars.

War was by no means the main theme of my husband's letters. It was literature. His literary exercises. I learned that along with subjects for two new short stories, a "marvelous third draft" of "The Lieutenant" was taking shape in his mind.

Even letters might interfere with this idea. Sanya asked which kind of letter would please me more: short and frequent ones, or long ones, but infrequent? He decided the question for himself: if he wrote me frequently, where would he find the time to work on his new story?

"Do you want me to become a writer or don't you?"

I consoled myself with the thought that if he found it possible to devote so much time to creative writing, his life must be a peaceful one and he was not overexposed to danger.

But the writer in him still had the upper hand. When he learned from me that Bronevitsky, our neighbor in Morozovsk, had acted as mayor during the German occupation, Sanya responded posthaste. The news about Bronevitsky disturbed and captivated him.

What a rich source of literary material! Sanya felt that this case guaranteed him a "brilliant short story" about a traitor. "I had such a theme in mind," he wrote, "but I needed the human being—what are they like, such people?"

In his words, once you have a flesh-and-blood person, you have a story. All that's left to do is write it.

In many ways Sanya still remained a little boy. With humor as well as pride, he described his new haircut, an idea which he had "transformed into life in three days' time," and he wrote that he had taken up smoking. "If it helps me write, why should I give it up? What's your opinion?"

Aware that my opinion carried no weight with him anyway, I tried, in exchange for my consent, at least to talk him into granting me the right to use lipstick. But I ran up against a stone wall. My husband was firm in his stand for "naturalness."

With the bravura of an old-time soldier, Sanya wrote me about vodka: "Imagine, it makes me merry, even if it's just a few ounces. Down the hatch—bottoms up!" His raptures on the subject of alcohol, however, lasted no more than three lines. Indeed, the paragraph ended with the sober conclusion: "Anyway, to hell with it! I'm not going to drink every day; it's harmful. I'll swap it for sugar."

Neither the smoking nor the vodka worried me, but something else did. The officer's status and the privilege of command were beginning to affect Sanya's character in a negative way. He wrote with unconcealed pleasure that no sooner did he finish eating the kasha from the mess tin than hands would reach out to take it away and wash it, while from the other side piping hot tea was being served up to him. He wasn't even given a chance to bend over to pick up anything that might have dropped to the floor.

But all this faded into the background as soon as we learned that early in July—after a long lull marked by the ritual phrase "no important changes at the front"—battles had erupted in Orel-Kursk, where Sanya and Koka were stationed, as well as in Belgorod.

And suddenly, in the very heat of the battle, there was a third encounter between the two friends. Koka described it briefly: "July 9, 1943. I was with him en route. We talked all through the night and at dawn I went back to my unit. Sanya has put on weight lately. . . . Sanya keeps writing all kinds of claptrap and sending it out for reviews."

But Sanya wrote about this differently: "These great battles he can't get out of his mind, what are they, anyway? Will they add a new page to history? Or perhaps they won't even rate mention in the Sovinform news summary?"

Lieutenant Solzhenitsyn's moods seemed to range from an exaggerated sense of power—to the point of overstepping himself—to a dull indifference, to a razor-edged tension.

As for me, at the beginning of August I was sent with my students to work on a collective farm, where I had to do quite a bit of battling with local authorities to assure my young charges more or less decent living conditions and nourishment. I was older than my pupils, but spending days on end with them made me feel quite young again. "Being close to children," I wrote my husband, "has turned me into the frolicsome tomboy I once was. They make me remember all the student games we used to play together."

When the news that Orel had been recaptured finally reached us, I was elated. I instantly dispatched a letter: ". . . Our forces are on the streets of Orel. Where are you?"

At that very moment Sanya was indeed in Orel, and on August 15 he was decorated with the Order of the Patriotic War, second grade.

What words can resurrect the extraordinary mood of those weeks? Only a year ago we had wished, whenever we opened a newspaper, that the news summaries would not mention any towns by name, because at that time they were being abandoned to the enemy. But now we felt miserable if we did not find reports about more and more towns newly liberated by our army, or about German retreats across more of our rivers. We almost began to take the advance of our armies for granted. And what was Lieutenant Solzhenitsyn complaining about now in his letters?

About forced halts, about no firing since morning—during the night the Germans had withdrawn to a new line. He and Koka had not seen each other again. Both were hoping and waiting. Meanwhile, instead of this longed-for encounter between the two friends, another one took place, with a former student of his.

A master sergeant who had lagged behind the unit was brought before Aleksandr. Place of birth "Rostov." Where do you live? "On Pushkin Street." Until what year? "Until August 1941." And then what? "I was evacuated to Morozovsk." (!) Where did you live there? "On Batratskaya Street." Did you study? Did you work? "I studied." Where? "At the Luna-charsky school." In what class? "In the ninth." (In *his* class!) Surname? "Popov."

And here it became clear to Sanya why at first glance the fellow's face had seemed so familiar. In *his* class. Popov had sat in the second row from the door, and had been "a rare gold-brick who showed up for class maybe twice a week." The fellow remembered neither his teacher nor the teacher's wife, but for some reason he did remember the Amplievs and Semochkin and Pyotr Ivanovich.

Sanya was very angry with this rare goldbrick, which Popov continued to be even in wartime. Everything about him, his manners and conduct, "exhibited so much looseness, and his speech was so foppishly affected, that no matter how pleasant it may be for me to have a fellow townsman and former student in my battery, I think I'll assign him . . . to counterintelligence. Then maybe he'll remember me."

I sensed that if Sanya's letters spoke a lot about literature, and postwar plans, it meant that things were quieter at the front these days. And I learned from the letters that Sanya was "charged with dynamite" after reading a biography of the great physiologist and academician Ivan Pavlov. Wouldn't Lieutenant Solzhenitsyn have been surprised if somebody had told him then that fifteen years later he would be teaching in the same building along whose corridors Vanya Pavlov used to run when he was a fledgling seminarian? Impressed by Pavlov's single-minded purposefulness, Sanya drew a conclusion for himself: he should stop flinging himself into everything that happened to interest him—mathematics, philosophy, psychology and pedagogy, foreign languages, political economy. For the time being, however, he continued to be interested in everything.

The short story "In the Town of M" was almost finished. It was based in part on impressions of Morozovsk (centering on Bronevitsky) and in part on later observations of liberated small towns. Sanya made an effort to go into every liberated town, even if it was out of the way from his main route.

When there was a quiet spell he used the few days for working on the short stories. Something was bound to jell. Sanya was planning to send the stories to Konstantin Fedin.

First of all, Fedin was a faithful pupil of Gorky; second, he was an old favorite of Sanya's (the war had prevented him from learning Fedin's opinion of "The Mission Abroad" and "The River Pointsmen"); third, Lida had recently written to Sanya praising Fedin's erudition and literary taste.

Sanya had great difficulty writing "In the Town of M." It seemed to break off before the ending, and throughout the tone and images seemed strained.

❧

In the middle of October the new term started at the technical school. My life suddenly became more lively and interesting than in the previous school year.

The day before classes began I was called in by the principal. He began by singing my praises and ended by foisting a mathematics class on me. After I had conducted myself in a completely sovereign manner as a teacher's assistant in trigonometry, the director and the principal decided that I had a marvelous grasp of mathematics. I came to my favorite group (the second-year chemistry class) and announced: "Well, after 'organic acids' we will now turn to—'progressions.'"

It seemed to me that I had found my true calling in teaching. I worked with interest and ease, and even the students noticed this.

Sanya, however, began persistently advising my mother and me to move back to Rostov. "The technical school pays a piddling wage; a harvest from the vegetable garden can be converted into cash; your aunt Nina Ivanovna works in the Regional Department of Public Education; sometimes just as much depends on a secretary as on some director of an institution."

Soon afterward I received another letter from my husband:

"We are standing on the frontier of the year 1941," he wrote to me elatedly. *"On the frontier between the patriotic war and the revolutionary war."*

Such a view did not disturb me in the least, even though the newspapers and radio broadcasts of the war years never carried an appeal for transforming the patriotic war into a revolutionary war. My husband had told me about a projected series of novels to be entitled either "LIUR" ("Love the Revolution") or "The Russian Avant-garde." The series was to encompass a vast historical period: from the beginning of the First World War to the complete triumph of the revolution on a global scale. It was in the light of this literary conceptualization that my husband viewed the war with Hitler's Germany. In the long run the patriotic war was to ignite a great revolutionary conflagration. But what was one to do about the anti-Hitler coalition? It was in another letter that he wrote me about the "war after the war."

I knew that he not only wrote these thoughts to me but also expressed them in his correspondence with Nikolai Vitkevich.

What a difference between all this and what Solzhenitsyn was to write in later days, in *August 1914* and *The Gulag Archipelago!* Particularly in his latest work he is once again up in arms against the anti-Hitler coalition, but this time from the other side of the barricades. Now he scolds Roosevelt and Churchill for not having launched a "war after the war" against the USSR.

❧

That autumn of 1943 I felt myself so much a mathematician that I even agreed to accept a tutoring job that turned up:

I have news for you: I have a private student—an extremely talented little boy with whom I must teach mathematics for the eighth grade. The first lesson was a surprise for me and I went wild with terror at the thought of having too talented a student—he demanded that everything be made more interesting, more difficult. Mother thinks my hourly fee is far too modest, but I hardly dared to ask even for that.

And, of course, when my own mathematical wisdom did not suffice, I turned for help straight to the front: Sanya, through his letters, taught me how to operate a slide rule. I got the gist of it quite well, but there were no slide rules in Taldy-Kurgan.

And one time a letter got through to the front with probably the only such request of its kind: "Solve the problem I can't solve. The director—a professional mathematics teacher —cannot solve it and, generally speaking, no one in Taldy-Kurgan is capable of solving it."

Sanya, of course, solved it. Then, on the very same day I sent the letter, I was returning home along icy roads, through mud and slush, thinking all the time about this ill-fated problem, and suddenly I myself figured out the solution!

As for the other, far more important request, to send me the short stories, this was more difficult to carry out. Sanya was wondering who would copy all this material. He had found one soldier in the battery fit to do the job, but he had his own work to do. Anyway, even after the copying was done, Sanya still had to make many corrections in the work. It was clear that in the future (for that time of calm, thoughtful, and voluminous work) he would require an assistant secretary who would have to be not only sensible and sensitive but accustomed to his way of writing—the punctuation, the logical stresses, the pauses, etc. Sanya paid me a compliment by saying that if I were not such a pronounced individualist he would sit me down and make me take on this task. But "never and not for any reason" did he want "to interfere with your development." He would have to bide his time in finding such a person.

Sanya did not foresee that in time he would indeed "sit me down"—a sensible person, accustomed to his way of writing —and that he would later do likewise with others.

Understandably, Sanya was concerned with the future and about the loftier matters of life, especially when he was with Koka. I received a detailed report after each such encounter.

In the last days of 1943 everyone was talking of the Teheran Conference. Our press, using the Western formula, referred to it as the Conference of the Big Three. It was natural, therefore, that the "wonderful discussion" between Sanya and Koka about postwar collaboration and a "war after the war" should be christened the Conference of the Big Two. "The more important details of our decisions are not being published for the time being," wrote Sanya, but he did report a most important development, that Koka had now become infinitely more close to him than had Kirill. What bound them together was a community of substantive thought and a community of perspectives in regard to future practical activities "in connection with Party-state affairs."

Again there was an obscure hint at some sort of plan that I did not know about.

Naturally, even Koka's literary opinions acquired greater weight. Sanya read everything to Koka the moment it left his pen: "The Lieutenant," "In the Town of M," "Letter No. 254." I was a little envious. Much less than everything was being sent to me.

On the other hand, brilliant prospects were again being opened before me. A place had been prepared for me since 1936 in the basic series of Solzhenitsyn's novels. I would be a native of St. Petersburg. In August of 1917 my first great love affair would come to an unsuccessful close, and so forth, but I was not supposed to know the vicissitudes to follow until the proper time.

Sanya was anxious about the fate of the earlier notes he had written in preparation for the future novel:

> Darling! Where are the notes from my bicycle trip? And where is the plan for "The Russian Avant-garde" and the first few chapters (on large white sheets)? They must be with you—aren't they? And the essay on "Black in Red"—the meeting between Severtsev and Olkhovsky? Don't tell me they're lost? If they are in Kislovodsk, then with whom? And back in Rostov, Maria Denisovna* has my poems. How can all this be brought together in one place?

When I replied that the drafts of "The Russian Avant-garde" were with me, as was the notebook with the three short stories, although some chapters had been left behind in Kislovodsk, Sanya wrote, "Thank you enormously for saving the three short stories for me—this is one of the most graphic expressions of love, which I shall never forget. After all, you were going on foot and you were carrying this on your person!"

The quieter it was on the front, the more frequent were the references to literature in his letters. One could sense Aleksandr's anxiety when he sent his works to Moscow. He even wrote to Koka (informing me of this later) that if Fedin should convince him that he possessed no literary talent, he would abruptly break with literature ("I'll tear my heart out of my

---

* Their neighbor in Rostov—Ed.

chest, I'll stamp out fifteen years of my life") and transfer to the History Department.

In another letter Sanya wrote about his hopes. His aim now was to receive the support of Fedin, Lavrenev, Timofeyev, and several others like them: "Yes, you have literary talent," "Yes, this is well written," "Yes, you did a good job."

And then, maybe, after having ideologically joined forces with some of them ("for support is no less important to them than their support is to us")—write, write, and write!

✸

Mother and I left Kazakhstan much later than we had intended. A totally unexpected obstacle arose—my mother's illness.

I had made my way to the Ush-Tobe railroad station to get the travel permit, only to find out that one had to wait three or four days for it. But then, finally, I held in my hands a small piece of white paper with a red stripe. The troubles one had to go through to get it! The permit was valid until March 25. By that time, of course, I would be home.

Suddenly Mother fell ill. She had been in perfect health in the morning, but by evening her temperature had risen to 104 degrees. Traveling was now out of the question. The only consolation was that this did not happen on the trip. Her temperature remained the same. Malaria was suspected. What relief if it really were malaria! But what if I had brought back typhus from Ush-Tobe? The days went by and quinine was of no help. My heart ached.

Finally Mother's temperature began to drop, and once again we prepared to leave. New applications, new passes and tickets—and that evening, once again, her temperature went up, to nearly 104.

Mother and I were now camping in the Ush-Tobe station among others like ourselves, and for several days in a row we vainly tried to get a seat on the passing trains, jammed to the hilt, which would take us as far as Alma-Ata. At long last a car was designated for those of us who were stranded in Ush-Tobe. Everyone, pushing and shoving each other, tried to crowd into it.

Happily, it took only a few hours to reach Alma-Ata. We arrived there the same day, on the very day that Sanya, on leave, had arrived in Rostov—where a disappointment awaited him.

A month later, when I reached Rostov, I was to find waiting for me a long letter in which he wrote that he hoped I could visit him at the front.

For ten days and nights the train carried my mother and me from Alma-Ata to Moscow, from Kazakhstan to Russia, from Asia to Europe.

Mother slept fitfully; she kept waking up to check whether our things were intact. It was only on the last night, exhausted by the long journey but rejoicing at having successfully managed to keep all our belongings together, that Mother fell into a deep sleep. But in the morning, the bundle with our most precious possessions was gone. It turned out that some man had sat on it all night long and, having persuaded himself that its owner was not worried about it, he stepped off the train with it at dawn, in Riazan.

Such was our first brief acquaintance with that town.

My mother wept—which happened very rarely. One would have to have lived through war, evacuation, fleeing on foot from the Germans, to understand what this loss meant. The one bundle had contained all my mother's clothes.

Mother had not been in Moscow since 1913. Back in the

years 1908–09, she had studied there in a finishing school for young ladies. She had not seen her brother, Valentin Turkin, who lived in the capital, for almost thirty years, and there had been no correspondence to speak of between them. All Mother had ever received from him was a telegram announcing the birth of his daughter and, once, a hundred rubles (with which we bought two quilts that served us both for many, many years).

How Mother had looked forward to the meeting with him and with his first wife, the lovely Veronica Nikolaevna, with whom I had stayed just after my marriage, and whom we were to visit now. And here, suddenly, she was humiliated—she had nothing appropriate to wear. But we found a way out. Mother was so thin in those days that one of my blouses fit her perfectly.

Veronica's daughter, Veronichka, was still a schoolgirl, sixteen years old. She wore her chestnut hair in two thick braids and there was about her the promise of future beauty. Her parents had divorced when she was only four months old, and although he lived on Strastnoy Boulevard, only fifteen minutes' walk from Patriarch Ponds, her father had not seen her since then.

We were met with the warmest welcome and every courtesy. There seemed to be no end to the conversations between mother and Veronica Nikolaevna.

When we went to visit my uncle, we rang the doorbell and Valentin himself opened the door. He put his arms around Mother and said, "All my thoughts have always been with you and Zhenya."

One had to know my dear uncle to understand that at this moment he sincerely believed in his sudden declaration. A few seconds passed, and it seemed as though there had never been a thirty-year separation, so tenderly, so simply, so affectionately did brother and sister converse with each other.

When my uncle started speaking about me, Mother asked, "But wouldn't you like to see your own daughter?" Uncle's face took on a helpless, hurt expression: "Then why doesn't she come to see *me*?"

It was decided that he would write his daughter a note inviting her to visit him.

Veronica's relatives, especially her aunt and grandmother, were opposed to this meeting, fearing it would be a nervous shock for her. It was no easy task for Mother to make them change their minds, but the next day she and Veronica went to see the professor.

Having lived in separation from her father, Veronica knew about him only through her mother, who continued to love him heart and soul and spoke only good of him. The fact that little Veronica's favorite book in childhood was Dickens' *Dombey and Son* was a clue to the place she had reserved for him in her heart.

The father ran out to meet the daughter and they embraced warmly. The professor began speaking to his daughter as though they had parted only the night before. And this was completely sincere on his part, for he was the kind of person who always lived spontaneously, guided by his feelings at any given moment.

Veronica, like a true daughter, immediately started to call him Papa and to address him in the familiar "thou" form.

The halo of specialness that had surrounded the father in the little girl's imagination and had endowed him with near-perfection was soon dispelled. She grew to know him and love him for what he really was: a highly creative person, extremely erudite, with a sharp, original, refined mode of thought and a subtle, kindly sense of humor. The years had not robbed him of the ability to wax enthusiastic over things and to evaluate them in his own way, passionately, deeply, and often paradoxically. Nor was Veronica in the least frightened by the professor's human frailties, which were far from few.

Thus my little cousin acquired a father. But the long years when she did not know him, when she was deprived of him, had left an indelible mark on her. Even fifteen years later, when my husband had left me, and she had to make a choice between my husband and me, she would be sorry not for me, but for an as yet unborn person—the child Sanya's second wife was expecting. "I myself grew up without a father," Veronica was to say to me.

From the moment I arrived in Moscow I couldn't wait to call Lida Ezherets. When I reached her she had just received the first comments on Sanya's short stories, not from Fedin, to be sure, but from Lavrenev.

He had said to her: "The short stories are engaging. I liked them." He was going to forward them to the editorial staff of the periodical *Znamia*.

How intertwined are joy and sorrow in life! On the day Lavrenev praised Sanya's short stories to Lida (he had been waiting so long for this appraisal—so much depended on it), Sanya learned about his mother's death: "Mamma died. I am left with all the good she has done for me and all the bad I have done to her. No one wrote me about the death. A money order came back, and on it was a mark indicating that the addressee was deceased. Apparently she died in March."

"The bad" was not just rhetoric. Sanya really felt guilty. Actually, he had been in no position to save his mother. But his annoyance with his mother's illnesses; his angry comments about "Mother's slowness," which, he said, was the cause of everything; finally, the fact that when he went to Rostov he had not gone to nearby Georgievsk to see her—now, of course, all this could not help but leave a bitter mark on his soul.

❧

When he received my first postcard from Moscow, Sanya wrote to me in Rostov, "You're so excited about Moscow that you don't write me about what is most important: when will you finally be in Rostov?"

In his reference to Lavrenev, the tone was somewhat restrained: "Lavrenev's appraisal gladdened me. Will wait for a more detailed account from Lida or from Lavrenev himself. But his promise to forward the short stories for publication surprised me. I didn't expect this at all and never gave it a thought."

I received this letter when I got home to Rostov and was waiting impatiently to be "called out" by Sanya's unit.

One night, around three in the morning, I was awakened by Mother's voice: "Natasha, a sergeant is at the door."

I jumped up, threw a bathrobe over my nightgown, and went into our front room. A young military man, wearing a greatcoat and a winter cap, with a knapsack on his back, was standing on the threshold.

We introduced ourselves, and Mother and I fed him and put him to bed to make up for lost sleep.

As for myself, I could not go back to sleep again. When dawn came, I ran out of the house and for a long time I wandered, happy, along our beloved Pushkin Boulevard.

The sergeant's name was Ilya Solomin. His parents were Jewish. Before the war they had lived in Minsk. Very few people had managed to leave Minsk in time, and Solomin had almost given up hope of ever finding his family alive. Perhaps this was why, even when he smiled, his dark eyes, slightly protruding from his serious face, never lost their sadness.

The sergeant had brought me a field shirt, a wide leather belt that went with it, epaulets, and a tiny star which I fastened to a dark gray beret. He handed me a Red Army pass issued in my name and certifying that I had already served some time in the unit. I was also given a furlough pass.

I was scared to death, of course. But I consoled myself with the thought that nothing would happen to a frontline officer for staging this little "theater performance." For myself, I was even ready to go to jail for the sake of a meeting with my husband. And I did not give a thought to how all this might appear to the soldiers. To me Solzhenitsyn was the most intelligent and the most decent human being on earth, and he certainly knew what he was doing.

That evening Solomin and I left Rostov. The sergeant was a quick-witted fellow. When the electricity went out in the ticket office, he managed to procure candles from somewhere or other. By way of "compensation" he obtained train tickets for us with seats in the car reserved for officers.

❧

And here we were, the two of us together. I was with my husband. In his dugout. Or was I dreaming?

The telephone rang. The division commander invited us over. I felt a little shy in the company of the other officers, but the vodka which I drank for the first time in my life gave me courage.

May was a cold month that year and we had to light a stove, but this made it even cozier in the dugout.

Evening. Logs crackled in the stove.

"Tell me all the details of your meeting with Koka," I asked my husband.

"I'd better read about it to you. *The Sixth Course* begins with this chapter." Then Sanya suddenly changed the subject and began to talk about his plans in general: his literary ones, and ones that were not strictly literary.

He spoke of how he saw the meaning of his life in serving the interests of world revolution with his pen. Not everything was to his liking today. Alliance with England and the United States. Dissolution of the Comintern. The national anthem changed. Officers' epaulets reinstituted in the army. He saw all this as a retreat from the ideals of the revolution. He advised me to buy the works of Marx, Engels, Lenin. It could even happen, he declared, that they would disappear from bookstores and library shelves after the war. One must be prepared to wage a struggle over all this after the war. He was ready for it.

After idling away my time for a few days, I began to get acquainted with Sanya's military work. It turned out to be easy to understand—the whole trick was to learn to work fast. I learned how to decipher the intricate sinusoids that were being typed out on the sound-range tape. Interesting!

In our free time Sanya and I walked, talked, and read. My husband taught me to fire a pistol. I began to copy Sanya's stories, "The Fruit Orchard" and "A Female Novel." In those days the greatest writer in my husband's eyes was Maxim Gorky. From time to time he would read aloud to me from *The Life of Matvey Kozhemyakin*.

Sanya was the complete master of his battery—even, one might say, the lord of the manor. If he needed Golovanov, the orderly, whose camouflaged bomb shelter was right next to his dugout, he would telephone the soldier on duty: "Send me Golovanov!"

SANYA

During one of his visits to our dugout, Pashkin, the deputy commander of the Political Section, announced that great changes were in the offing. Their artillery battalion would cease to be an independent unit and would be attached to brigade. The brigade commander would be someone called Colonel Travkin, who, it was said, was not inclined to tolerate the presence of women in his unit.

For the first time we started talking about my departure.

I told Sanya that I had read an announcement in the newspaper that applicants were being accepted for postgraduate work in physical chemistry at Moscow University. The specific field was chemical kinetics and catalysis, just what I loved. Maybe I should take off for Moscow? Then after the war we could start living together in the capital!

"Well, that's not a bad idea."

We tried to imagine our life together after the war. But all the pictures we drew were much too hazy, and we did not see eye to eye with respect to whatever we did discern in this haze. This divergence in our views was to be reflected in the letters that followed my departure. I would be trying in every way possible to see the future through Sanya's eyes, to feel with his feelings.

Thus I had spent three weeks with my husband.

❧

I was on the way back to Rostov when the formidable Red Army advance was launched in Byelorussia.

Sanya wrote me later that during the nine days of the advance he barely had the time to jot down, using short phrases only, all the impressions that were piling up on him. How sharp the contrast between the four summers, the four stages of this war! The summer of '44 was swift, headlong, and triumphant!

On July 9 I was registered at Rostov University as a temporary laboratory worker.

By this time I had established a regular correspondence with both Koka and Lida. "Lida and I have become very intimate," I wrote my husband. "We grew closer together in Moscow. Nadya Simonian is going to Leningrad. I have already written Lida: Why not give Nadya the mission of looking for a place for us all to live?"

This was a joke. The basis for it was a project Sanya had proposed, that after the war we would set up a "community" in Moscow or Leningrad. It was to include all the members of our group—"the five."

Sanya wrote that for some reason or other his correspondence with Koka was becoming irregular. Many letters were not reaching their destination, or were being delayed. As for Sanya's creative writing, this had to wait upon the future. He had no time for it now. But just think how many people and things he would have to write about later!

"I'm sketching in more and more new details of Pashkin —oh, when will I be able to sit down to write 'The Sixth Course'? I will write it so magnificently! Especially now, when the battle of Orel-Kursk stands out in such bold relief and can be seen so vividly through the prism of the year 1944."

Sanya did not let any literary novelties pass him by. He singled out Tvardovsky's *Vasily Tyorkin* in particular:

I ran across the first truthful (along my lines) little book about the war: this is *Vasily Tyorkin*, by Tvardovsky. If this poem is read carefully, one can glean many things no one has touched upon before. In gen-

eral, Tvardovsky is one of the best (or is he *the* best?)
Soviet poets. Some day I must get a letter off to him
expressing my appreciation.

And along with his discussions of literature came my husband's reaction to the new, stricter marriage law that had
just been promulgated: "The new marriage reform will, perhaps, surprise many people. Some will be pleased, others distressed, but it is entirely consistent—it's one of a whole series
of others like it—with a policy of tightening the screws from
all sides."

Ever since our meeting at the front I had been unable to
shake off the alarming feeling that Sanya and I had different
views about happiness. I tried in every way to conform my
concept of happiness to his. But this was not simple or easy,
and Sanya, also sensing our divergence, upbraided me for this
in his letters.

When you were with me at the front you once said to
me: I cannot imagine our future life together if we
don't have a child. Practically anyone is capable of pro-
ducing a child and bringing it up. But to write a history
of the post-October years as a work of art is something
that perhaps I alone can do, and even then only by
dividing my work with Koka, and perhaps with somebody else. That's how much this work is beyond the
brain, body, and life of one person!

Another letter from those times reminds me of how we
lived then. I wrote my husband on my name day, September
8, 1944. The trace of a little quill remained in the right-hand

corner of the letter—ink dots marking the outline—and on the other side of the page, a few stitches:

As usual, I am not celebrating my name day, but I am receiving presents. This time they are quite unusual: Mother fixed my old briefcase and presented me with an American (!) hot-water bottle; from my aunt I got a jar of honey; from Shura*—two little quills. One of them is my favorite, the other one is for you. That's the one I am sending you. I have sewed it in so it won't fall out and I hope the censor will sympathize with the frontline scribbler who found himself without one, and will let my little quill reach its destination.

Besides the American hot-water bottle I also own a pair of American overshoes. They are just lovely (Mother got them on a coupon).

Am writing you from my laboratory in complete solitude. I am working nervously, feverishly, because I must obtain all the data by the fifteenth.

Sometimes even a little quill can become the victim of the strangest fate. The fault lay with a change in the box number of Sanya's field address. Five letters were returned all at once. Thus the little quill, after having made a grand tour, was once again dispatched to the front.

Sanya and Koka were now farther apart geographically than ever before. My husband complained that now they were even on different fronts.

Sanya had evidently learned about Koka's relocation from someone else; there were still no letters from him. "Do you

---

* An acquaintance—Ed.

hear anything from Koka?" he asked me again. "The son of a bitch has been silent since June."

Meanwhile, the bridgehead on the Narev River, where Sanya was, had widened. ". . . In the first days of this month the counterattacks were repulsed not by us but by neighboring battalions on our left."

But a lot of fighting still lay ahead. Sanya made his vehicle warmer by upholstering the interior with captured blankets.

Still, one could sense that the end of the war was approaching, if only because of the fact that Sanya kept returning to the theme of our postwar life. He wrote details of how our "community" in Moscow ought to be arranged for the first few years. The immediate problem to solve for this commune would be finding several possible locations for apartments. To this end, it would be helpful to have the assistance of influential people—such as Lida's father, Aleksandr Mikhailovich, or perhaps Sanya's former teacher, Anastasia Sergeyevna Griunau, who was now working in the Moscow Department of Public Education.

Why there was no correspondence from Koka was still a total mystery. Sanya complained continually about the absence of letters from his friend.

In the meantime I received another letter from Koka, enclosing a snapshot. He had lost weight, and he had the typical frontline fighter's expression that Solomin had worn but that I had never glimpsed on my husband's face.

Sanya, where was your mathematician's perspicacity? Why didn't it ever occur to you, or to Koka, that your letters about postwar plans might be of interest not only to the two of you?

Things reached such a point that I forwarded Sanya's letter to Koka. And this, of course, produced the predictable reaction: "Dear Natasha, I have received Sanya's letter from you.

Only *he* is capable of such things. He's just 150 kilometers away from me, but he sends his letters via Rostov."

My husband already felt himself to be a writer, so much so that he didn't hesitate to pass judgment on others:

In the periodical *Novy Mir*, issue No. 9, 1943 . . . I read a play by Aleksandr Kron, *Long-Range Reconnaissance* [*Glubokaya Razvedka*]. The first three acts so enthralled me that I was ready to write Kron a letter of congratulations. But in the fourth act he abruptly lost the thread and revealed that, although his talent is extraordinary, he's quite ordinary as a thinker. (Would very much like to know your opinion about this play. Lida doesn't like it.)

Meanwhile Lida was prodding Lavrenev for a written appraisal of Sanya's short stories. Finally this appraisal was in Sanya's hands, and in mine I held a letter in which my husband reported that he had been twirling Lavrenev's appraisal around in his fingers for ten hours without being able to make head or tail of his attitude. There was every reason to be displeased, but at the same time there was a pleasant lightness of tone, a hint of satisfaction. First of all, Lavrenev had remembered everything that had been sent to him back in May of 1941 ("The Mission Abroad," "The River Pointsmen," "The Nikolaevsky Couple"). He said they displayed "a rudimentary skill in putting his thoughts and observations into literary form." All the "praise" was contained in the following two sentences:

1. The author has traversed a long path (since 1941), he has matured, and now one can start speaking about literary productions.

2. I can have no doubts about the author's aptitude for literary work and I believe that in an atmosphere of calm, after the war, when he can devote himself totally to the work which he evidently loves, the author will be able to achieve success.

Lavrenev had given Sanya pause—pause for reflection.

The same postcard in which Sanya relayed Lavrenev's appraisal to me contained a completely unexpected postscript in the margin: "Maybe I'll go to see Koka around the twentieth of December!"

This idea was developed further in the next letter: "I'm all set to see Koka. Travkin's permission has been received, I've only been waiting for Captain Stepanov's return from leave...."

But, alas, Stepanov returned three days late, and for this reason Travkin did not let Sanya go. When would they have a chance to meet again? And on what front?

On New Year's Eve the officers' club gave a dinner with the soldiers. It was followed by group singing and dancing. Outside, it was a moonlit night. According to Sanya, he spent the night walking, looking around, smoking, and thinking about his plans. Later he was to write facetiously that his life appeared to him as a piece of cloth sufficient for a whole family: how does one cut out of it both a man's coat and a skirt, both a lady's jacket and a little boy's trousers! And so, one had to comprehend the incomprehensible . . .

Sanya's letters were becoming more and more complicated, difficult, contradictory. It was as if he were attacking me, but then he would retreat, trying to smooth over his harshness: "My last letters probably depressed you. Put them away, somewhere far, those great words of wisdom, or burn them up altogether. Let nothing confuse you."

But then came another letter, which made me wince: "You complain that I seldom write to you. The truth, dear, is not that I write you seldom, but badly."

To understand each other at a distance during any long separation required development in the same direction, along the same path and at the same rate of speed—so thought my husband. But all his life he had developed "painfully, one-sidedly"—first his right side, then his left—and just where life was pulling him he himself did not know. Every month his literary plans and intentions were being "captured, drawn into, absorbed, carried away by the vortex of Politics."

I felt that in these moments of reflection he needed another person, not myself. And this was confirmed in his letters. Koka was "the only person in the world" who could send him a letter even after an interruption of a year, the only one with whom Sanya felt a sense of seamless continuity, "like two trains that are traveling side by side at the same speed, and one could step from one to the other while they are moving."

Involuntarily, I felt that these words not only expressed Sanya's satisfaction with the complete mutual understanding which he and Koka enjoyed, but were also meant as a reproach to me.

No doubt the tone of these letters was influenced by the nervous tension under which generals, officers, and soldiers alike lived during those weeks in the boundless reaches from the Baltic to the Carpathians. Each one felt: Something has to begin! Perhaps it will begin this very night! And each one thought that this great, irresistible advance was going to be the last one. The caterpillar tracks of tanks and artillery, the wheels of trucks and weapons carriers, the feet in frontline boots, all would come to a stop only in Berlin! And although, of course, each man tried to put this thought out of his mind, it would still creep through: the individual soldier was asking himself, "But will *I* ever get there?"

Churchill's well-known message to Stalin* accelerated events. The First Ukrainian Army, coming to the rescue of the Allies, who were in disarray in the Ardennes, broke through the enemy defenses in southern Poland on January 12 and pushed on westward, advancing a good hundred kilometers a day. On the thirteenth, its neighbor, the First Byelorussian Army, began its march on Berlin. On the fourteenth the other armies had their turn to move.

And now there was no time for painful reflection about an abstract future. It was hard to imagine how Captain Solzhenitsyn managed to snatch a few minutes to dash off a note:

Today we *have begun*, we pushed off, we went tearing, tramping off. Am replying on the run. The last mail suddenly showered on me, like three handshakes, like three wishes for victory and life—three letters: yours, Lida's, and Ostrich's.** And for five (!) hours I couldn't open a single one of them—you can imagine from this what's going on here.

Every evening the radio program "Latest News" resounded with new names, unfamiliar to the Russian ear. I could only vaguely guess the direction in which the recently promoted General Travkin was moving his brigade.

---

* This was Churchill's telegram of early January 1945—Ed.
** Kirill's nickname in school—Ed.

The Front

It was ridiculous, of course, to think of any kind of personal wishes when battles like this were raging, but I very much wanted Sanya's premonition to come true, for his division to turn north, to the frontiers of East Prussia, where Solzhenitsyn had mentally traveled more than once, ever since he conceived of the novel that was to begin with General Samsonov's catastrophe at Tannenberg in August 1914.

And then, suddenly, another of those inexplicable premonitions, which so often are confirmed in life, came true. Sanya's mad idea of the year 1939, to spend some time in Neidenberg, materialized after six years. Sanya was there, standing in the middle of the burning town. What was most interesting about that was that when General Samsonov entered Neidenberg in 1914 it was also burning—and that was just what the novel was planned to describe.

"Tramping through East Prussia for the second day. A hell of a lot of impressions."

"Am sitting not far from the forest where Olkhovsky and Severtsev were surrounded! . . ." (Those were the names of the heroes of *August 1914* in its original version.)

The very last letter my husband wrote me from the front again heaped a mountain of suffering upon me. With one hand he seemed to push me away, and with the other he drew me even closer, even tighter to himself.

He did not indulge in illusions: our future was not completely clear and the decision would depend on me. "In the spring of 1944 I saw how egotistical your love still was, how full of prejudices you still were about family life." And I received an irritated sermon:

> You imagine our future as an uninterrupted life together, with accumulating furniture, with a cozy apart-

ment, with regular visits from guests, evenings at the theater. . . . It is quite probable that none of this will transpire. Ours may be a restless life. Moving from apartment to apartment. Things will accumulate but they will have to be just as easily discarded.

Everything depends upon you. I love you, I love nobody else. But just as a train cannot move off the rails for a single millimeter without crashing, so is it with me—I must not swerve from my path at any point. For now, you love only me, which means, in the final analysis, you love only for yourself, for the satisfaction of your own needs.

I must, he wrote, realize that our interests had to be as intertwined as, for example, Sanya's and Koka's—which formed the bedrock of their friendship—and it was suggested that I rise above my "completely understandable, completely human," but nevertheless "egotistical" plans for our future, and then "real harmony" would reign.

And there was the postscript again: "No letters from Koka, but I see that General Kolpakchi* is heading right for Berlin."

The confusion this letter threw me into soon gave way to worry, fear, despair, and finally a sense of hopelessness.

It is always difficult to wait for a husband to come home from war. But the last months before war's end are the most difficult of all: shrapnel and bullets take no account of how long a man has been fighting.

It was precisely at this point that letters from Gleb stopped arriving.

----

* Commander of the 47th Army—Ed.

Nadya would run outside to look for the mailman. She wrote her husband, she wrote his friends, she wrote to his superiors. Everyone maintained a silence, as though enchanted.

In the spring of 1945 hardly an evening went by without salutes blasting the skies. One city after another was taken! Taken! Taken!—Konigsberg, Frankfurt, Berlin, Prague.

But there were no letters. The world dimmed. Apathy set in. But she must not let go of herself. What if he is alive and returns? He would certainly reproach her for having wasted her time! And she consumed herself with long-extended days of work—nights alone were reserved for tears.*

I received my husband's last war letter early in March of 1945. Hardly a week had gone by when suddenly, instead of the expected regular letter, my own postcard was returned to me. It bore the notation: "The addressee has left the unit."

I panicked. Immediately I wrote to Sanya; to Pashkin, who after our acquaintance last spring had become Arseny Alekseyevich to me; to Ilya Solomin. They would certainly reply, if Sanya himself could not.

Lida wrote inquiries to the two commanders, Pashkin and Melnikov. If they too failed to answer, she consoled me, this would probably mean that the field post-office number had been changed and that everything was clearly all right.

Kirill Simonian, now a captain in the medical corps and also somewhere in East Prussia, not very far from Sanya, tried to console me too: "Our army is not trained so delicately as

*From *The First Circle*

to conceal from the family the truth about the fallen. If Sanya were wounded, the postman would have written on the letter: Wounded—or killed—on such-and-such a date."

A month passed after my postcard was returned, a month during which no one could recognize me. I lived like an automaton. I did what had to be done; I tried to do everything well and conscientiously, knowing and understanding that Sanya would not forgive me if I conducted myself otherwise. But no one heard me laugh any more, or saw a smile on my face.

Zoya Braslavskaya, a lecturer—we had become very attached to each other—kept asking, "Natashenka, when will I hear the old lilt in your voice again?"

In the daytime I kept myself under control, but in the evenings I cried, burying my face in the pillow.

On April 10 or 11 the postman brought a letter from Solomin. Ilya was writing not to me but to Mother, which in itself struck me as strange. The opening lines of the letter were frightening.

"Circumstances are such that I must now write to you. You are, of course, interested in Sanya's fate, why he's not writing to you, and what has happened to him . . ."

But further on in the letter he tried to be reassuring: "He has been recalled from our unit. Why and for what reason I cannot tell you now. I only know that he is alive and in good health, and nothing else. Also, that nothing bad will happen to him."

What was this—a special mission? I had heard that such things happened.

But why the alarming note that crept in again? "I ask you, please, not to worry, and to help Natasha."

But we could not help worrying. Even if this were a special mission, there were many kinds of special missions. Sometimes they were quite dangerous indeed. Still, Ilya had assured us that Sanya was alive and healthy, and that nothing bad would happen to him.

> The human heart, never ready to reconcile itself to what is irreversible, began to create fables: perhaps he had been sent off on a top-secret intelligence mission? Perhaps he was on special assignment? A generation nurtured on suspicion and secretiveness fancied mysteries where none existed.*

Then came May 9, 1945:

> Wild with joy, people ran through crazed streets. Someone was firing a pistol in the air. And all the media of the Soviet Union combined to broadcast victory marches across a wounded and hungry land.*

How unspeakably happy this day would have been for me—if only . . . But there was still the hope that Sanya would let us know about himself.

But another month passed, and there were no letters. And for a suspiciously long time Koka's mother, Antonina Vasilyevna, had not heard from her son. Why?

There were no anwers to her inquiries either, and she too was terribly worried. Once she quoted me the question Koka's grandmother had asked: "Why both of them?"

Why both of them?

---

* From *The First Circle*

SANYA

I was thinking about this at the very moment another letter from Solomin arrived. I expected it to solve the riddle.

"The departure was sudden. . . . We could not even talk to each other, that's why you mustn't be surprised that he could not have reported anything to you . . ."

"Could not?" If Ilya had written "did not have time to" it would have been more understandable. But what did "could not" mean? Had someone forbidden it? Who?

"Don't wait for letters from him, for he is in no position to write you. Don't make any inquiries either, for this, at best, would be useless . . ."

"Well, thank God, everything is over with now." (He was speaking about the end of the fighting.) "By the way, this played no role in Sanya's departure."

This meant that Sanya's disappearance had no connection with his service, the battles, the war. The only thing it could have been, perhaps, was . . .

I pounced on the letters I had brought back from the front. They were neatly filed in a little homemade carton, labeled "Letters from My Wife." Here too I found a batch of letters from Koka.

The first letter I read told me what Ilya had left unsaid.

The only thing that remained now was to wait for the next news. What kind? And from where would it come?

4

The Muscovites

On February 9, 1945, Master Sergeant Solomin, holding a piece of blue velours, dropped in on his battery commander.

Many years later, Solomin, now a middle-aged engineer, told me about this episode as he recalled it:

"I said I didn't have anyone to send it to, anyway. 'Let's send it to Natasha,' I said, 'there's enough here for a blouse.'

"At that very moment, two men entered the room. One of them said: 'Solzhenitsyn, Aleksandr Isaevich? We want you.'

"The three of them went out.

"Some strange force prompted me to get up and follow

them. He was already sitting in the black *Emka*.* He looked at me long and penetratingly, or so it seemed to me.

"He was driven away and I did not see him again until twenty years later.

"I myself don't know why I ran to his car. Inside it I found a German ammunition box. I opened it. Books. He was collecting our books from the 1920s. Under them, something-or-other in German. I opened one of the books and found myself staring at a portrait of Hitler.

"Can you imagine? Of course, to him this was just a war memento, but then there were the wartime laws, you know.

"I took the box to my quarters and later burned everything. I spared only your letters, which I brought to you subsequently. Do you remember?

"About an hour later those two men came back again and demanded Solzhenitsyn's things. I handed over his suitcase and his greatcoat. 'Isn't there something else?' they asked. 'No,' I said."

While they were fetching Solzhenitsyn's belongings, he himself was already in a cell, still unable to believe that everything that had transpired in the general's office was real.

General Travkin had asked the captain to hand over his revolver. Solzhenitsyn promptly unfastened his holster and placed it on the table. But the general made no move to check whether the battery commander's personal weapon was in order.

What happened next was unbelievable. A harsh voice pronounced the words: "You are under arrest."

"This cannot be!" Solzhenitsyn cried out. "For what?"

"You are under arrest."

---

* Russia's equivalent of our Dodge limousine—Ed.

"Wait a moment!" ordered Travkin. He stopped the counterintelligence men with an authoritative gesture and then, looking at his former subordinate, he asked simply, as though nothing of moment was happening, "Solzhenitsyn, do you have a brother in the First Ukrainian Army?"

He could say no more, but this was sufficient. The "brother" must be Nikolai Vitkevich. Koka. Could all this really be because of their correspondence? . . . Or was it his "Resolution No. 1"? But how could anyone know about that?

The counterintelligence men started to lead him to the door.

"Halt!" It was again the general's voice. "Solzhenitsyn, I wish you—luck—"

They got into the car and off they went. This time, not from east to west but from west to east.

Flatcars loaded with tanks and cannons sped by in the opposite direction to their train. A stream of people, weapons, provisions, ammunition was pouring relentlessly toward those last battle fronts, which would be stormed without the artillery captain who for two years had advanced with his army from the heart of Russia—from the Orel region—to the Reich itself, and who now was being so senselessly withdrawn and returned to the rear.

The other passengers in the train suspected nothing. Three military men were traveling together, that was all. One of them was not wearing epaulets. Nothing strange about that. A gentleman's agreement had been reached between Solzhenitsyn and his two escorts: they would not treat him as a person under arrest, and he in turn promised not to do anything foolish.

On one occasion, after they had crossed the former border, Aleksandr struck up a conversation with a girl. They were making small talk and the escorts did not interfere. Suddenly

SANYA

Solzhenitsyn asked the girl not to register fright, not to change the expression on her face. But this did not come so easily to her. One of the escorts, suspecting something, changed his seat to move closer to them. But by then Aleksandr had had the time to apprise her of the essentials: he was under arrest, his wife must be informed that he was alive, that he had been seen. Rostov, 27 Sredny, Reshetovskaya.

The girl had such a good face. Such kind eyes. But now the eyes showed fear. Would she write? Would she be afraid to? Maybe she had not properly committed the words to memory, or had not heard them properly. Or out of sheer fright she simply might not have grasped what it was all about.

Perhaps she did write, but the letter never reached its destination. This was wartime. Anything could have happened.

The last few steps in freedom . . . then the heavy doors opened before him and slammed shut behind him.

❧

From my husband's accounts, and from the few official documents available, I tried later on to piece together how the proceedings went, especially the interrogations. I had to do some guesswork, of course, and make some assumptions based on my husband's psychology, which I felt I knew rather well. But a well-rounded and fairly coherent picture, though sparse in details, formed in my mind, and for many years it remained unchanged.

But one evening I heard a chapter from the *Archipelago*, one about the interrogation, over the radio. There was nothing new in it for me; the text was very familiar. But there was something in it that struck me, and made me stop and think. What seemed a smooth, cogent picture began to dissolve.

It was not until 1974, when I learned from a radio broadcast that Nikolai Vitkevich had had an interview with a correspondent of the *Christian Science Monitor*, the American newspaper, that I found myself forced to look at those distant events with different eyes and to try to give them another interpretation.

But first let us recall the little that Solzhenitsyn has revealed in *The Gulag Archipelago*, which coincides almost completely with his earlier accounts of the interrogation. Aleksandr had acknowledged making all the statements attributed to him and had tried to explain, just as Nerzhin was to do in *The First Circle*, that all this was "pure theory," infinitely far removed from life, and just as in the novel, "the pretrial investigator did not believe that my indictment under Article 58 could be traced all the way back to my first studies of dialectical materialism."

Other ways to reach the heart of the interrogator had to be found. Aleksandr had already, as he wrote, "crossed himself off the list" and "with a muddled mind" had to "weave something credible" concerning his meetings with friends. And not just concerning the meetings. Concerning everything. And this "weaving" had to convince the interrogator of Solzhenitsyn's "simplicity, humility, and utter frankness."

The thought that through Sanya harm might come to others had never entered my mind. That not Sanya alone, but Koka too, had suffered punishment seemed only natural to me, because the basic cause of their troubles, as I believed and as Sanya confirmed, was the nature of their correspondence with each other. That Nikolai received a more severe penalty (ten years instead of eight) I considered sheer accident.

In later years we rarely talked about these interrogations. Subsequently, when I became familiar with the material of *Archipelago*, some of the new details merged with what my husband told me at our meetings, as we sat together on the little bench at the camp on Kaluzhskaya Square in Moscow.

The interrogations took place in the spacious study of the investigator, Captain Yezepov. Besides the two captains, there was the mute presence of the Supreme Commander-in-Chief— a huge portrait of him, full-sized, in full-dress uniform, occupied almost the entire wall. On occasion, a friend of Yezepov would drop in; he too was evidently an investigator. The two of them would sit on the sofa chatting about something, while Aleksandr considered his next reply.

As he familiarized himself with the charges, Solzhenitsyn learned (from a text typed on the file folder of his "case") that he had the right to submit written complaints about any improper conduct during the proceedings. He expressed his dissatisfaction with the harsh, bureaucratic formulations in which the investigator had clothed his replies. Yezepov made no objection. He told him to go ahead and write his complaint. But in veiled warning he said: "All right then, let's begin all over again."

Begin all over again? No. Somewhere it was May. The first beam of sunlight fell on the bronze clock on the mantelpiece in the study. Ahead of him there was still a promise of some kind of life . . . and Solzhenitsyn signed the paper which stated that he, the subject under investigation, had no challenges or complaints to file, that he acknowledged his guilt under Paragraphs 10 and 11 of Article 58 of the Criminal Code of the Russian Soviet Federated Socialist Republic. The first of these paragraphs provided for punishment for anti-Soviet agitation; the second, for organizing or attempting to organize an anti-Soviet group.

Thus the investigation came to a close. Solzhenitsyn was brought to the Office of the Procurator, Lieutenant Colonel

Kotov. He was a nondescript, blond man whose duties included that of ensuring that due process was observed by the investigator. Lazily Kotov leafed through the file containing all the protocols and material evidence, pausing occasionally for small, tired yawns. Kotov's weariness rubbed off on Solzhenitsyn and, in his words, he limited himself to one request: cancellation of Paragraph 11. What kind of group could there have been? After all, only two had been indicted in the case, and they were not even being tried together. Kotov elucidated: "Even one and a half persons are more than one. Which means a group."

About twelve years later, I decided—or rather, circumstances compelled me—to talk once again with my husband about these months of investigation. I had learned from Lida Ezherets that Kirill Simonian knew of some kind of testimony Aleksandr had given against him and that he was still indignant about it. I asked Sanya what this was all about, certain beforehand that I would hear him say, "Oh, it's just another falsification."

But to my surprise, Aleksandr did not deny that he had cast a shadow on Simonian. He had been in a difficult position; he had had to explain the source of his anti-Soviet attitudes, as the interrogator called them. He offered versions of how he had become "overread," of how his bookishness had made him too smart for his own good. Yezepov found this explanation unacceptable. Aleksandr, demonstrating his "simplicity, humility, and utter frankness," decided to give the impression of being a pathetic man in the street, with petty complaints about the authorities—harmless, essentially a grumbler and a whiner. He said he had never bothered with "high-level politics" and that he was now horrified at the thought that he might have caused a stir.

Aleksandr went so far as to tell the interrogator that he was glad he was arrested "at the beginning of 1945, and not in 1948 or 1950," because he knew how deep in the hole he would be then with Article 58, Paragraphs 10 and 11, what with living in the capital and frequenting literary and student circles. This was precisely what Solzhenitsyn had told me when we first discussed the interrogations. Now, in regard to his testimony about Kirill, Solzhenitsyn said that he had tried to portray him, too, as a mere grumbler, unhappy about a few details of his life.

As he was telling me about it, my husband added, "Maybe it wasn't such a good idea. But I wanted to make the best of a bad situation. After all, nothing terrible happened. Kirill wasn't imprisoned, was he?"

Many years after that, when Kirill and I renewed our acquaintance, I asked him about this old and unpleasant story.

"Well, it wasn't quite harmless," he recalled. "I was summoned several times and questioned about my relations with Sanya. And then I was shown a school notebook filled with what may have been his handwriting. You know what a characteristic hand he has. Some of the details described were things both Sanya and I knew. For example, we are sitting on the window sill with our feet dangling in the air over the street below us. But the content of the conversations is sheer invention. The notebook implied that I, Kirill Simonian, was an enemy of the people and that it was incomprehensible why I should be walking around a free man."

When the interrogators asked Kirill how he could explain such testimony, he replied that as a physician he saw it this way: the person was suffering from what might be called a "dislocation of consciousness." Sanya "was in prison; I was free; therefore many of his perceptions and judgments had undergone a kind of hypertrophy."

"But maybe you were deluding yourself too?" I rejoined.

"At that moment you were shaken by the testimony and, over-reacting, you attached far too much significance to it. Whereas in reality it was just a lot of nonsense to which no one paid any attention. After all, everything turned out well, didn't it?"

Kirill shrugged and did not answer.

Then came the evening in February 1974 when I tuned in to the Voice of America. A familiar surname came through the noise and crackle. For an instant I thought I had not heard correctly.

". . . Nikolai Vitkevich . . . accuses Solzhenitsyn of having falsely denounced him during the investigation . . ."

It was part of a brief news summary and no more details were given. I had to wait for the full newscast.

I had not seen Koka for almost ten years. False denunciation! I could not disbelieve him, but I did not want to believe him either.

The American news program came on. The faraway announcer repeated what I had already heard, but now added Vitkevich's assertion that Solzhenitsyn, during the investigation, had also "exposed" his wife. Again no details were reported. Perhaps Nikolai had withheld the details?

I listened to excerpts from *The Gulag Archipelago* on the radio: the investigation proceedings. Everything was exactly as I had imagined it for many years—the conversations with Yezepov, the spacious study with the enormous portrait on the wall, and my husband, with shaven head, seated alongside the interrogator's table.

"Don't cast stones at those who turn out to be weak under interrogation." This phrase, which I had heard and read and typed and retyped many times, echoed again, and suddenly I caught myself feeling that this somehow did not jibe too well with some other statements by Aleksandr Isaevich.

Only very recently he had vehemently attacked Yakir and

Krasin for "caving in" after their first trial. And indeed, could the injunction not to cast stones be reconciled with Solzhenitsyn's impatience with human frailties, his demands for sacrifice from each and every one, his unwillingness to forgive people for the slightest even unconscious lapse?

"Thank God I avoided sending anyone to prison. But it was close."

And at that moment, from the depths of my memory a day long ago came back to mind, a day when I wanted to shout for pain and joy. It was the day in Rostov when, after many long months of silence, the first letter arrived, scratched out with a poorly sharpened pencil and folded into a tiny triangle.

And, of course, joy, not sorrow, won: he is alive, he will stay alive, he will be able to write, we will meet, he will return.

Mother rejoiced with me. Then suddenly, as she read the letter, she became frightened. She was struck by the sentence: "What indescribable joy the sheets written in your own hand gave me . . . in this way I found out that you are alive, healthy, and free."

"Free? What does he mean?" she exclaimed. "Does he mean that you too could have been arrested? Why shouldn't you be free?"

Sanya's words had not disturbed me. It had seemed only natural that my husband would be anxious. He had feared for me and now he was reassured.

I sorted through the batch of old letters from 1945. Here was the little triangular one. Rereading it once more, I found: "To this day I don't know whether or not 'sir' has shared my fate." "Sir" was Nikolai Vitkevich (since their Three Musketeers days, Sanya, Koka, and Kirill had referred to themselves as "the sirs"). In mid-August, then, Solzhenitsyn had not known whether Nikolai had been arrested. But according to

Archipelago, he was at that time telling the procurator, Kotov, that two were indicted in the case. And he would go on to say that they were not being tried together. So, without knowing whether Nikolai had been arrested, he already knew that he would be tried, and separately at that. How did he know?

And then another letter. And still another.

Sanya, who had made contact with Aunt Veronica in Moscow before he was allowed to write to me, had bombarded her with questions about us all. Where was Kirill? Where was Lida? What did she hear about Nikolai? "Answer me briefly, just bare essentials . . ." "For ten days I have been waiting impatiently for news." Why might we have disappeared? Why such concern about us in July and August? Back in May, after all, he knew that two had been indicted. Might there be more?

What could have developed during the investigation?

I tried to put myself in the place of the people in Moscow, unknown to me, reading the letters between the two friends in 1944 and early 1945.

What could these letters have contained? Some reflection of their correspondence, their disputes, their views must, after all, be in these two packages, letters to me from Nikolai and from Sanya.

Koka's letters contained, one might say, nothing of special import. "Sanya keeps writing all kinds of claptrap and sending it out for reviews." "Only immediate, local events concern me now."

Letters from my husband. Phrases I had once paid no attention to now acquired an entirely new ring: "the beginning of a colossal Party-literary struggle"; "the frontier between the patriotic war and the revolutionary war"; "the war after the war." My husband's monologues when I was with him at the front came back to mind.

Finally there was the letter that spoke of "the first Marxist document. Resolution No. 1." Solzhenitsyn had this paper with him in a little map case and it was confiscated at the time of his arrest. I had read this "Marxist document" when I was with my husband at the front. Among other things, it stated that for the purpose of achieving their goals, it would be necessary after the war to seek the understanding and support of student and literary circles, to attract influential people to their side. This required an organization.

Yes, it was quite probable that in 1945 such ideas might not have appeared so harmless.

I imagined myself as the investigator on whose desk these documents lay. So that was where the indictment under Paragraph 11 came from—the intent to organize a group. It had not been cited simply because "even one and a half persons are more than one. Which means a group." Worse, Solzhenitsyn could not have sustained his claim that only two people were involved. After all, at that very moment Kotov was leafing through a dossier in which both "Resolution No. 1" and letters in the same vein were filed. The dossier thus contained my husband's "allegations" against all of us.

Why was there, in my husband's accounts, never a mention of the principal reason for the charges against him—an attempt to organize us into a group? Is it possible that this was because Solzhenitsyn found himself in the role of a person repressed unjustifiably because of his criticism of Stalin?

Further, why wasn't Nikolai charged under Paragraph 11? Was this due to the confusion of wartime, or were the charges against him and Solzhenitsyn different? But there must have been a common charge. The two men were, after all, "*odnodeltsy*"—"one-casers"—indicted in the same case. And incidentally, where was this term "*odnodeltsy*" first used for them? That was how they were referred to in the Marfino Prison four

years after the trial, and also in my husband's words. It looked
as though he were interested in a simple version that would not
give cause for reflection: Together we sinned, together we are
judged. For what? For a correspondence with each other. But
how about the "group"? Was it an error by the investigatory
machinery that Vitkevich was not sentenced in conformity to
Paragraph 11? Why had Solzhenitsyn received eight years and
Vitkevich ten? Well, there were all kinds of injustices and
judicial vagaries in those days.

A few days after the radio broadcast I read the text of
Nikolai Vitkevich's official letter. He wrote that the day he was
rehabilitated, when he was allowed to read the protocols of
the proceedings, was "the most horrible day of my life." He
could not believe his eyes when he read that the members of
our "fivesome" were named as having been engaged in anti-
Soviet activities ever since our student days. Not only had the
five been named, but also someone by the name of Vlasov. I
happened to know who this Vlasov was: a naval officer with
whom Aleksandr had struck up an acquaintance during the
war. They had traveled in the same compartment of a Rostov-
Moscow train back in the spring of 1944, and later they had
exchanged a few letters. Leonid Vlasov had actually been discussed during the investigations. I knew this from my husband.

My husband had told me that Vlasov had "saved" himself
by a letter he wrote to Solzhenitsyn that arrived in the unit
after his arrest and was subsequently forwarded to the investi-
gators. Captain Yezepov himself read this letter to my husband. "I do not agree," wrote Vlasov, "that anyone could
further Lenin's cause better than is now being done by Josef
Stalin." That was why Vlasov was never even questioned.

At the time it had seemed to me that this move by the
investigator was akin to the presentation of new evidence
against Solzhenitsyn, as if to say: "So you see what Vlasov's

point of view is—that means you must have had an opposite one." Now an entirely different thought occurred to me. Might this have been Yezepov's rebuttal to allegations against Vlasov?

If one must drink the cup of bitterness, then it should be downed to the dregs. I arranged a meeting with Vlasov and showed him Vitkevich's statement:

> . . . Solzhenitsyn informed the investigator that he had planned to recruit into his organization a fellow passenger he had casually met during a train trip, a navy man by the name of Vlasov, who, he said, not only agreed to join but even offered the name of a friend who shared the same anti-Soviet attitudes.

Vlasov suddenly exclaimed, "That was Kasovsky!"

How did Vlasov know this? He had guessed the name instantly. He had indeed talked about his friend to Solzhenitsyn during the train ride and had mentioned his name (it goes without saying that only a madman or a person bent on suicide would have talked about anti-Soviet attitudes in an officers' car in 1944). Some years after the war, when Vlasov renewed his acquaintance with Solzhenitsyn, he could not understand at all why the latter still remembered the name of Kasovsky, a man he had never met. (This name crops up in the very first letter Solzhenitsyn wrote to Leonid after he had "found" us again in 1959.)

Now this was quite understandable. The whole picture, sketched in a few lines in Nikolai's letter, became clear:

> . . . end of the protocol of the first interrogation. The investigator reproached Solzhenitsyn for insincerity and

unwillingness to tell everything. In reply, Aleksandr declared that he wanted to tell everything, that he was concealing nothing, but that some things might have slipped his mind. He would try to remember by the next session.

He seemed to have remembered "everything" down to a name casually heard.

It was all too easy to reconstruct the scene now. By having to admit that he was preparing to create an organization, Solzhenitsyn inevitably allowed the investigator to evince an interest in those he had planned to recruit into it. When names were mentioned, the question naturally arose as to why he had considered these particular people fit for this purpose. He had to show motivation. On the other hand, the investigator must not be provoked to anger. It had to be proved to him that the accused had only "simplicity, humility, and utter frankness." Thus the good impression that had to be created in the mind of the investigator was thrown on one side of the scale, and the fate of five or six human beings on the other.

When Vlasov read about Solzhenitsyn's "slandering" other people, among whom he was included, the words "Some character!" escaped his lips involuntarily. We began to leaf through the letters Solzhenitsyn had written to him after they reencountered each other. One sentence in particular leapt to the eye: "Under the personality cult, the situation was such that the very best person, out of the very best motives, could ruin an innocent man." This was the germ for Solzhenitsyn's short story "An Incident at Krechetovka Station."

Later, as we talked, Leonid Vlasov reconstructed the situation logically: Wanting to preserve himself, Solzhenitsyn, the future great writer, did all he could to attain his hope of receiving the shortest possible sentence. Those whom he had to slander might not be destined for such an intense and difficult role in life.

It may be that I still don't have a fully coherent picture of all the interrogation proceedings. But one thing has become clear. They did not transpire in exactly the way that Solzhenitsyn has written of them.

What happened to Vitkevich is described in this same official letter. He was arrested about a month after Solzhenitsyn told the investigator that Vitkevich "had tried to create an illegal organization . . . From 1940 on, he conducted systematic anti-Soviet agitation . . . worked out plans for effecting a forcible change in the policy of the Party and of the state, cast aspersions upon Stalin," etc.

Vitkevich received a sentence two years longer than Solzhenitsyn's. The others were lucky.

Paradoxical as it may be, it was nevertheless a fact that some of the prosecutors were forced, at the same time, to defend people against the slanders produced from my husband's words. This, of course, does not conform with Solzhenitsyn's "theory" that in those days it sufficed merely to name a person, saddle him with accusations, even the most absurd, and presto, the poor wretch would end up in a camp. But I trust he does not regret that his theory was not entirely foolproof, and that we remained in freedom.

Everything ended relatively well. And probably neither Vitkevich nor I would ever have addressed ourselves to events long gone by had Solzhenitsyn not discussed these matters in the *Archipelago*, the same *Archipelago* so full of pretensions to being "the voice of truth" and even "the unadulterated truth."

I recall the words of Adam Roitman, one of the personages

in *The First Circle:* "With whom does one begin to reform the world? With oneself? Or with others?"

⟡

The standard quarters in Moscow's Lubianka Prison were not like the "boxes" used for solitary confinement. Although the windows were barred, a patch of sky was still visible. In the evenings, at that time, this patch of sky was increasingly shot through with shafts of scarlet, golden, and emerald hues, with showers of stars and sparks from fireworks glittering like so many fountains. The hollow rumble of cannon reverberated in the cell. It was the sound of salutes announcing victorious battles. Another step toward the West! What of it if a great army had been deprived of an artillery captain? It would reach Berlin without him.

And finally came the day that, even in prison, stood out from all preceding days. Routine was entirely out of whack, including the schedules for breakfast and lunch. Lunch was brought late, and dinner followed immediately afterward. By evening, conjecture became certainty when the roar of salutes continued without letup and the patch of sky itself was blanketed by the endless rapid-fire volleys spat out by the can-nons. It had come—VICTORY!

It was far from the way my husband had imagined he would meet this day when in August of 1944 he wrote to me: ". . . the first instant—the news of the war's end—will be the brightest, the most blissful day in everyone's life."

And in 1946, on the first anniversary of the victory, he wrote in a letter from camp that he remembered how six of the prisoners in Lubianka, already in bed, gazed at the tiny patch of sky above the window, ablaze with fireworks, criss-crossed by the violent beams of the search-lights, rejoicing that they had remained alive and reverently remembering those who had laid down their lives for Russia and had not lived to see this day.

From Lubianka, Sanya was transferred to the Butyrki Prison. He was taken there in a closed van and therefore did not see the brick wall of the fortress that so awed and frightened passers-by. Inside this particular prison, however, it wasn't unbearable. The hours went by in interesting discussions and the inmates shared one life story after another. People who could have been beginning to work with enthusiasm for a faster restoration of a war-devastated country were now, instead, playing chess, reading, reminiscing, telling jokes.

No one was forced to work, and the prisoners were fed quite adequately. "Health Spa 'Bu-Tiur'" was stenciled on the clothes issued to them.

It was here, on July 27, that my husband heard his sentence read out to him: "Eight years in corrective labor camps pursuant to Article 58, Paragraph 10, and Article 58, Paragraph 11."

In the Butyrki he was permitted to write relatives in Moscow, if he had any, and to tell them that they were allowed to bring parcels. There was no particular need for the parcels here, but it was a means of letting someone know you existed. He remembered the address of my aunt Veronica:

Veronica Nikolaevna Turkina

42/14 Malaya Bronnaya, Apartment 10

❧❦

They were *arrested, both of them* were arrested—because of their letters to each other, I thought, holding the batch of envelopes in my hands. The "sirs" had outwitted themselves.

That was the denouement of their meetings at the front, the meetings that had filled our hearts with such joy.

None of the commanders had answered me. Pashkin was silent. Melnikov had not replied to Lida. Only Sergeant Solomin had had the courage to write.

I was working hard preparing for the postgraduate examinations, trying to surmount the sorrow I did not know how to conceal. Everyone knew that my husband had disappeared: the graduate students knew about it; the whole faculty knew, as well as my instructors. Previously I had often paraphrased Sanya's letters for them; at times I had even read excerpts aloud. Everyone sympathized with me.

Somehow my examinations got bunched together. I had to take all three of them at the end of June and the beginning of July.

On June 25 a telegram arrived, marked "Urgent": SANYA ALIVE WELL DETAILS LATER—VERONICA.

Could it be that all our apprehensions were false? To me the telegram sounded optimistic.

Perhaps Sanya had passed through Moscow in some special echelon. Since he was not allowed to write, either he had somehow managed to visit the Turkins on Malaya Bronnaya or he might have asked someone else to tell them his whereabouts.

I revived. Once again life acquired meaning for me.

Two days later a second telegram arrived: SANYA MOSCOW UNFREE ARRIVE OR ORDER TELEGRAPHIC TELEPHONE CALL MY ADDRESS—VERONICA.

Should I rejoice or despair? Did this mean he was under security restriction, or what? Had my premonition been wrong?

I remember the tormenting wait for the telephone call,

and then my aunt's words, which buried all my illusions: "I took him a parcel today."

So that was what SANYA UNFREE had meant.

My heart was breaking. But the brain still worked. Those I had told about the first telegram must be asked to keep silent. I had to forewarn them to prevent the news from spreading around town, so as to avoid any difficulties for myself as the wife of a political prisoner. I had to tell everyone, and believe it myself, that Aleksandr had been reported missing. Thus a deep secret began to worm its way into my life.

I walked down the street trying to hold back the tears. Pity and compassion for my husband filled my whole being. I imagined him, only recently a successful man, full of self-confidence, a brilliant, decorated officer, now deprived of everything, languishing in solitary confinement in a cell with a barred window.

But the next morning I waked with a joyous heart: he *is* alive—nothing else matters!

Those who did not know that my husband had been found were perplexed. One day Shparlinsky, who taught German, met me on the street. I was animated, and I looked it.

"News from your husband?" he asked.

"No," I replied, trying to mask my face with sorrow.

"Such is woman's constancy!" said Shparlinsky, but he was no longer addressing this to me.

Just about that time it became known that Professor Trifonov, my postgraduate adviser, was being transferred to Kazan, where he was to become chairman of the department. Since he felt responsible for me, he offered me three choices: first, to go to Kazan myself—but with the knowledge that he himself would not yet be fully established there, and therefore could not assure decent conditions for me; second, postgraduate work in the Polytechnical Institute at Novocherkassk, where I would have a suitable adviser; finally, I could try to transfer to postgraduate studies at Moscow University, where Professor Frost was head of the Department of Physical Chemistry.

"You are one of Stepukhovich's students. Stepukhovich was a student of Frost. Thus you turn out to be a sort of academic granddaughter."

Could there be reason for surprise that immediately, without any hesitation, I chose the third possibility, the most unrealistic and, one might say, the most fantastic? To Moscow! Of course, to Moscow!

Everything became interwoven into a whole. Everything gravitated toward Moscow. I had to leave at once. I had not yet taken the postgraduate examinations. No problem! I would take the textbooks along with me. Trains were hard to get. I went by plane.

I took with me to Moscow some scraps of the "golden" dress I had worn the day we signed our marriage certificate, so that Sanya would feel that I still loved him as before and that I was ready for anything for his sake.

From Malaya Bronnaya to the subway up to the Byelorusskaya. Then by Tram No. 5 to Novoslobodskaya Street.

Butyrki—essentially a cheerful prison, with mild regulations—gave cold shivers to the wives. They saw the fortress wall, high as four men standing on each other's shoulders, stretching for one full block along Novoslobodskaya Street. They saw the iron gates between two invincible-looking concrete pillars. Moreover, the gates

themselves were most unusual: they slid slowly, me-
chanically, opening and closing their jaws to let the
patrol wagons in and out.*

Relief from suffering lay in incessant activity. Parcels.
Visits to the Information Department of the Ministry of
State Security at Kuznetsky Bridge.

At that time the Department of Physical Chemistry at
Moscow University was in a house, hidden in the recesses of
a yard adjoining the oldest building of the university. There I
found Professor Frost, still young and handsome. All his postgraduate appointments had been filled, but he would raise no
objections if I were to be taken on by Professor Kobozev, head
of the Catalysis Laboratory. Because of illness, Kobozev was
seldom seen at the university, but he could be reached by
telephone and could be visited at home.

I found myself in Nikolai Ivanovich Kobozev's study, beside his antique writing table. After listening to a brief recital
of my academic qualifications, he pronounced me a *tabula
rasa* and suggested that I acquaint myself with his works.

Accordingly, I began to read Kobozev's articles in the
Journal of Physical Chemistry in the reading room of the
Lenin Library. His "theory of ensembles" seemed to me ex-
tremely original and bold.

Later came a visit to the Ministry of Higher Education.
Transfer from one university to another required agreement
of both rectors.

Next I saw Professor Przhevalsky, assistant dean of the
Chemistry Department.

The first contretemps: "You still haven't passed your ex-

---

* From *The First Circle*

aminations—number one. You must change your thesis—
number two. You won't get it in on time—number three!"

Another parcel to Novoslobodskaya Street. I have only one
short letter to Mother from this period of my life:

Dear Mamochka!
  Nothing new. It could happen that that's just what
I'll come back to Rostov with. Yesterday I sent the
second parcel. In addition to foodstuffs, I sent clothing,
a towel, socks and handkerchiefs. Don't forget to register me at the dining hall, and to turn in my work card
to Rostov University.

The "theory of ensembles" fascinated me. I said so frankly
to Professor Kobozev and I asked him some questions about
it that had occurred to me.

"These are the very questions I propose that you answer
yourself," replied Nikolai Ivanovich. Thereupon, on a separate
sheet of paper, he wrote that he agreed to accept responsibility
for acting as adviser in my postgraduate research. It was dated
July 18, 1945.

The first victory!

Professor Frost confirmed the agreement.

After I had mastered the "theory of ensembles," I began
to prepare myself, in subway cars and trolleys, in reception
rooms, wherever possible, for the examinations I was to take
in Rostov.

It was almost on the eve of my departure from Moscow,
at the beginning of August, that I was told in the reception
room of the Ministry of State Security on Kuznetsky Most that
my husband had received a sentence of eight years in correc-
tive-labor camps.

"Will it be possible to write?" I asked immediately. It seemed that this would be my only comfort.

"Yes. With the right of correspondence."

I walked out of the ministry with a mixed feeling of bitterness over the length of the term and joy at the expectation of letters. I immediately called Lida. She had been sharing all my inner ordeals; she had walked with me under the "fortress walls" of the Butyrki, and she had helped in getting parcels to Sanya.

"And we were just going to invite you to the theater to see Priestley's *The Inspector Calls,*" she said in a downcast voice.

"I'll go!" I replied resolutely.

I had to muster an enormous reserve of strength. *Eight years* of waiting lay ahead. One had to get used to living with it.

Back in Rostov I took all three examinations, one after the other. I studied as if inspired. Philosophy fascinated me most of all.

We had chosen a new method of taking examinations. Instead of answering questions, we had to write an essay, whose subject Professor Reznikov gave us a week in advance: "The Physics and Philosophy of Newton and Descartes." We had first to write about each philosopher individually and later draw a comparison between the two, which was by far the most interesting part.

From Lida came a brief communication: "Write to the following address: Moscow, 22, Krasnopresnensky Transfer Point. Well, what else can I tell you? Everything is all right."

Everything is all right? About to be transferred. No longer behind the awesome wall. But where to now?

A letter from Aunt Veronica also arrived: ". . . Saw Shurochka* just once. She was returning with her friend from

---

* Sanya's code name—Ed.

a job unloading firewood on the Moscow River. She looks marvelous, she is sun-tanned, energetic, cheerful, smiling from ear to ear, teeth sparkling! I'm very glad she's in good spirits."

Six months ago I had read the last letter from my officer husband. Now I received the first letter from my prisoner husband.

I opened the tiny triangular letter: four tightly crammed pages written in hard pencil in a minuscule hand.

He wrote that he was confident he would not have to sit out the eight years to the end—all his hopes were pinned on an amnesty, about which there were many rumors. If this amnesty did not materialize, however, Aleksandr felt duty-bound to grant me "complete personal freedom" for the entire term of his punishment. He wrote about his great love for his "beautiful woman" whose youth, since the age of twenty-three, had been spent only in waiting. And now what? Was she to wait until the age of thirty-four? He was also worried about Nikolai, whose fate was still unknown to him.

The future was completely enshrouded in fog, but Solzhenitsyn could not help building plans. In the army he had dreamed that after the war we would live in Moscow or Leningrad. In prison an entirely different dream took shape: after his return to freedom, he wanted to go with me to live in a "remote, but thriving, well-provisioned, and picturesque village"; the village would have to be far away from a railroad, maybe in Siberia or in Kuban, or along the Volga, or even on the Don. We would both teach in a high school there, and during the two-month summer vacation we would travel and enjoy ourselves in Moscow, in Leningrad, in Rostov.

He dreamed of a life that would be happy, peaceful, close to nature, and safe from such "accidents" as the one that had happened to him on February 9, 1945. How this could be combined with my future professorship never seemed to enter

Aleksandr's mind, but at all events he advised me to "by all means hang on to the postgraduate studies."

As regards age, my husband realized after these six months that he had overestimated its importance. He had seen people who wanted to begin a new and happy life at the age of fifty-five, and even at sixty-five.

What did the author of this letter have in common with the author of the 248 wartime letters? And what did he have in common with the Solzhenitsyn of today? How many abrupt changes of direction had I observed in my husband, tireless in my efforts to follow him, trying not to stray from his zigzag course, even if these sudden turns so far were taking place only in his imagination?

Meanwhile, Aunt Veronica, on a regular Friday, went to Krasnopresnensky to deliver her regular parcel. She was not admitted. He had left. Where to they would not say. They told her to come on Tuesday, then on Thursday—and it was not until Friday, August 24, that Veronica Nikolaevna wrote me:

> It's the truth, you were born under a lucky star! Nata-shenka, my golden one, how many envious eyes were fixed on me yesterday! You can calm down. Every Sunday you will be going from Moscow to New Jerusalem. This is a resort place, in a magnificent natural setting; it used to be called the "Russian Switzerland." You will see each other there.

"Russian Switzerland." If you walk left from the railroad station along the Volokolamsky Highway for about a mile, on the right-hand side you can see a small brick factory surrounded by white, two-story houses. This, then, was the camp to which my husband had been sent. He was glad that he had not landed somewhere in the far north, like Pechora or Kolyma, but instead was close to Moscow, in good climatic conditions. But the work was strenuous.

"The work loads of an unskilled laborer are beyond my strength. I curse my physical underdevelopment," my husband wrote.

But Sanya's address was changed before I could leave Rostov to visit him. It turned out that he was back in Moscow proper! The address was:

> 30 Kaluzhskaya Plaza
> Construction Site No. 121
> Moscow 71

I had no word of this latest transfer, and I was absolutely flabbergasted by Aunt Veronica's words when she met me at the railroad station: "Sanya's already in Moscow. You will see him tomorrow. He is waiting."

Few Muscovites walking past the house under construction noticed that several rows of barbed wire stretched above the wooden fence.

High over the masonry, some people were puttering about in dirty, tattered clothes. But construction workers everywhere looked like this, and none of those who walked past this site or drove by it guessed that these were—zeks.*

And anyone who did guess would keep quiet about it.

. . . Buses and trolleys stopped at the end of the railing around Neskuchny Gardens, which was exactly

---

* Prisoners, slang from the Russian *zaklyuchenny*—Ed.

where the guardhouse of the camp was located. It resembled an ordinary entrance gate to any construction site.*

This was the guardhouse that I approached, and I spoke to the guard on duty.

I spent a few minutes alone in an empty, low-ceilinged room with wooden benches along the walls.

I heard the sound of steps. There in the doorway stood my husband, smiling at me! He held his cap in his hands, revealing a shaven head.

This was our first meeting *à trois*—the two of us and the guard.

At that meeting Sanya asked me, "The last letters I wrote you were all right, weren't they?"

Now he wanted them to be that way. The former Sanya had not known how to stop to consider the pain he might be causing others, but there was something about the new Sanya that already made him far more sensitive to the beat of another's heart. He wanted to cross out the lines in his old letters that had insulted me.

The work on his projected big novel about a student at war, *The Sixth Course*, had been interrupted by the arrest, which, without preparation or study, without examinations, graduated Solzhenitsyn to the next, "The Seventh Course." Never again did he express a desire to resurrect the chapters of *The Sixth Course*, which he had once sat over night after night, working till dawn. On the other hand, everything he experienced during this new period of his life, everything

---

* From *The First Circle*

learned in this "Seventh Course," was to form the foundation of almost all his future work, whether stories, novels, plays, or screenplays.

Time (only three weeks in all) had gone by quickly in the first camp, connected to the brick factory in the Moscow suburb of New Jerusalem. Here Solzhenitsyn tried to apply the leadership ability he had acquired at the front. Somehow or other we always strive to continue our accustomed way of living, not to lose our way, or, if we have been deflected, to return somehow to the beaten track.

Solzhenitsyn did not yet understand that his beaten track was bound to fall away from him in the new and unfamiliar terrain. He was trying to transfer the laws and concepts of a world he knew into a totally unknown world, antithetical to everything he had experienced before.

His first attempt to integrate himself into the new world in the role he had enjoyed at the front quickly ended in failure. At the end of August my husband wrote that he had already been bounced from from his command functions and was working on various assignments as an unskilled laborer, but he was still aiming at getting into "some small, comfortable office job or other. It would be wonderful if I could."

One had to live it out. One had to find one's place in this new, incomprehensible world. And indeed, it was no great sin to start out by living a little as a "halfwit."* In his letters to me my husband complained that although he worked only eight hours a day, there were only about three hours left which he could use for reading or any other kind of useful pastime. He

---

* Assistants to the prison guards, drawn from among the prisoners, were called "halfwits"—Ed.

was bothered by spiritual fatigue, his head was clogged up with a viscous jumble of dullness. The noise in the room disturbed him, and there was a lack of books and paper.

But then the optimist in Solzhenitsyn won. He made plans, more plans, and then more. He gave serious thought to studying English; he asked for clean sheets of paper, pencils, pens, ink in spillproof bottles, English textbooks and dictionaries.

But before these requests could be granted, Sanya was already on his way to the construction works in Moscow.

Solzhenitsyn spent a little over ten months in the Mocsow camp on Kaluzhskaya Plaza, which he later immortalized in a play called *The Love-Girl and the Innocent*.

In this camp where political prisoners as well as ordinary criminals, zeks as well as free people, men as well as women, worked side by side, Aleksandr Solzhenitsyn began his life arm in arm with the hero of his play, Rodion Nemov. Both of them were recent frontline men, and moreover they had both been students at MIFLI. Both wore officers' field shirts bearing traces of former decorations and long greatcoats down to the floor; in camp slang they were "caribou," the innocents.

Solzhenitsyn's literary double says: "Citizen Commandant, I am a frontline officer. I have experience of leadership. I will try to fathom the business of production." And he is appointed supervisor of production.

Two tables stand in the small bare room with a door made out of fresh, unpainted plywood. On the wall over each table hang little placards. One reads "Production Manager," the other "Foreman." At the first table, wearing an officer's woolen field shirt, sits the Production Manager. The camp commandant has gone, leaving him as deputy, with instructions to do whatever is necessary to increase labor productivity.

Nemov is quick to find resources. Cut down the routine services of the camp by half. Send all the extra hands from the bookkeeping department, the kitchen, the bathhouse, the hospital, to work.

In a matter of a few days, labor productivity has increased by 8 percent.

"The loafer dental technician, put him on general duty! Tighten the screws on camp services! Redistribute the extra rations!"

But thanks to the joint intrigues of the bookkeeper and the doctor, Nemov is removed from the post of Production Manager.

Solzhenitsyn too was thrown out of the same post. He ceased to be a chief, but for a while he continued to sit behind a desk.

Solzhenitsyn, the zek, spent less than a year in the camp on Kaluzhskaya Plaza, but to him it seemed much longer. He had been suddenly uprooted from his fixed place in life, forced away from the goal he had set himself. From this stemmed his total rejection of what had happened to him. Prison—and the camps that followed it—was perceived by Solzhenitsyn as the most absurd series of events in his life, as a wholly foreign body that had rudely intruded into his being and caused him incessant pain. As with any foreign body, the prison had to be excised from his life. It should remain no more than a vexatious memory.

He was unable to rid himself of this thought. But he himself was powerless, he couldn't eject the irritant. For this reason it was easy for him to succumb to illusions, to become infected with "latrine rumors," of which the prisons and camps were never in short supply. They aroused hope, lifted the spirits, instilled faith. People who found themselves helpless in a situation that changed the course of their lives had no recourse save that of consoling themselves with false hopes.

On May 9, 1945, the Day of Victory, an old Armenian from Rumania in one of the cells of Lubianka Prison was praying: "Oh, amnesty, amnesty, oh, amnesty!" The other five people sharing his cell did not know how to pray, but the same longing for amnesty also filled their hearts. Among them was my husband.

On July 7, 1945, an amnesty was indeed announced. Alas, it did not apply to anyone imprisoned under Article 58. But still the hope, even the certainty, that at any moment the amnesty would come to pass remained with many, and it remained with Solzhenitsyn.

Beginning with the very first of his prison letters, this expectation of amnesty was to lengthen into a long thread of hope. "The basic hope is for an amnesty for those convicted under Article 58. I still think that this will happen." (This was written from New Jerusalem.)

But the November holidays of 1945 came and went, and there was still no amnesty. Faith in it began to fade.

Hope revived in the spring of 1946. "I am 100 percent sure and still convinced beyond doubt that the amnesty was prepared long ago, in the autumn of 1945, and that it was approved in substance by our government," he wrote me in March of 1946. "But then, for some reason, it was postponed."

Here it is curious to note a characteristic expression of Solzhenitsyn's: "I am convinced beyond doubt." It did not take much even then, as on other occasions, to convince him beyond doubt. The main thing had always been that he either accepted something or rejected it. This seemed to be the criterion of truthfulness.

Months passed. New hopes were voiced in almost every letter.

"Today we were waiting very hard," he wrote me on the first anniversary of victory. "Although the rumors were conflicting about the ninth, still, from the ninth on, we are giving it another week or two of time. Such a weariness has descended upon us all, it's as though the newspapers had promised the amnesty for this day, today."

It was only after one and a half years of internment that Sanya confessed, "Whenever they start talking of amnesty—I smile crookedly and go off to one side."

5

Marfino and Mavrino

*F*rom letters and from conversations during our meetings,
a rather full picture gradually took shape in my mind about
Sanya's life in the Marfino special prison, called "Mavrino"
in *The First Circle*.

He worked in a well-ventilated room with a high-vaulted
ceiling. He had a roll-top desk with numerous drawers, the
kind one used to see in offices. It stood next to a window
which was kept open day and night. Beside the desk was a small
block of wood mounted with four electric sockets. A desk
lamp was plugged into one of them, and another was for his
electric hot plate. The third socket was transformed into a

clever electrical gadget for lighting cigarettes, to reduce the wear and tear on the cigarette lighter I had given him; and a portable lamp for illuminating bookshelves was plugged into the fourth. Soon the room was wired for radio with an outlet right next to his working place.

Sanya spent the better part of the day here, from 9:00 A.M. until the end of the work shift. During the lunch break he lounged in the yard, sprawled out on the grass, or napped in the common quarters. In the mornings and evenings he went for walks, most often under the linden trees, which he grew to love. And during his days off he would spend three to four hours outside playing volleyball.

The common quarters were an enormous semicircular room with a high-vaulted ceiling which at one time had been the chancel of this converted church. Double-bunked beds, spreading out as in a fan, were arranged along the radius of a semicircle. On a night table near Sanya's bed stood a lamp which he had fixed so that the light from it fell only on his pillow, so as not to disturb his comrades. Sanya would read until midnight. At five minutes after twelve he would put on his headphones, turn off the light, and listen to a night concert.

Sanya soon came across a new pair of headphones and returned his old earphone to me. As a joke, I called it my "lover," because it always lay next to me on my pillow.

Every morning my husband would awaken to a blast from the headphones. This was the bugle reveille, so familiar to him from childhood, with which the broadcast "The Pioneers' First Light of Dawn" began.

"In regard to the details of everyday life, I have probably never lived with such orderliness as now," Sanya wrote me in September of 1947. Strange as it may sound, his letters of that time exuded a feeling of comfort, well-being, and calm. I hoped that Sanya would remain in this institution on the outskirts of Moscow, adjoining Ostankino Park, for a long time to come—preferably until the end of his term.

The Marfino special prison was an ancient building, formerly a seminary. For a long time it had been used as an orphanage. Shortly after the war, the building had been occupied by the Scientific Research Institute of Communications, which began to assemble a qualified prison labor force. Among the prisoners here were physicists, mathematicians, chemists, and representatives of practically all the scientific professions.

The idea of using the labor of prisoner specialists for scientific research arose back in the early thirties. Professor Leonid Ramzin, a renowned heat engineer, had been sentenced to death at the hands of a firing squad for heading the counter-revolutionary Industrial Party. The sentence was commuted to a ten-year prison term and Ramzin was put in charge of the heat engineering laboratory in the first such special prison. Someone offhandedly dubbed it a *"sharashka."* The expression caught on and, in time, other special prisons also began to be called *sharashki*. The conditions of life in those prisons, and the treatment of prisoners there, were indeed special.

The Marfino Institute specialized in research in radio and telephonic communications. Sanya worked there primarily as a mathematician. His duties, however, did not take up all his time, as anyone who has read *The First Circle* knows. He was able to carve out time for reading and for independent studies.

Sanya's work did not demand any special effort. Rather, it provided a certain rhythm to his life and helped to make the time of confinement seem shorter. His mood was usually equable and cheerful. The daily routine was strictly measured off, and for this reason work days passed very quickly. In one of his letters to me he wrote: "The work so fills time and thoughts that weeks flit by like telephone poles past a moving train."

We know from *The First Circle* that the residents of the *sharashka* were quite adequately fed. Not only that, but the prisoners could buy extra food. Sanya, for example, bought potatoes for himself. Sometimes he boiled them and sometimes he fried them on his hot plate, or took them to the kitchen to be baked in the oven.

In those days parcels were more symbols than necessities, and were timed for our family celebrations. As for things, Sanya had warm clothing and felt boots, but he wrote that he could use a watch. His had been confiscated when he was arrested, as usually happened, but here, strangely enough, Sanya's watch was returned to him.

Sanya tried to use the years spent in Marfino to broaden his knowledge, and to some extent the *sharashka* was a continuation of his MIFLI line of education. Lev Zinovyevich Kopelev, a former assistant professor at MIFLI, later introduced in *The First Circle* under the name of Lev Rubin, was Sanya's neighbor in the laboratory and became his closest friend. The discussions with Kopelev, the range of Kopelev's readings and of his literary interests, had considerable influence on Aleksandr.

The library in Marfino was fairly adequate, and one could sometimes receive other books by placing a request order with the Lenin Library. The problem was not so much finding a good book as selecting what one required from an enormous quantity of available books.

Sanya listed everything he read in his letters to me: Vasily Klyuchevsky, Mommsen's *History of Rome*, Pyotr Struve's *Reader on Ancient History*, books about the history of Western literature, Darwin's essays, Timiryazev's works, and others. He was going to take up languages again, but he had come upon "so much reading matter in the Russian language" ("a full two years wouldn't be enough to digest it all") that no time was left for foreign languages.

As for fiction, Sanya, exercising "the most stringent selectivity," read only the very great masters.

"Am slowly savoring the third volume of *War and Peace* and along with it your little chocolates," he wrote me in October 1947.

Here in the *sharashka* he made a full discovery of Dostoevsky. He directed my attention to Aleksei K. Tolstoy, Feodor Tyutchev, Afanasi Fet, Apolloni Maikov, Yakov Polonsky, Aleksandr Blok. "You don't know them, after all," he wrote, immediately adding in parentheses, "Neither do I, to my great shame."

He read Anatole France with enthusiasm, singling out *The Revolt of the Angels*. In those days Sanya considered him superior to all other French writers and believed he had lost much by not having understood France in his adolescence.

He was also carried away by Ilf and Petrov's books, *The Twelve Chairs* and *The Golden Calf*, and, with his love for classification, he categorized these authors as "the direct heirs of Chekhov and Gogol."

One of the carefully and precisely chosen directions he pursued was the regular reading of Dahl's *Dictionary of the Living Russian Tongues*. Volume III of Dahl came into his personal possession—"It fell like gold from the heavens! Indeed, as the saying goes, the quarry comes running to the hunter!"

Reading the Dahl Dictionary had an enormous impact upon Sanya. He wrote that he used to be "a flat, two-dimensional creature," and then, suddenly, "stereometry opened up" before him.

On one occasion Sanya wrote me that he could visualize himself in the future only as a teacher. On the other hand, when he learned that Ilya Solomin still had some of his books and notes, he asked that Solomin "preserve, come what may, the little volume of poems by Esenin and the notes on the Samsonov catastrophe of 1914—until they can be sent from hand to hand to Moscow, or they might get lost on the way." Did this mean that he had not abandoned his dream of writing a historical novel?

At that time only his closest friends in the *sharashka*— Kopelev and Dmitry Panin—knew about Solzhenitsyn's "secret" occupations. But Solzhenitsyn has not concealed them from his readers of *The First Circle*. In the evening, "surrounded by paraphernalia, under Simochka's glances of concealed love, and to the good-natured mumblings of Rubin," Nerzhin, in minute handwriting, was making excerpts from history books, and jotting down his own thoughts in the smallest hand on the tiniest scraps of paper "that went unnoticed amid his camouflage of officialdom."

Gradually these occupations were to compete with his basic work, so that, willy-nilly, he began to dawdle, or, as he put it, to do some "stretching of the rubber." Sooner or later this was bound to end up badly.

Taking advantage of the opportunity to listen to the radio, Sanya also began to fill in the gaps in his knowledge of music. Never before had music played such a role in his life as during the years he spent in the *sharashka*.

He eagerly shared his musical discoveries with me, and he tried to list for me everything he particularly liked. Once he wrote me that hearing the second part of Chopin's Second

Concerto, the "Dumka" by Tchaikowsky, his beloved "Walpurgis Night," and a cycle of Rachmaninov's symphonies and concerts, had given him special pleasure. He also liked very much the second part and the brilliant finale of Rachmaninov's Second Concerto. On another occasion he wrote that he had listened with pleasure to Tchaikowsky's Violin Concerto, Scriabin's "Waltz," and Khachaturian's "Toccata." A subsequent letter reported his discovery of two marvelous sonatas that he had not known: Beethoven's Seventeenth and Schumann's F-Sharp Minor.

In time, the residents of the *sharashka* were shown movies on Sundays. Sanya had missed movies so much (he had not seen one for more than six years) that he sat through two showings in a row of the first film, *Legend of the Siberian Land*.

What was sorely missing was the theater. True, he once heard a radio performance by the Moscow Art Theater of Aleksei K. Tolstoy's play *Czar Feodor Ivanovich*. "An excellent piece, and what language!" he wrote me. "Will it ever be possible to see this on the stage?"

He asked eager questions about my impressions of the theater: about the Moscow Art Theater, about Leo Tolstoy's *Resurrection* and how its stage version had come off. He himself was skeptical about it: "Old Man Tolstoy was opposed to any such adaptations."

"I can just imagine," he exclaimed ironically, "if he were made to sit and listen to the opera (!) *War and Peace*—it's precisely in *War and Peace* that he poked fun at the conventionality of the operatic art." He could not have imagined in those days that Prokofiev's *War and Peace* would in time become a jewel of the first stage of our country. Twelve years later, Solzhenitsyn himself would be hearing it, in a state of

continuous rapture, at the Bolshoi Theater, with Mstislav
Rostropovich, then a friend of both of us, on the conductor's
podium.

Finally, Solzhenitsyn also found the people with whom fate
had thrown him at the Marfino Institute objects of very
serious study. If someone's life story struck him as unusual, he
retained it in his memory, upon which by that time he had
had to begin to rely.

"It is natural that men outstanding in intellect, education,
and life experience," as Solzhenitsyn described them, "should
make a big impression on a young man who was, generally
speaking, provincial, not having seen very much before then."
It occurs to me that their influence can also be traced in the
development of that peculiar system of views which was to find
its fullest expression in *Archipelago*.

The internment situation has its own historiography and its
own attitude toward politics, its own myths and its own
hagiography. Here the "sciences" are of necessity not written
but based exclusively on oral tradition. The role of documents
and quotations must be played by tales of "old-timers," "eye-
witness testimonies," even rumors and anecdotes.

Thus, for example, for decades there circulated around
the camps the tale about the miraculous rescue of Mikhail, the
Czar's brother, and there were "exact" versions of Stalin's
biography. Then there were stories about seeing in prison the
Socialist Revolutionary Doria Kaplan, who had made an attempt upon Lenin's life, and who had been executed in 1918,
and discussions of the Octobrists Party, which had disappeared
long ago.

From their "bell tower," the "outstanding" men, now outside of events, continued to evaluate those of more recent date,
such as the victory over Germany and the postwar tension in

Europe, from the point of view of the import such events might have for their own fates. One of the basic criteria for arriving at an evaluation was, inevitably, its divergence from the official or the commonly accepted version. Anyone who expressed thoughts coinciding with what could be read in an ordinary book or a newspaper, or with what could be heard on the radio, could be certain that he would be scornfully dismissed as a slow-witted novice, a primitive, if not something worse. And it almost seemed that the more a point of view deviated from what was commonly accepted by those "in freedom," the more it could be trusted, and thus the more its author's prestige increased in the eyes of those around him.

To take one such example, Aleksandr firmly believed—and wrote about this subsequently in *Archipelago*—that every one of the Soviet prisoners of war who had been in Hitler's death camps was, upon repatriation, dispatched directly to a camp behind barbed wire. When I told him of some people who had gone through German captivity and returned to freedom, Solzhenitsyn found this very strange. He regarded such cases as exceptions. War prisoner images glide through the pages of all of Solzhenitsyn's books.

I read *Archipelago* as I typed it. I have a definite opinion about this book, and I am somewhat perplexed about the reaction to it in the West. There *Archipelago* has been accepted as the solemn, ultimate truth. This should not be so even from a formal point of view. The book's subtitle is "An Experiment in Literary Investigation." In other words, Solzhenitsyn does not suggest that this is historical research, or scientific research. Obviously the method of research in the arts and the method of scientific research are based on essentially different principles. The material for *Archipelago* was in multiple ways furnished to Aleksandr Isaevich through conversations he held in the *sharashka*, in transfer prisons, and in the camps. The information he received bore a folkloric and, frequently, a mythical character.

The central purpose of *Archipelago*, as I saw it in the process of its creation, was not to portray the life of the country or even to depict daily life in a camp, but, rather, to present a collection of camp folklore. Moreover, at the time I became familiar with these notes, they were not destined for publication. This was merely "raw material" which my husband was planning to use in his *future* productions.

Nevertheless, in the West, on the basis of this unscientific analysis, there is a tendency to draw conclusions bearing on global problems. I am left with the impression that the significance of *The Gulag Archipelago* is being overestimated and wrongly appraised there.

I would say that in *Archipelago* the dominant feature of Aleksandr Isaevich's character once again came to the fore: his will to believe in what he would like to believe in, in what accords with his preconceptions. Aleksandr has always believed unqualifiedly in any tale that did not contradict them.

Here I should like to remember Professor Kobozev. What amazed me about him was that he loved any results that did not accord with his theory. They would stimulate his thinking, force him to make new assumptions, new hypotheses, to search for new paths in science. On this level Aleksandr Isaevich seemed to be his complete opposite. Directly he came upon an idea, he was interested only in confirming it. The rest he simply brushed off.

It was an enormously satisfying experience for me when I found a confirmation of my thoughts in a signally important book by Professor Kobozev, *Research in the Realm of the Thermodynamics of the Processes of Thought and Informa-*

tion, which was published in 1971 by the Moscow University Publishing House.

> The most common properties of reality are regularity and irregularity, definiteness and indefiniteness, chaos and order. . . .
>
> Every event is dual. It contains within itself a certain vectoral, directed component and a certain Brownian, chaotic component. . . .
>
> The Brownian component plays a dual role. Not only is it the component of irregularity, it is also the *component of search.* The Brownian dispersion, the deviation of the organism from the designated vectoral trajectory (perhaps even designated erroneously) causes it to collide with new elements of reality that could be useful to it, i.e., they report a variety of information to it. . . .
>
> A certain moderate dose of the Brownian dispersion and the receipt of additional information at its expense is as essential as a marked degree of directedness.

Kobozev leads us to the conclusion that the object must come into contact with a sufficient variegation in the elements of reality so as to combine this with a directedness of its action—and that is how life and work ought to be structured, whether for a scientist, a writer, an artist—in short, for any human being who happens to be a creative personality.

Ivan Denisovich Shukhov was punished for having been a prisoner of war. The investigator did not want to create unnecessary difficulties for himself and simply recorded that Ivan Denisovich was a "spy" without specifying concrete details of the crime. Evidently Solzhenitsyn had more than once heard from people, who may have had something to conceal, the working hypothesis that the very fact of their having been prisoners of war was sufficient grounds for conviction.

Incidentally, it is precisely the "outstanding" men who, rather than emerging as full-dimensioned living personages, merely flit through the pages of *The First Circle*. The main characters, on the other hand, are merely those who were closest to the author behind those walls. They include Nikolai Andreyevich Potapov, known to us by that name in *The First Circle*, as well as Nerzhin, who was one of the "founders" of the *sharashka*; then there were Dmitry Mikhailovich Panin (known as Sologdin in *The First Circle*), who arrived there soon after Solzhenitsyn; Lev Kopelev (Lev Rubin); and the artist Sergei Mikhailovich Ivashev-Musatov, renamed Kondrashev-Ivanov in *The First Circle*.

When in 1948, by some tortuous, mysterious path, Nikolai Vitkevich made his way from the remote region of Inta to the selfsame Marfino Institute, the friendship between the one-time "sirs" was not renewed. On the surface they were friendly —they chose beds next to one another, each knew what the other was doing, they shared the day-to-day routine of living— but there was no longer that all-embracing friendship which had reached its apogee at the front.

The books Sanya read, the films he saw, often aroused a stream of associations that weighed on his conscience. Once he wrote me about his impressions of Pushkin's *The Mermaid*. He was deeply upset by the first scene, in which the prince behaves so heartlessly toward the miller's daughter. Sanya sank into thought about her and could not help but feel it was "an agonizing reproach to myself." He reproached himself for his cruelty to me, and although this cruelty "was motivated by other reasons and assumed different forms," he was still ready to pass judgment on himself: Did this make it any less cruel? And he asked sadly, "Indeed, must one live through a life ten times, from beginning to end, so that it is only on the eleventh time that one could live through it as one should—without regrets, without agonizing over one's past actions?"

Solzhenitsyn began to become susceptible to the suffering of others. After seeing the film *Michurin* he sent me two letters voicing sympathy for the wife whom the biologist had tyrannized. He felt "infinitely sorry for Michurin's wife," whereas four years previously "I would not have been able to comprehend so deeply the whole tragedy of her life as I comprehend it now."

In another letter, discussing another movie, *The Village Schoolteacher*, which had also impressed him, he interrupted his comments to return to the film about Michurin. He asked whether he had written me that he had "sat through some of the scenes in Michurin—the fate of his wife and the history of their relationship—with an incurable, irredeemable—or is it still redeemable?—anguished ache" in his heart.

Sanya found a justification for his unhappiness in the mellowing of his character, the thawing of his heart: "Years go by, yes, but if the heart grows warmer from the misfortunes suffered, if it is cleansed therein—the years are not going by in vain." . . . "Perhaps, if it should happen some day that I start living happily, I will become heartless again? Although it's hard to believe, still, anything can happen."

How I wish that Solzhenitsyn's own apprehensions had never been confirmed! That he had not also turned in for incineration, along with his prison garb, the highest, noblest impulses of his soul!

Solzhenitsyn did not as yet have a religious faith, but he had superstitions. Since he was a mathematician, his superstitions had a mathematical twist. He believed in the mystical significance of numbers. In the case of dates, of course, their significance must be confirmed by many recurrences, and such confirmations had already occurred in his life. Although the dates were not always happy ones, they were nevertheless significant and marked turning points in life. For him the recurrent dates were 9, 18, 27; that is, dates divisible by 9. Sanya even went so far as to predict that he would probably die at "9 + 18 + 27 = 54 years of age," that is, in 1972.

Over those years Solzhenitsyn learned to live differently from before in still another respect. At the end of 1949 he wrote me that his mood was even-tempered, that there was nothing left "of the former hurried-convulsive attitude toward life." At last Solzhenitsyn was living *in harmony with time.* Thoughtless actions, rash decisions, heartlessness were now, he felt, things of the past.

Alas, this "hurried-convulsive" attitude toward life, to which Solzhenitsyn bade farewell in prison, would gradually return to him as the prison-camp years receded. In Kok-Terek, where he was to live in exile after his prison term, he remained at peace with himself. But later, in the period of our "quiet existence" together, manifestations of his former attitude became discernible. And with the arrival of fame, it was difficult to say what there was more of in Solzhenitsyn's life: hurriedness or convulsiveness.

❧

Probably the happiest time during our years of unhappy separation was that short period when we both became "Muscovites" again, the two years from the summer of 1947 to the summer of 1949.

We exchanged letters constantly and somehow each keenly

felt the life of the other. Sanya took all my affairs to heart, gave me advice, encouraged me. And I felt that everything I was doing I was doing not only for myself but also for him. It was so pleasant to cheer up Sanya with my little triumphs: an examination passed with flying colors, a successfully read test lecture, a complimentary remark by a professor. The letters warmed us and sustained our feelings for each other, and our meetings became celebrations in themselves.

When a forthcoming meeting was announced to Sanya, he would surrender himself wholly to the "pre-rendezvous mood." Once he wrote to me that in the evening, after work, he walked in the yard for a long time, gazed at the moon, imagined the conversation that was about to take place between us, and thought about how I, too, was probably thinking about him "more than about the dissertation."

I was not the only one who worried about appearances before our meetings. Sanya wrote me once that after washing his hair he walked around "in a towel rolled up like a turban so that my hair would set properly by tomorrow." He wrote that he would polish his shoes and shave the evening before.

I had hoped that our meetings would take place in Marfino itself, and was bitterly disappointed when the permission I received for the first meeting after Sanya's transfer to Marfino specified the Taganka Prison.

I arrived at the prison a little early and was told that the meeting would take place in the club for prison employees. The club entrance faced directly on the street. Several women were already standing there. After a while, it was not some kind of "fearsome machine" that pulled up but, rather, a small-sized bus from which our husbands stepped out, quite properly dressed and not looking a bit like prisoners. Each of them went straight to his wife, before we all entered the building. Sanya and I, like all the others, embraced and kissed each other and quickly pressed our letters into each other's hands, thus escaping censorship.

Just as one is drawn to share a heavy sorrow, so too one wants to share a great joy. And so I went to visit Lida and Kirill. They had been married for three years by then. After talking my heart out, I listened to music; they had several marvelous records. And when I returned to my hostel in the Stromynka district, I found a telegram from Mother saying that her vacation leave had been granted and she would soon come to visit me. I was in seventh heaven. How could one possibly feel unhappy when one had such a husband, such a mother, and such friends?

While waiting for that first meeting, I had made the acquaintance of Evgeniya Ivanovna Panina, the wife of my husband's friend Panin, and we later made several trips to Ostankino Park together. The address of the Marfino Institute was not supposed to be known by the prisoners' wives, and so when we wandered around it we had to be extremely cautious. But it seemed we were not cautious enough. We once had to run for our lives.

We were walking leisurely along the highway overlooking the little recreation yard of the *sharashka,* which had a volleyball net stretched across a special court, and every now and then we would peer at the volleyball players. Suddenly a man walking behind us caught up with us, asked to see our passports, and told us to come with him. I replied that this was not wartime, when one was obliged to carry a passport on one's person, and I was slow to follow him. When he moved a safe distance away from us, we suddenly turned off in the direction of Ostankino Park and then took to our heels.

After that we were even more careful. But we could not

totally deny ourselves the pleasure of "calling on" our husbands. Instead of walking along the highway, we would creep
into the little yard adjoining the *sharashka,* wait for the lunch
break, and then, through a crack in the fence, observe the zeks
in repose: some were simply strolling or lying on the turf,
others were playing volleyball. Squinting, we tried to seek
out our Mitya or Sanya.

Once, on our way back, we were caught in the rain. We
waited it out in a little house not far from the *sharashka,* in
which lived a young family: a husband, a wife, and a child.

"Here it is, real happiness!" I said to my companion.

It turned out that both the husband and the wife worked
in Marfino. We did not conceal from them that our husbands
were there. "Don't worry about them," the woman consoled
us, "they feed them well in there."

Evgeniya Ivanovna and I talked about many things during
our walks and meetings, and we turned out to be alike in many
respects. Both of us had read in the very first letters from our
husbands that they offered us freedom, feeling that they should
not wreck our lives, but neither of us considered taking advantage of this.

In this regard, neither Solzhenitsyn nor Panin was an exception. Almost all the men who received long-term prison
sentences considered it their duty to state in the very first letter,
or at the very first meeting: "Don't wait for me. Divorce me
and marry again." And most often the wives would reply on
the spot that they had no such intention and that they would
wait. But after this, different men would begin to behave in
different ways. Some demanded fidelity as a part of the waiting.
Others dropped the subject and it was never discussed again.
Still others tried to think of the best alternative arrangement
for the period of waiting.

Probably the correct approach to this problem would have been to discuss nothing, not to advise, not to touch on this matter either in letters or during visits, if any took place, and to leave everything to the natural course of life.

Our husbands approached this matter rationally. Panin agreed that Evgeniya Ivanovna should wait for him, but only on the basis of unfailing loyalty. Solzhenitsyn filled many pages on the theme of whether to wait or not to wait, and how to wait, offering sundry advice, often mutually exclusive, and ending with the admission that he had got himself "entangled in contradictions," that he did not know any more "what is best."

I replied to Sanya that we must "stop chewing on this theme," that my loyalty to him was to his credit, not mine, that I could have started building life anew if my feelings for him "had not overwhelmed me for the rest of my life."

Evgeniya Ivanovna also considered her husband an extraordinary man.

Neither she nor I was capable of duplicity. What distinguished us both was that wholehearted love which, one might say, did us a disservice. But the most important thing was that we loved our husbands very much and we believed in their feelings for us. This determined our conduct. The awareness that we were loved gave color and light to our lives from a source concealed from everyone, visible to no one but ourselves.

Just as for zeks the most important thing was to hold out until freedom, so the greatest dream and the overriding goal of loving wives was to wait out the days for their husbands. How could it ever have occurred to these women that their future would not be in any way determined by whether they waited or not? It seemed that everything depended on oneself, that

one needed only to wait it out. That the husband would return
—and then everything would be marvelous.

For the woman, the husband's release was seen first of all
as his return to her, to the family. For the husbands, however,
their release would mean not only return to the family, to the
wife. This was only a particle of what would be restored to
them. Their release would also signify a return to the life
which for the woman had been a familiar daily routine, but
for the husbands, who had long forgotten it, would be a whole
new world that would overwhelm and inundate them with
waves of fresh, long-absent impressions and even temptations.
They would encounter many practical difficulties in the initial
period, but they would also find much that would appear
attractive.

So the husband would return to a wife who had aged over
these years and who had lost her past appeal. All the tears and
suffering she had undergone would have left their mark on her
face, cast over it a shadow of weariness and grief. But on the
streets and at work, young, joyful, smiling women's faces would
flash across his line of vision, and he would be drawn to them
involuntarily, as though to a life that was beginning anew for
him. It would be fine if he had a kind of heart that would not
permit him to abuse the one to whom he owed so much. It
would be fine if he had an integrity that would leave no room
in him for any feeling other than the one that, at one time and
intending it for the rest of his life, he had given to this woman.
But what if the man possessed neither the one nor the other?
Then the wife's feat of endurance would lie as a heavy burden
on the man, and it could happen that sooner or later (better
for her if it were sooner!) he would cast off this burden.

How life was to turn out for Evgeniya Ivanovna and me
will be seen in the pages to come. But what of the wives of

other Marfino zeks? The wife of the artist Ivashev-Musatov would wait in vain. Kopelev would live with his family for only a little over a year after his release. Potapov's wife, Ekaterina Vasilyevna, of all the wives known to us, would be the only one truly rewarded for the long years of waiting. Such a warm-hearted, truly collected person as Nikolai Potapov not only could never have left his wife, who had loved him faithfully and devotedly all these years, but would simply have been incapable of starting to love someone else. After living through those years of waiting, Ekaterina Vasilyevna would later travel with her husband from one construction site to another. While she provided him with all the homelike comforts, she managed at the same time to become an excellent dispatcher for him, always knowing where he could be found at any given moment, and helping those who telephoned to get in touch with him. Aleksandr Isaevich and I would observe her in this role with our own eyes in the summer of 1962, during the construction of the Votkinsky Hydroelectric Station on the Kama River.

I also know of other examples of a happy married life between people who were reunited after a separation forced on them by imprisonment. I will relate only one case, which has no resemblance at all to the one just described.

Here too there was a devoted woman, there was the concern, there was the waiting, but there was not a trace of a monastic life, and there was no faithfulness in the fullest sense of the word. However, the dream of waiting it out to be ultimately reunited with her most beloved, who had temporarily released her from her vow, had never left her. ("Temporarily" in this case turned out to be ten years!) She felt that she had to preserve herself for him, and that she also had to live a full life—even though her real, her true life lay ahead, with her

Andrei. Meanwhile she would be doing everything possible to make his life easier. Parcels were sent, and Vera Ivanovna packed them carefully, sparing no effort, just as if she were "decorating a Christmas tree." Letters were written: "I love you more than anyone in this world. The moment you call me I will abandon everything and come to you!" But he couldn't very well call for her while he was behind bars, and in the Potma camps not even visitations were allowed. Vera Ivanovna was living with another man when she learned that her husband, after having served half his term, was being "released because of illness." And she, still a young, beautiful, energetic woman, left at once and brought back with her to Moscow an old, sick man, frightening to behold—a skeleton.

But could anyone have doubted for a minute that this woman, from the very start of his imprisonment, would have abandoned Moscow and gone to stay in Potma if only she had been permitted to live there with Andrei? We can form an idea of her boldness, resourcefulness, indeed her daring, from her behavior upon her arrival in Potma, where she went as soon as she learned that her husband was there. After being refused permission to meet with him, she bravely walked to the prisoners' work site. By showing Andrei's photograph, then asking for him by his surname, she finally managed to reach the spot where her husband was working. He was sitting on the roof of the barracks making repairs. She pointed to the man she wanted to see, as the astounded zeks looked at her, their eyes popping. Her Andrei turned around and was struck dumb at seeing before him, inside the forbidden zone, his Vera.

On another occasion, at home in Moscow, she went to the telephone and placed an order for a connection with Potma. She gave the proper number of the detention camp and de-

manded that so-and-so be paged. Probably there was no prece-
dent for a situation such as this. Her husband was in fact
called to the telephone. "Andrei?" "Vera, you?"

They lived together for sixteen years after his release. In a
real sense, only death could part them. One day, shortly before
he died, Andrei said to Vera, "If I had my life to live over, I
would marry you again."

Generally speaking, however, there are as many fates as
there are people. And in each case it is the confluence of a
great many causes and circumstances, a combination of many
forces, that determines the vector of life, the life of two human
beings.

❧

My mother spent all of August 1947 with me in the
Stromynka hostel. Relieving me of domestic chores, she en-
riched my diet, so to speak, and in general spoiled me in a way
that only she knew how to do. During this time I got stronger
and made considerable progress with my dissertation.

Still, I had to face up to the fact that I could not possibly
meet the deadline, which was September 1. It turned out that
I would even have to do a little more work in the laboratory.

I managed to get the deadline postponed to November 1,
and as a result, both my Moscow residence permit and the
right to live in the hostel were extended for another whole
year. But even this proved far from enough.

I could not find a way to solve the problem of how to remain at the university. From November 1 on, I would face
destitution and unemployment. My postgraduate grant would
end, and I had neither money nor ration cards. I tried in every
way to economize, and that is why, on the critical date of
November 1, I still had a reserve of two loaves of bread as

well as some coupons I had saved. But one could not live this way forever. Later I bought myself a ration card, which helped me skimp along until the middle of December. Who knows what might have happened then? On the very same day I used up my last coupon, the entire rationing system was abolished once and for all.

I marked the last day of my postgraduate life by accompanying Shura Popova, one of my roommates, on the piano at a party given by the members of the History Department on the anniversary of the October Revolution. I went to the party directly from the dressmaker, wearing a new dark green cashmere dress, with full sleeves in the Japanese style (I had somehow obtained the cloth on a coupon). Everyone liked the dress very much. Now if only the dissertation were finished, I had something to wear in which to defend it.

I was writing the dissertation with everything I had, and, thank heaven, it was coming along well. I sat over it through all the November holidays; I did not even go to see Lida. But in return, right after the holidays, I had about a hundred pages for Professor Kobozev to look through. Meanwhile, I continued to write and learned to do mechanical drawing all over again. I had not done any since schooldays, but now I had to do all the illustrations for the dissertation.

I was in such feverish haste that it was no wonder I was extremely absent-minded about everything else. Sanya noticed the enormous number of mistakes I was making in my writing; either a word contained extra letters or else some letters in it were missing. I even skipped entire words in my letters to him. But it didn't stop there. I also had to explain to Sanya why he had suddenly turned into Aleksandr Davidovich and why certain sketches were being demanded of him!

I had written Sanya's address on a postcard that should

have been addressed to Aleksandr Davidovich Stepukhovich, under whose guidance I had completed my course work at Rostov University and who was now an assistant professor at Saratov University. Stepukhovich needed some special glass apparatus for his doctoral dissertation and I was helping him order it from the university's glass-blowing department.

During one of his regular trips to Moscow, Stepukhovich, interrupting his story with Homeric gales of laughter, reproduced the scene that took place when he received his missent postcard. Stepukhovich, knowing that my Sanya had "been reported missing," was more than a little surprised to find out that I had apparently entered into a very tender relationship with yet another Sanya!

By the end of November the whole dissertation was in Kobozev's hands. He approved what he had read. There were almost no comments.

I worked feverishly. I rushed. After all, I was still unemployed. If I was not accepted at the university, I could still find some sort of job for myself in Moscow, but right now there was no time even to breathe. And Mother still had to continue bailing me out.

Before the New Year I turned in the dissertation to Kobozev for the last, final check. It was all typed, including the tables and the appendices. All that remained to be done was to get it to the bindery and, meantime, photograph the drawings.

In my elation I bought a small Christmas tree, to the general rejoicing of all my roommates. We decorated it with anything that was handy. On the top was a silver stopper from a bottle of wine; below was a bagel, a garland of sugar cubes, carrots, tangerines, some pretty buttons, onion bulbs, drawing curves and T squares, pencils, fountain pens and cigarettes. The base was covered with cotton wool, sprinkled with silver. It turned out to be simply charming.

It was around this tiny tree that we greeted the New Year.

After the food rationing was abolished on December 17, my life took an abrupt turn for the better. Everyone breathed a deep sigh of relief now that there were no more ration cards. You could buy anything you wanted, whenever you wanted, and wherever you wanted. You could dine in any cafeteria.

Soon after the reform I dropped in on my aunt Veronica, on Malaya Bronnaya, and they fed me as I had not been fed since 1940.

In January I was taken on as a scientific worker in Kobozev's laboratory. My wages were less than the postgraduate grant, but still, some money was dribbling in. I asked Mother not to help me any more and to start taking better care of herself.

Kobozev was in no rush to give me a new assignment. First of all, I had to complete everything connected with the dissertation. Photocopies of the drawings had to be inserted in each of the four bound copies. An article on the same theme had to be written for a scientific journal. A lecture had to be delivered at a forthcoming conference.

At the beginning of April the dissertation, nicely bound, was delivered. Soon thereafter it was in the hands of the two scientists who were assigned to challenge it. I almost managed to rest as I waited for their reactions. I was even able to start reading books, to make music with Shura, and to play a little chess.

The comments of the challengers were received at the end of May. My defense was scheduled for the end of June.

One unresolved problem remained: What should I wear at the defense? By this time it would be summer, after all, and the cashmere dress simply wouldn't do. Of course it was Mother who again came to the rescue when she managed to get a piece of gaily colored crêpe de Chine for me. I adored the dress when it was made, but I was afraid it wasn't exactly the thing to wear for the defense; it seemed slightly on the frivolous side. Why not wear my new cream-colored, rib-knit sport dress instead, and save the silk one for the banquet my laboratory colleagues were arranging for me?

My mood was one of elation. For some reason, I had no fears whatsoever. Only three days before, my husband had wished me a successful defense! We had seen each other again in the Taganka Prison on Sunday, June 20, after a very long lapse. (Visitations were getting more and more difficult.) That was the day he told me the startling news that Nikolai Vitkevich had arrived at the *sharashka* of Marfino from faraway Inta.

On the day of my defense, June 23, the temperature stood at ninety-five. Moscow had not experienced such a heat wave in seventy years, or so said the radio. Nevertheless, Professor Kobozev did not cancel his plan to attend my defense. This was the first scientific conference of the Chemistry Department that Professor Kobozev had attended in thirteen years. For this reason my defense turned into a day of celebration for our whole laboratory. The big chemistry auditorium was packed. They were not so much interested in listening to me as they were in taking a look at the mysterious Kobozev.

Stepukhovich was present—he had delayed his departure from Moscow five days for this occasion—and there were three other ex-residents of Rostov. I had done postgraduate work with one of them under Professor Trifonov; I had worked with the second, a woman, at Rostov University; I had begun my studies under Trifonov with the third; and now we were working together under Kobozev. These four people somehow provided me with a sense of continuity between my present and my past, and this was particularly pleasant. Lida and Kirill also came, as did Veronica with her husband Ruslan.

Academician Balandin was the chairman of the conference. In my "secondary ensembles" he saw a resonance to his "multiplets." He could not help being impressed by these "secondary ensembles," inasmuch as one of them contained six atoms, which was a characteristic of "multiplets"! I was told later that I had spoken well and had answered the questions briskly and to the point.

The results of the secret balloting were twenty for, two against. As consolation for the two "no"s I was told that I owed them to the fact that Kobozev's theory of ensembles had met with some opposition. Thus the negative votes were aimed not at me but at him.

I was showered with bouquets after the results were announced.

The department dining room was reserved for the banquet. We had two rooms at our disposal. In one we ate and drank to our hearts' content. In the other we danced. Besides the homemade mulled wine prepared by my colleagues, there was also champagne, which Lida and Kirill brought.

The memory of this day, which my friends and colleagues turned into a really grand and festive occasion, will remain with me for the rest of my life.

The celebration of my candidacy continued in the Stromynka. Shura prepared "straws," a thin, crisp pastry sprinkled with powdered sugar. Another roommate, Zhenya, the archaeologist, baked a pie.

Shura inherited my dissertation table. It was now her turn to tackle her thesis.

After my summer vacation, I received a new research subject from Kobozev. Three students were assigned to work under my supervision and I immersed myself in the project with pleasure.

During the summer I played a lot on my Becker piano and

decided to resume my musical studies with Undina Mikhailovna Dubova at the Moscow University Club. Since I was not
tied down to a strict schedule at the laboratory, I managed to
combine chemistry with music rather successfully. I needed
only to run across Herzen Street to get from the laboratory to
the club, where I practiced piano daily.

Soon I began to play in amateur concerts at Moscow University, and in addition to the university itself, our amateur
group performed before the most varied audiences and in the
most varied places: in the House of Scientists, in the Hall of
Columns of the House of Unions, in the Kremlin Club, in the
Theater of the Soviet Army.

Once I played in the University Club for a meeting of the
electoral district. The concert was organized jointly by the
Moscow Conservatory, the drama school, and the amateur
groups of the university. Thus, on the same day, on the same
stage, and on the same piano, works of Chopin were performed
by the well-known pianist of that time, Yakov Zak, and by
Natalya Reshetovskaya! Zak played two waltzes in the first section, I played two Etudes in the second. For the first time,
Undina Mikhailovna kissed me in congratulation and told me
that conservatory teachers who sat next to her in the audience
had said I played better than their own students.

Undina Mikhailovna had been a pupil of Heinrich Gus-
tavovich Neuhaus, and from time to time she would show off
her charges to him. I too had to play for Neuhaus in his apartment, in a room where two pianos stood side by side. Neuhaus
made some comments about my musical temperament and expressed surprise that a "chemist" could play that well. As I
remember, he advised me, in one passage of Chopin's Twelfth
Etude, to make an abrupt transition from loud to soft at the
point of passing from one bar to the next, instead of effecting
a diminuendo.

When I had attended the Rostov Music Academy I was used to being praised for my technique. Now everyone was emphasizing my temperament. Kirill remarked, "Natashka suffered a little and then began to play well!"

That year Kirill and I were carried away with playing four-hands piano. Most of all we played Beethoven, his symphonies and the "Egmont" Overture. We especially loved the Second Movement of the Seventh Symphony.

Sanya was thrilled when he learned about my return to music, which he had always considered my true calling. He even saw in it the "real meaning" of my stay in Moscow, because it was only here, it seemed to him, that I could come out onto "the big road of music." "Become a great, brilliant pianist in these years!" he urged me, without stopping to consider my abilities.

Everything, it seemed, was turning out successfully. Then, suddenly, all-out security restrictions were clamped on the entire laboratory, without regard for the kind of research being conducted, whether open or classified. There were new forms to fill out, forms I dreaded.

Professor Kobozev was hospitalized in the Skilfosovsky Institute with a bleeding ulcer. The physician treating him chanced to be Kirill Semyonovich Simonian. Kira at once arranged for me to visit Nikolai Ivanovich.

Kobozev was not the only person to whom I turned for advice. I consulted my relatives, my closest friends, and even a lawyer. But I had to decide for myself. When Sanya and I got married, we chose to retain our own surnames. Now this gave me an option: should I declare my relationship with Sanya? Or should I conceal it?*

---

* EDITOR'S NOTE: Soviet law provides for three alternatives in registering a marriage. The wife may take the husband's surname,

SANYA

By another coincidence, during those same days Evgeniya Ivanovna Panina was asked to fill out the same special form. We talked, we racked our brains. What was one to do? In the end, both of us saw only one way out—to fill out the form and apply for a divorce.

For several months afterward I lived in a state of painful uncertainty, finding consolation only in music. "I live and breathe music," I wrote my mother.

At the next visitation—it fell on December 19, again at the Taganka Prison—I told Sanya that I had to obtain a formal divorce from him or lose my job.

In a New Year's letter to my mother, Sanya wrote that he was very glad I had stopped being stubborn and finally decided to divorce him. "This is the correct, the sober thing to do; it should have been done three years ago," he concluded.

When the New Year 1949 came around, I met it with Lida. As I sat at the festive dinner table I was suddenly struck by the realization that all the members of our one-time "fivesome" were right here, in Moscow. But we were not all greeting the New Year together—and the separation would go on

---

or the husband may take the wife's. Or each may retain the surname used prior to the marriage. This last was the choice that Solzhenitsyn and Reshetovskaya took in 1940. In the fall of 1948, when she filed court papers declaring the dissolution of their marriage, Reshetovskaya was able to refer to Solzhenitsyn as a *former* husband on the form she had to fill out. Thereafter, the case lay dormant because she did not pursue it. In 1952, she once again instituted proceedings in the divorce case. At that time, divorce procedure required filing a declaration in court, placing a divorce announcement in the newspaper, and accepting the judgment of a court examination of the case. The placing of a newspaper announcement of a divorce was abrogated toward the end of the 1950s.

much longer. I felt so sad that I couldn't control myself and broke into bitter tears.

Kirill stopped me. He told me very severely, "You chose to bear your cross—now bear it!"

More time passed, and finally, to my great joy, I was cleared and admitted to secret research.

One success followed another. During vacations I went with the university amateur group to Leningrad, where I had never been before.

Daily concerts alternated with visits to museums. We performed on various stages including those of Leningrad University and the Vyborg House of Culture. I wrote Sanya a letter as I sat in the greenroom of the House of Culture among my innumerable mirror reflections. We were a success. So was I; I even played an encore.

In answer to my letter "with snapshots of Leningrad and with a fountain of impressions about Leningrad," Sanya wrote that he was especially glad I had now developed "a professional *présence* in making appearances" and that I had made my way to Leningrad, not simply as a tourist but "as a victor among the instrumentalists."

Sanya began to believe so much in me as a pianist that he advanced the slogan: "Less chemistry and more music!" And he started to build fantastic plans about how I could bypass the conservatory and become a professional performer. Sanya's tendency to erect fantastic mental constructs without taking due account of reality lent comical overtones to his enthusiasm. For example, he asked me whether I couldn't take part "in a regular competition of performing artists and musicians," and in the next sentence exclaimed, "Oh, how I would like to live to see the day when they start having you play for the radio!"

This wish, however, turned out not to be so improbable as it sounded at the time. On April 26, the eve of our ninth marriage anniversary, I played in a concert in the Soviet Army Theater for delegates to the Tenth Congress of Trade Unions. I had written Sanya about this concert, and for some reason he got the idea that it might be broadcast over the radio. It was only after I had played Chopin's Twelfth Etude that I learned that the concert was indeed being broadcast. It turned out that many of my friends, acquaintances, and relatives had heard it. But most important, so had Sanya. "Somehow I just knew it. It was just as I thought it would be, Chopin and not Rachmaninov," he wrote me the same evening. "I listened, and my heart was pounding. How I wanted to catch a glimpse of you at that moment!" Nevertheless, he felt in his soul "as though we had seen each other on the eve of our anniversary."

How does one explain such a coincidence? April 27 was our favorite day in the year. If Sanya and I could not get permission to meet on that day, I still tried to go to him, even if it was just to leave a little parcel or take him a gift of something. And this time, on the eve of April 27, it happened that I played Chopin for him.

This concert led to my reconciliation with my uncle, with whom I had quarreled three years before because of my husband. At that time I had asked him to read Sanya's statement in which he requested a mitigation of his sentence. I had expected some help from my uncle, some advice. Instead, Valentin Konstantinovich loudly began to berate Sanya, calling him a little brat.

Now, all of a sudden, my uncle's second wife, Nina Andreyevna, made an appearance in the judges' room during the rehearsal for the concert, and after the performance she sought me out.

One day in May I visited the Turkins. A richly laden table awaited me. There was a freshly fried chicken, and ham and crayfish. There was cheese, halvah, and even beer. Among his other accomplishments, Professor Turkin was, after all, a great gourmet and also an excellent cook.

After our long-standing quarrel, my uncle reached out to me with special tenderness and solicitude. He had listened to me play over the radio and had liked the way I played, he said. They were proud of me. He even invited me to spend the summer with them in Tarusa. Thus peace was fully restored.

My "concert season" was crowned by two events: I received the first prize in a university competition and I was awarded a two-week stay at Moscow University's House of Rest, in Krasnovidovo, for July.

Present in the audience at my last appearance on the Moscow University stage was Antonina Vasilyevna, Nikolai Vitkevich's mother. She had come to Moscow to see her son. It seemed incredible, but it happened that she and I were given appointments to meet with our "sirs" on the same day, May 29.

Antonina Vasilyevna and I arrived for the visitation together, both of us with flowers.

This meeting took place in the Lefortovo Prison. Walking up a narrow corridor and fastening my eyes on the wide-open doors on the right-hand side, I caught sight of Nikolai, standing upright by the table. He stood behind the light, and it was just a split second, but I was still able to discern that he was now sporting a mustache. Nikolai, too, managed to see me in time, and to recognize me.

For Sanya and me, there was a special, radiant quality about this meeting. I had not been allowed to see him since December, when I had told him about the divorce. It was only in the letter written on the day of our meeting in May that my husband confessed to me that in December he had returned to the *sharashka* in a mood of "darkest despair." This time, on the other hand, he returned to Marfino in high spirits, carrying a bunch of lilies of the valley in his hands, and feeling "an amazing sense of relief."

All the next day, Monday, May 30, I was filled with complex feelings. I conducted experiments in the laboratory, I thought my own private thoughts. I was delighted when a fellow pupil of Undina Mikhailovna called me up and said that he happened to have an extra ticket for Sviatoslav Richter's concert. There was little time left. I quickly cut short my experiments and ran off to the conservatory.

The next day Kobozev's deputy for the Economic Section reproved me and gave me a warning notice, claiming that the day before I had left the premises without shutting the *fortochka*, the small, hinged windowpane used for ventilation.

Quite possible—but after all, I was far from the last one to leave that night. There were still people in Kobozev's office, and since they had to go through my laboratory to get out, whoever was the last to leave should have closed the little pane. Moreover, wasn't the whole window barred anyway?

The reply I received was that in the evening the laboratory had been visited by representatives of the Special Section, who took a very serious view of all of this.

I went at once to the head of the Special Section. Yes, he had the report in question. I explained the entire situation to him. He heard me out in silence. In the belief that I had convinced him, I calmed down and went back to the lab. Apart from routine matters, I was also working very hard on a philosophical paper I had to read at a forthcoming faculty conference on theory.

Suddenly, on June 6—completely shaken, not believing my own eyes—I read an order dismissing me from the university "on the grounds of a slipshod attitude toward work, expressing itself in the fact that, upon leaving the laboratory, she left ajar the window and the door"!

The Moscow University lawyer at first received me with an attitude of distrust. But later, when I made a sketch of the room arrangement and explained that I could not have locked the laboratory from the outside without locking up my co-workers who were still inside, he concluded that I had every right to protest the order and to demand reinstatement.

In a state of terrible anguish I went to see my professor, who was now hospitalized in the Uzkoe Sanatorium, just outside Moscow. Nikolai Ivanovich had not been aware of my misfortune. When I told him, the man who had always given me support in the past, who had considered me a member of his scientific school, this time advised me that I should leave the university. Whatever the outcome, I would not be allowed to work in peace there, and since he was seldom in the laboratory because of his illness, he was in no position to protect me. It stood to reason, however, that I should not leave with the damaging, vicious formulation of charges against me. He would take care of that.

The order was reworded to read that I was released "in accordance with a personal request."

What was I to do? From whatever evil that comes crashing down on us, we must try to extricate as much as possible of what is useful, if not good. By this time I had realized that I missed the work of teaching, which had so captivated me during the war. Perhaps I could win a competition for a teaching job in one of the institutes in the suburbs. Or perhaps even in Moscow itself. There were still three months to go before the academic year began, so there still was time to submit applications and take the exams. But how was I to live through the summer without any income? Would that mean that I must turn to my mother again? But I could not write her about everything as it really was. I had no right to worry her needlessly.

Accordingly I wrote her that I had decided to change to teaching as of the fall. I told her that in order to do so I had to leave the university for the time being: I was at the point of finishing my research assignment, and if I were to undertake another project they would not let me go by fall. Only material considerations disturbed me.

Mother sent me the money without even waiting for my next letter, in which I requested a loan. And at this point, out of the blue, a music student turned up. At least a tiny income was assured.

Losing no time, I started to make the rounds of institutes near Moscow—but either there were no vacancies or I was late after all. I also betook myself to the Ministry of Higher Education to find out which institutes were announcing competitions for the kind of position that would be suitable for me.

A newly opened Agricultural Institute in Riazan seemed to afford the most practicable and tempting prospect. It was quite close to Moscow, which meant close to Sanya and to Undina. The opening was for an assistant professor. Moreover, from my experience in Taldy-Kurgan, I knew how interesting it could be to work in a newly founded institution where the teaching staff was in the process of being assembled, where, at least in the initial period, the faculty were close-knit, where the work demanded a great deal of initiative, energy, and a total dedication of one's resources.

The documents were submitted. Among them was a very

favorable reference from the university and a brilliant recommendation from Professor Kobozev. I was almost certain I would be selected.

Forced to take a "vacation" against my will, I threw myself into music with even greater fervor. I even made an appearance on television somewhere during that time.

What if I were to switch to music? But how? Undina Mikhailovna thought I would have a good chance of enrolling in a conservatory. But would this mean becoming a student all over again? And being a burden to my mother once more?

Sanya was enthusiastic about the idea of my trading in chemistry for music. He believed that if one were to stay in Moscow for music's sake, then one perforce must find "an absolutely exceptional, but a quick and sure-fire method of becoming a professional," by-passing the conservatory. "You will say there is no such way," he wrote, "but it must be found." Once again fantastic constructs. But life is life. One has to work. One has to earn an income.

In July I spent my two weeks in the House of Rest near Moscow, the vacation trip I had won at the same university that had dismissed me.

I was not the only one who had won the trip for successful amateur performances. There was a great deal of music-making, singing, and even amateur whistling. I struck up an interesting acquaintance with a pianist who had just graduated from the Moscow Conservatory. His advice was by all means to enroll. This pianist, Oleg Boshnyakovich, now has many admirers.

A pleasant group was formed. We shared music, walks along the Moscow River, heart-to-heart talks, tomfoolery. And for a time, concern about my fate receded.

I wrote Sanya from the House of Rest that I would probably be working in Riazan. After thinking it over, he was gladdened by the news. When I got back to Moscow I found a letter in which he wrote that inasmuch as I was not a native Muscovite, it was just as well that I was leaving the city, because "it would have taken many more years of huddling in corners and leading a semihomeless existence." He thought that I would be better off peacefully settled in some quiet town. Then Mother could move in with me, "together with the aunts and the whole ménage, including the piano."

But there was as yet no decision regarding the position I had applied for.

I resorted to translating articles from English. I began tutoring the daughter of a well-to-do family to meet the entrance requirements in chemistry at an institute. All this was interesting and the pay was not too bad.

A large package arrived from Riazan. Alas, it was my documents. I had not been accepted for the opening.

I went back again to the Ministry of Higher Education. Once more I made the rounds of various departments. Gorky University was looking for laboratory assistants in my specialty. Professor N., chairman of the department, happened to be at the ministry at the time. He was prepared to take me despite my admission that "I am divorcing my husband, who is imprisoned." And this assistant's position in Gorky presupposed access to secret research.

On August 19 I arrived in Gorky, and on the same day I was taken on the staff as an assistant in the Department of Physics and Chemistry. But only as of September 1. If the rector had taken me on as of the day of my arrival, then I would have stayed in Gorky. This seeming trifle determined my future.

I was guaranteed a substantial salary and expenses; I was

promised a room on the campus after a certain period of time. Meantime, I had a single room in a centrally located hotel on the waterfront, with a wide window that opened on a view of the Volga. All this seemed like a fairy tale after the Stromynka hostel. The solitude did not bother me; instead, it permitted me to experience even more fully the present, which was attractive because of its novelty, and the future, which seemed to hold out the promise of something.

I threw open the window. A gossamer pre-evening mist stretched along the Volga. Here and there a few lonely lights began to glimmer on the opposite shore. A fresh, cool breeze wafted in from the river. Then the lights were joined by others, and the river itself was gradually dotted with the moving lights of ships slowly sailing by. I was overwhelmed by a feeling I had not experienced for a very long time, the feeling of inner peace.

I visited the university, I prepared for the laboratory practice course, I reread the two volumes of Aleksandr Brodsky's *Physical Chemistry* that Sanya had used to further his self-education at the camp on Kaluzhskaya Plaza. I strolled around town; I treated myself to *pelmeni*, meat dumplings. I went to the movies. And I was in no hurry to go to General Delivery to ask for my mail; it was too soon, after all, to expect replies.

It turned out, however, that a telegram from friends in Moscow had been waiting for me for several days: RIAZAN OFFERS POSITION ASSISTANT PROFESSOR.

Once again I was thrown into confusion. It was not only the question of an assistant professorship, although giving lectures was far more appealing than conducting laboratory practice sessions. Riazan was closer to Moscow. And most important of all, there I would not need to bother at all about getting a divorce!

I sent a telegram to Riazan, but it was too much torture to wait for a reply. I shared my news with the chairman of the department. Did giving lectures appeal to me? Well, then, he would let me lecture a special course.

I asked for permission to go to Riazan.

"But you have to prepare for the lab course. There are only a few days left before classes begin."

"But I've been accepted on the staff only as of September 1."

There was nothing the professor could say against that. I could go.

In Moscow no one in the ministry knew anything about changes in the openings at the Riazan Institute of Agriculture. I called Riazan long-distance, and was told that the position was open, I was being awaited. Still, I urged, I'd like to see things with my own eyes. "You are welcome."

I arrived in Riazan on August 27. I liked the town. In those days it was a quiet place. Ancient monuments and landmarks were preserved. The Institute building, a former boys' secondary school, followed the strict lines of classical architecture.

The director led me to the apartment of the chairman of the Chemistry Department. When we broke in upon him he was preparing lectures in physical chemistry. He was delighted that I would take them over. The reason the position of assistant professor of chemistry turned out to be vacant was that the person who had been selected did not want to accept the post of assistant professor; his aim was to be head of a department.

I was assigned a cheerful white-and-blue room right on the premises of the Institute.

On September 1 I was back in Riazan. A carter loaded my belongings onto a wheelbarrow and, at a slow pace, we proceeded across the town to the Institute. The Riazan of those days had only two very ancient buses, and residents preferred to walk rather than wait for them.

I let the deputy director know I had arrived, and soon a note from him was delivered: "Your lecture is scheduled for tomorrow at 10:00 A.M." The signature, Naumov, was the same as the one on the telegram to Moscow that had offered me the position.

I was tired. I wanted to sleep, but I could not permit myself. The lecture had to be ready by morning. Thank goodness I had been making notes on it all through the journey. This would be an introductory lecture, so there was much that had to be said. Lying in bed, I finished writing up the lecture in a sleepy, scrawling hand.

Although Naumov had arranged a substitute for me, just in case—an assistant professor of anatomy—there was no need for it. Present at my lecture, in addition to the 150 students, were the department head, the dean and several other faculty members. This baptism by fire took place in the Assembly Hall of the Institute, a former court of justice. The speaker's rostrum adjoined the stage. It was here that the jury used to pronounce the verdict: guilty, not guilty; execution, pardon.

"You'll do all right. Well begun, half done," Dean Bolkhovitinov told me after the lecture.

This was how Riazan came to be an integral part of my life, and to remain so for a long time to come.

Sanya wrote me: ". . . for the first time, after all these years, a marvelous awareness has come upon me that somewhere, out there, a family home awaits me. . . . There is no home for me without you, home is only where you are the mistress of the house—there, where you live."

Thus in life some things happened differently from the way

they did in *The First Circle*. I was the first to leave Moscow, and not my husband, who was a Moscow "resident" for almost a full year longer.

The timespan of the action in the *Circle* is approximately midway between the date of my departure from Moscow and that of Sanya's departure from Marfino. While the scope of people and events is broad indeed, the timespan is restricted to only three days and three nights: from five minutes after four on December 24 until the end of the lunch break of the Marfino zeks on December 27, 1949. Thus, Aleksandr Isaevich's desire to condense time in life was transferred also to his creative work. No time vacuums! At first, the reader shares Stalin's sleeplessness. Next, he stays up with Yakonov—who meets the dawn by the Church of St. John the Baptist (the church described is actually the one named after the martyr Nikita). But the same dawn is being observed by Sologdin, who was already up and is now standing by the saw-horse to cut logs. On the following night it is Rubin who is suffering from insomnia. At half past three in the morning the reader parts with him, only to land at once in Roitman's bedroom. He, too, is unable to sleep, because of the torments of a guilty conscience. He just then hears the full-bodied sound of a single, heavy stroke of the wall clock—announcing the same half past three in the morning.

One passage in the *Circle* typifies Solzhenitsyn's method of dealing with reality versus fiction. For years his brain would shelter "precious ideas" for which he sought a place in his productions. These "precious ideas" could be individual thoughts or concepts or merely autobiographical episodes. For example: Once, little Sanya Solzhenitsyn had voiced some crude anti-Semitic remarks and offended a fellow schoolboy, a Jew. A stormy discussion of this event took place at a class meeting called for the purpose. Several little boys got up to speak and severely berated Sanya. Thirty years later, Solzhenitsyn incorporated this little scene into *The First Circle*. It goes without saying that Oleg Rozhdestvensky (this is the name Sanya gave the protagonist—himself) is portrayed in touching colors, whereas his persecutors are depicted as fiends from hell. It is curious to note that thirty years later these little boys were identified by their real names. He had avenged himself, albeit with some delay.

Roitman was not among them; here we do have a fictional hero. And even though the "victim" Solzhenitsyn could remember this episode after thirty years, it is doubtful that a real Roitman would have exhibited such a flash of exceptional memory and then suffered a bout of insomnia because of a guilty conscience, all the more so since the righteousness of the young anti-Semite is somewhat doubtful. But to Solzhenitsyn this seemed an appropriate place for an inserted novella.

And evidently without any further reflection, he repeated his infantile reasoning thirty years later. How so, why can't I call a person a "yid" if we have freedom of speech? The thought that his opponents also might have the freedom to express their attitudes about this does not enter the mind of either the boy or the writer. If Solzhenitsyn was criticized, it meant that this was no longer freedom, but "persecution"!

Another example: In 1950, in his first letter after leaving the *sharashka*, he wrote me from the deportation point in Kuibyshev that on May 19 he had left Marfino "completely unexpectedly as far as I'm concerned." He had not thought this would happen so soon; he had wanted very much "to live there until next summer." (It was customary to exclude prisoners from secret scientific work some time in advance of the expiration of their term.) "Step by step, circumstances were speeding up the departure and making it inevitable," he wrote, and in the same breath assured me that he had left "on perfectly good terms."

In another letter, written not to me but to someone else, he attributed his departure from the *sharashka* to the fact that he had simply stopped working. That is, he had been "stretching the rubber," even though he suspected that the upshot would be "a transfer to other places." It is natural that at some point he would have started to occupy himself more with his favorite pursuits than with his assigned duties.

Even in his conversations with me Sanya never depicted his departure as a consequence of some heroic deed, or of a stubborn refusal to carry out a task assigned to him. However, I know of still another version of what actually transpired, which Solzhenitsyn reported to Leonid Vlasov: he had been the victim of a quarrel between two superiors who "would not share him between themselves," and the senior of the two, who had the authority, summarily sent him off "to that torment."

These apparent searches for the best explanation of his departure from Marfino revealed a basic characteristic of Solzhenitsyn—a tendency to pass for both a hero and a martyr—which was then only in an embryonic state but which gradually came to occupy a central place in his life.

To be sure, a prison, no matter how easy the conditions of confinement may be, remains a prison. And even the relatively unburdensome life in the Marfino *sharashka*—with work in one's field of specialization, with books, music, with Rubin's pranks, arguments, intellectual discussions, with butter at breakfast and meat at lunch—nevertheless unfolded within prison walls, and its evenness, monotony, and atmosphere of predestination were oppressive. So the work that was his duty was gradually neglected. More and more attention and time were devoted to his "own affairs," thus creating the impression that he was lazy and a malingerer. And ultimately this led to Marfino being replaced by Ekibastuz.

❧

An ebullient, active life, quite unlike my two years in Moscow, began for me in Riazan. I gave two lecture courses and conducted laboratory practice sessions—so I had a very tight teaching schedule.

This required a lot of preparation. One day in October I wrote Sanya, "Today is Sunday, I am sitting buried in physical chemistry, preparing a lecture on thermodynamics which I must cover thoroughly in the space of two hours—which doesn't make it any easier; on the contrary, it's much harder."

Nevertheless, I still found time to participate in amateur performances. I accompanied a student choir conducted by an assistant professor of anatomy. The anatomist had a good tenor voice; we rehearsed operatic arias with him and performed at holiday parties. I did not play solos as I felt this would not be a proper thing for someone in my position to do.

Sometimes it happened that I had to prepare my lectures at night, especially when they came on successive days and we had evening rehearsals. I don't remember a single occasion in my student years when I had to stay up all night studying for an examination, but here I was continuously complaining to Mother that I was sleeping only four or five hours a night, and that once I was up till four in the morning preparing a lecture. Six months after I went to Riazan I was promoted to head of the Chemistry Department.

At first I lived alone. Later Mother came to stay with me for her vacation, and Aunt Nina stayed with me the whole winter and spring.

Little by little my favorite personal possessions moved in with me from Rostov. They were mostly old things: an antler for hanging towels; a white ink well that could be turned up-side-down without spilling; a cast-iron ashtray; pretty frames for photographs; a small antique writing desk.

Although Moscow was close, I did not go there often—there simply was no free time. I managed to get there only once in a while, on holidays. Having been transformed from a poor relation into a "rich" one, I now went to the Turkins' as a gift-bearing guest, with apples or fresh mutton from Riazan. I also visited my Stromynka girl friends who had not yet bidden farewell to the university.

Sanya wrote me a letter that winter which upset me very much. He advised me to pursue the divorce proceedings, which had been started a year ago, to the end and to stop writing to him. He spoke of "this illusion about family relations which long ago ceased to exist." He declared that my well-being was more precious than these nonexistent relations, and that he did not want to cast the slightest shadow on me. However, he breathed a sigh of relief when in my return letter I totally rejected this advice, which had been prompted by reason while at the same time his heart "shrank with fear—could this possibly come to pass?"

I, on the other hand, was happy precisely for the reason that, because I had traded Moscow for Riazan, I could now drop my divorce case and continue to be wife to my husband not only in my heart but also under law.

Sanya and I saw each other only once during my first school year in Riazan. Our meeting was in March, and it took place in the Butyrki Prison, where he had been brought for the occasion. It was a joyous meeting for us both, but toward the end a cloud suddenly passed over it: Sanya said he regretted that we had no children together. This saddened me and I replied that in all probability it was already too late to think about this.

6

With
Ivan Denisovich

*T*he east-bound trains moved along at the regular speed. But the occupants of the cars, with gratings on the windows, had their own stops to make, pre-fixed for them alone: the prisons of Kuibyshev, Cheliabinsk, Novosibirsk.

The prisoner transport was unhurried, but then the prisoners themselves had nowhere to go and no reason to rush. Thus Sanya had time to get interested in the life histories of those with whom fate had thrown him into deportation.

Sanya's mood could in no way be compared to the inner despair that had marked the summer of 1945 when he was still a "green" prisoner. Now he did not have such a frighteningly enormous load of prison years ahead of him. He felt at ease in the prisoner car and, in general, adjusted to the ambience. He looked well and strong, and he was relatively pleased with the last three years of his life. Of course the rest of the prison term might turn out to be quite onerous—"Where will I land and what will the situation be?"

They were fed during the period of travel and in the stops at the transit prisons. The food, of course, was not as good as in the *sharashka*, and Solzhenitsyn tried to stop smoking to compensate for this deficiency.

The first acquaintance with Asia: for the first time he could admire the "majestic beauty of the Urals"; for the first time he was traveling past the "EUROPE-ASIA" obelisk.

Finally the prisoners arrived at their destination, the Ekibastuz camp, in eastern Kazakhstan. It was a bare, desert area with few buildings. In the middle of August 1950 a life began there for Sanya which resembled the one he had led five years before, when he was in the camp attached to the brick factory in New Jerusalem.

But if at that time he had tried "convulsively, hurriedly, and with errors compounded" to improve his situation, to "arrange for more intelligent work," now he was inwardly prepared for anything and was much less demanding of life. The "antlers" were broken off now, but the "deer's legs" still performed for him. How he would manage himself here no longer seemed a matter of importance to Sanya. "Let things take their natural course," he wrote in one of his first letters from the camp. And he confided to me that he had begun to believe in destiny, in an inevitable alternation between good and bad luck, adding that "if in the days of my youth I boldly attempted to influence the course of my life, to change it," now "this often seems like sacrilege."

And indeed there had been a time when everything came

A group of ninth grade students from School 15 in Rostov-on-Don, 1935. Standing in the center are Nikolai Vitkevich and, with the striped tie and very blond hair, Aleksandr Solzhenitsyn. Sitting in the center are Lida Ezherets (with pigtails) and Kirill Simonian. At right is their literature teacher, Anastasia Sergeyevna.

Taisia Zakharovna
Solzhenitsyn
(nee Shcherbak),
Aleksandr's
mother.
This photograph
was taken in
the late '30s.

The author
as a student in 1937.

Aleksandr
Solzhenitsyn
and Natalya
Reshetovskaya,
just married,
1940.

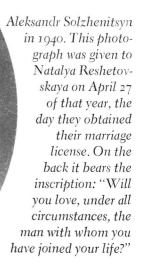

Aleksandr Solzhenitsyn
in 1940. This photo-
graph was given to
Natalya Reshetov-
skaya on April 27
of that year, the
day they obtained
their marriage
license. On the
back it bears the
inscription: "Will
you love, under all
circumstances, the
man with whom you
have joined your life?"

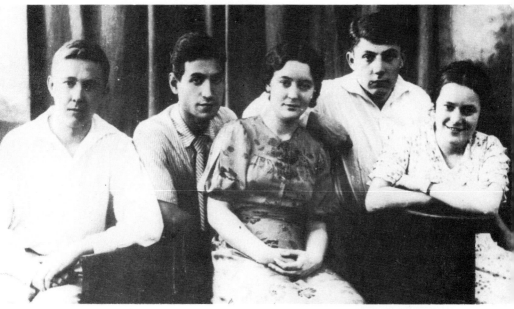

"The Five" in May 1941.
From left to right:
Aleksandr Solzhenitsyn,
Kirill Simonian, Natalya
Reshetovskaya, Nikolai
Vitkevich, Lida Ezherets.

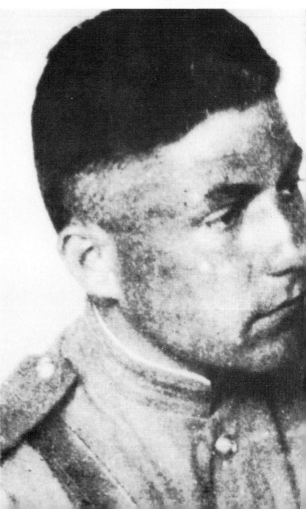

Nikolai Vitkevich
and Solzhenitsyn (right)
in 1943.

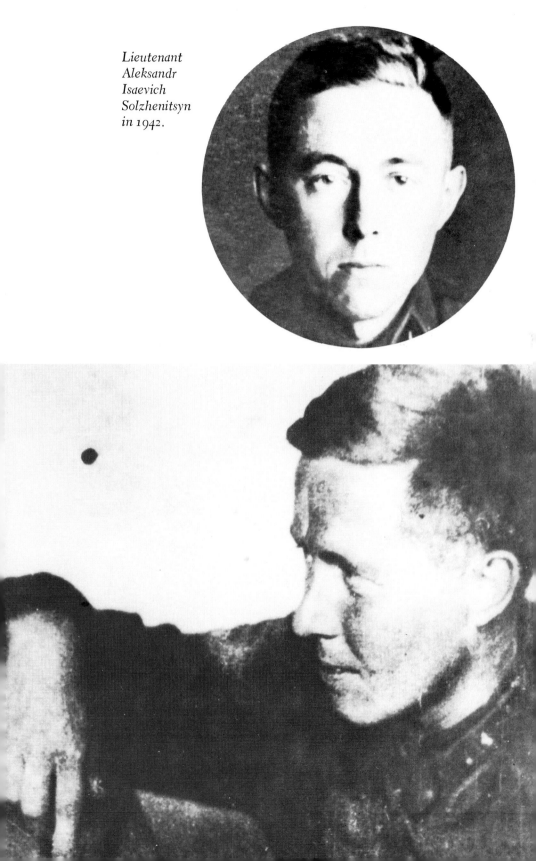

Lieutenant Aleksandr Isaevich Solzhenitsyn in 1942.

Husband and wife
in a brief reunion at the front,
in the spring of 1944.

Solzhenitsyn in exile
at Kok-Terek, 1954.

Riazan.
In a garden on Kasimovsky Lane,
in the spring of 1957.

Solzhenitsyn on his first visit
to Riazan, December 31, 1956.

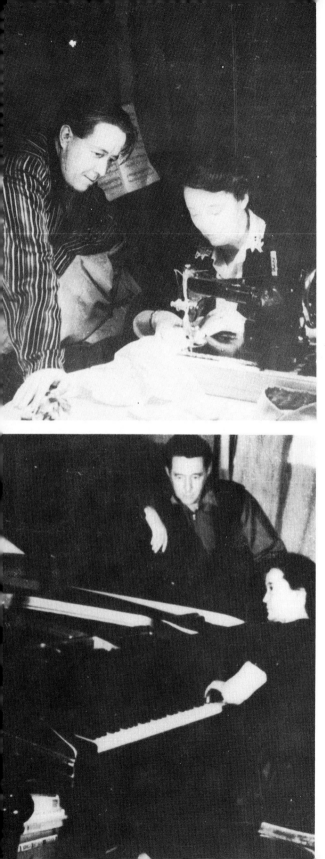

Solzhenitsyn
and his wife
at home
in Riazan, 1958.

At home
in Riazan, 1958.

The Solzhenitsyns near their home on Kasimovsky Lane, Riazan, 1958.

*Solzhenitsyn setting off
on his cycling tour of
the Riazan and Moscow regions, 1960.*

*At Lake Baikal
in the summer of 1962,
during their trip
through Siberia.*

Solzhenitsyn and Reshetovskaya sawing firewood in Riazan, 1961.

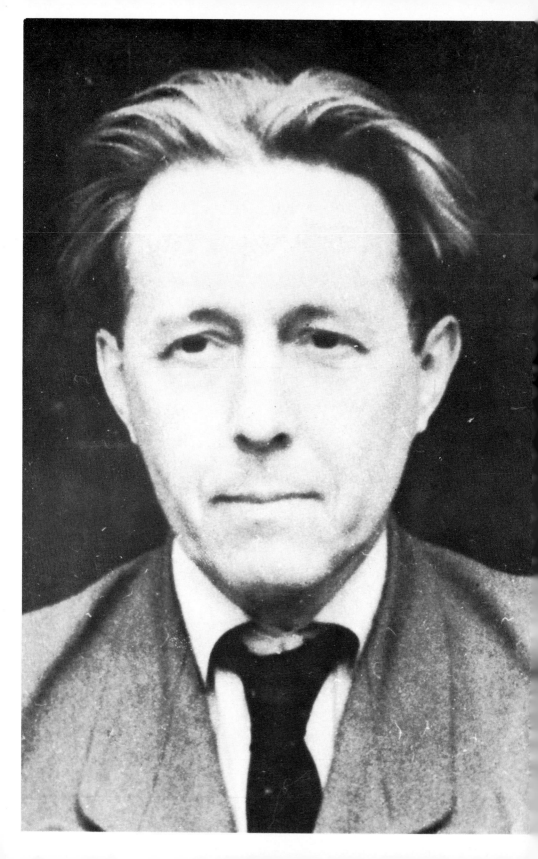

Solzhenitsyn working
at Solotcha in
the spring of 1963.

The author took
this photo of Solzhenitsyn
in the fall of 1962.

Solzhenitsyn and the author
at Solotcha, 1963.

easily to Sanya. All he had to do was lift a finger. At the front, even though Captain Solzhenitsyn was eager to know the people, he lacked the requisite capacity. The people who were entrusted to him, his soldiers, apart from performing their direct military duties, also had to serve their battery commander. One copied his manuscripts, another made his soup and washed his mess tin, a third contributed touches of intellectuality to the crude life on the front. It could have seemed to him that these people did not live independent inner lives of their own.

But here he suddenly understood that in the given circumstances he was but a human being like thousands of others, with their meager, almost insignificant capabilities. This was the source of his new resignation, of his "what is to be will be."

Sanya was again a common laborer, as once before in New Jerusalem. "The abrupt change in the way of life has made me extremely tired," he wrote. Nevertheless, he hoped gradually to get used to it, to pull himself into the routine. During one "last gasp of August" he became more suntanned than he had ever been before. He was quartered in the Ninth Barracks, he wrote, boxcars equipped with double-decker bunks.

My state of mind in many ways and for many years had been determined by what Sanya wrote to me, what he said at our meetings, what I read in his eyes. In the past few years a certain rhythm of life had been established which had made provision for meetings, even if only once every so many months, and the intervening time had been filled with remembrances of the last meeting and anticipations of the one to come.

Up to now, only time, nothing else, had separated Sanya from me—the gulf of time between one meeting and the next, between one letter and the next. And somewhere in the distance the mind's eye could see the letter that would come from the discharge point, and the meeting in freedom.

But when the first letter came from faraway Ekibastuz, I learned that now we were not to see each other at all. Now there would be no meetings, and letters would arrive only twice a year. Now we were separated not only by time but by distance.

Gradually, a feeling of another kind of remoteness was added to my awareness of this geographical expanse. It was explainable not only for the reason that Sanya's letters were infrequent, but also because they were written by a person expressing moods entirely different from those I had known, by a Sanya who was completely new to me.

I knew my husband as a person who had actively arranged the events of his own life. But he was now conveying the idea that he could, of course, apply for employment at Rybinsk, where he had worked as a mathematician before. Probably they would take him back. But—was it worth it?

This would have been so unlike him before. Instead of a stormy will, passive waiting: what is to be will be. Resignation . . . submission to destiny . . . fatalism. "Perhaps this faith in destiny is the beginning of religiosity?" He answered this question directly after posing it: "I don't know. It seems to me I'm still far from having reached the point of believing in a god."

Although the word "god" was still not capitalized, it nevertheless began to crop up with increasing frequency. In a letter of December 1950 he wrote, "Haven't been ill here yet, thank god, and may god grant that no illness befall me in the future."

Solzhenitsyn's "precious ideas" appeared repeatedly in his letters as well as in his productions. One of these thoughts had been born at the front. It was carried around in his head for all those years until it finally found its consummate expression in *The First Circle*, in Chapter 34, "The Muted Tocsin."

> In her letter Nadya writes: "When you come back . . ." But that was the whole horror of it, that there will be no *return*. It is impossible to *come back*. . . . One can only arrive *anew*. A new, unfamiliar person will arrive, bearing the name of her former husband, and she will see that the man, her first and only one, for whom she had waited, withdrawn into herself, for fourteen years—that man is no more. He has evaporated, molecule by molecule.
>
> It would be fine if in that second life they would once again come to love one another.
>
> But what if they shouldn't?

When I first read, in one of my husband's letters from the front, excerpts from his "The Fruit Orchard"—a short story in the form of a letter from a husband to his wife—saying that there would be no "return," but only an "arrival," and that I too would find a different person coming home to me, I did not believe this.

A feeling of great oneness in our inner beings was sustained in me from 1945 to 1950, and it even seemed to intensify. It was sustained by letters, by our rare meetings, by our inextinguishable love, about which we never wearied of writing to one another. No matter how rare our meetings in these years, not a single time had I encountered a person who seemed in any way a stranger to me.

But gradually a completely different person began to appear in those rare letters from Ekibastuz. This person could still arouse great sympathy, but he could no longer maintain to the same degree that inner glow without which my life lost its color.

For me Sanya increasingly became an unreal figure; he turned into a distant, beloved image—an image evoked by memories, an image evoked by hope, but an image nevertheless.

I continued to write to him about once a month. I wrote about work, about my involvement in amateur groups, about reports I had delivered either at a philosophy seminar or in the newly organized chapter of the Mendeleyev Society, where I spoke on my thesis subject. I wrote that early in 1951 I would be receiving one or two rooms in a new house which our Institute was building for its teachers and that I would then be able to move my piano over from Riazan.

❧❦

A torrid summer in Ekibastuz was followed by a dry, warm autumn. Suddenly the area was hit by a cold wave that sent the thermometer down into the thirties, and overnight it was winter. And what a winter! Never before had Sanya experienced temperatures of more than forty below zero.

Sanya worked as a bricklayer throughout that fall and winter. "A physical way of life has always been of benefit to me," he wrote. He said that he was not getting sick, and that he looked fine. The only trouble he was having was with his mittens, which had "literally burnt out" at work. He owned two pairs, his own and a government issue, but he barely managed to keep either pair patched up.

Work on the construction of the heat and power plant was proceeding briskly. Sanya, to be sure, was not completely proficient at his job, but even he could become so involved in the work that on occasion he did not notice that it was quitting time.

My husband assured me that he was in no sense despondent. His spirits were high. He was looking forward to "many good things in the future," and this anticipation eased his "life of today."

The request to send him the poems and dramatic trilogy by Aleksei Tolstoy, the plays of Aleksandr Ostrovsky, Aleksei Koltsov's poems, and the lyrics of Aleksandr Blok corresponded to his subdued, calm, and somewhat fatalistic mood. Meanwhile, each day he would read a short page from Dahl's Dictionary.

Many of his fellow inmates at the camp remembered Solzhenitsyn in just this way: "a man with Dahl's volume under his armpit who kept company with Panin and I. V. Karbe."

Sanya now mentioned things that had never come up in his Moscow letters. The Ekibastuz camp was nothing like the *sharashka*. Accordingly, it was not only spiritual nourishment that one had to worry about. Next to his requests for Tolstoy and Blok, Sanya's letters asked for sugar, salt pork, biscuits.

I was not able to send parcels in my name. Riazan was a small town, and such mailings could come to the attention of my Institute. And after all, I was now the family breadwinner. I had been able to free my mother from helping us and even to stop working. I was able to help my aunts. And now I also had to help my husband. Aunt Nina, in Rostov, selflessly took upon herself the job of coping with all the cares and worries about Sanya's packages. By this time she was over seventy, and my older cousin's husband helped her carry the parcels to the post office.

SANYA

Every month Sanya was sent sugar, salt pork, biscuits, tobacco, and sometimes even butter, as well as sausages, onions, and garlic. And not only foodstuffs. Felt boots, a knapsack, woolen socks, mittens, and many other items went into the packages: a wooden spoon, a tube of toothpaste, needles and thread, a sponge, plastic dishes, a spillproof ink well.

Every time Sanya received a parcel it was a great occasion for him. Letters could be written only twice a year, but postcards confirming the receipt of a parcel were permitted. Here is one of them: "Your parcel of 6/13 has been received by me. Many thanks. Everything's perfect. Send me some pencils. I kiss you all. Sanya."

For us these postcards were missives that filled up the long intervals between letters.

"Your parcels are a source of life for me," Sanya wrote in December 1950. He was very grateful to Aunt Nina and considered himself indebted to her, with "a debt too great to be repaid." Inasmuch as he realized that Aunt Nina was doing everything for him out of sincere concern and love, he did not mind writing her that he "would particularly like to have some pastry and something sweet," that there was "no more need for dried fruit," and that it would be better not to send No. 3 *makhorka* tobacco, but either No. 1 or No. 2. "No. 3 is just too mild."

After a while Aunt Nina got to know Sanya's tastes so well that she even managed to please him with the tobacco. "The baccy you sent was out of this world, just as if you yourself smoked!" ". . . the Saratov *makhorka* was particularly good." And he was overjoyed at receiving her homemade sweets. "Anything sweet that you send is a feast for me," he wrote Aunt Nina.

Later, Sanya would also need protective glasses against dust, little wooden or plastic boxes (no ironware or glassware was permitted among personal possessions), paper, notebooks, writing pads, a kit bag, oatmeal flakes (because it boiled faster) instead of grain, slippers. . . . And all this would appear before him as in a fairy tale. "You are caring for me like my own mother," he wrote to Aunt Nina.

The camp had a library. Sanya read the metropolitan newspapers, but with a long delay: "It takes them many days and nights to reach us here from Moscow." As for the radio, he did not hear it at all. Which meant that he was not hearing music, and he missed it. "When I read the radio programs in the newspapers, I get sick at heart," he wrote me. In the library Sanya got acquainted with those who used the reading room. Some of them were to become his friends.

And now the first Ekibastuz winter was coming to a close. Pleasant spring days arrived, alternating with still-freezing weather.

Sanya's face was lean, but fresh and ruddy, he wrote. "Such is the beneficial effect of these freezing winds in the steppes."

❧

Professor Vilensky, an acquaintance of my professor, Nikolai Ivanovich Kobosev, was the leading spirit behind the organization of the Riazan chapter of the Mendeleyev Society. He was also head of the Department of General Chemistry in the Pavlov Medical Institute, which had just opened that year in Riazan. The assistant professor of physical chemistry, V.S., eagerly undertook the task of helping him.

The Medical Institute in Riazan was founded as an extension of the Third Medical Institute of Moscow. For this reason its staff of scientific workers was of unusually high caliber. Now there were three higher educational institutions and four departments of chemistry in Riazan, more than enough chemists to organize a Mendeleyev Society.

Soon the Riazan chapter of the society was formally opened. Professor Vilensky was elected chairman, and Assistant Professor V.S. became executive secretary. The meetings were held on the premises of the Medical Institute. Gradually the chemists in town became better acquainted with each other. Assistant Professor V.S.'s wife had recently died, and it was because of this that he had moved to Riazan. His closest co-workers were greatly concerned about him.

In February 1951 Mother came to live with me, and she and I moved into a house on Kasimovsky Lane (where *One Day in the Life of Ivan Denisovich* would later be written). We had obtained two adjoining rooms in a three-room apartment.

My birthday was not far off. It was decided to combine a birthday celebration with a housewarming party. Among our guests were the dean and his wife; my assistant with her husband; a woman physician, also with her husband; and Olga Nikolaevna Ulashchik, a teacher of English, who had been my next-door neighbor in the Institute building but had now moved into the house on Kasimovsky Lane too.

The woman physician proved to be the most cheerful guest of all. She was bubbling over with life and tried to amuse everyone. But it was impossible not to notice that nothing could cheer me up, that I was very sad that evening. No one at work was used to seeing me this way, and for this reason my behavior visibly astonished them all. But I could do nothing to help myself.

I had not even received a letter from Sanya for this day. He had wished me a happy birthday back in his December letter, in which he also sent his New Year's greetings and good wishes for the dawn of the new half-century. In his very first letter from Ekibastuz, Sanya had suggested that whenever I felt particularly lonely without his letters, I should reread his old ones—especially the letter he had sent me for my thirtieth birthday, in which he wrote that even when I became sixty he would love me "the same way" he had loved me at eighteen, so that on the morning of February 26 it would seem to me as though he had "just then spoken those words, leaning over your pillow."

Involuntarily I remembered my birthdays in Moscow, which had been celebrated in the Stromynka hostel. Why had I not felt this infinite sorrow then? Why hadn't I felt so terribly unhappy then? Was it because I was invariably revitalized, cheered up by the generous attentions of my friends in the hostel? Or because I was waiting impatiently for Lida and Kirill to arrive, and then laughing heartily at Kirill's witticisms?

Perhaps I was so sad because the Stromynka girls, whose futures were also unsettled and uncertain, were not with me on this birthday. We had grown accustomed to one another, even if ours was only a crossroads coexistence. We had met on the crossroads, and it would be there that, inevitably, we would part. Each one of us had to find her own haven, her own harbor, her own corner on earth. But in the meantime each one of us had had her own unsettledness. Living among them, I came to feel as if I were sitting and waiting at some transfer point and would never reach the end of the line.

All this was no more. Instead, I saw all around me many happy families. It was then that I suddenly felt something I had not felt all these years—my incredible loneliness while surrounded by people, the loneliness felt on a crowded street, or in a packed auditorium. This, then, was probably the turning point, the most difficult period of my life. It would probably have been easier for me had I been able, then and there, to say, to shout out for all to hear, that I had a man I loved, for whom I was waiting, and for whom I would continue to wait. Only help me wait it out for him!

I had written to Sanya. A year had passed since we had last seen each other. I wanted very much to go to him. I wanted this very, very much. I could not exist without it. Perhaps in the summer? After all, I would be getting a two-month leave.

The reply arrived in March. "My dear little girl," Sanya wrote. "Coming to me here is completely useless, because a meeting is absolutely impossible." He wrote that "we can see one another only in the third summer from now," that "there is no point in thinking about the future, because this only weakens one," that "one has to find the meaning of existence in day-to-day living."

❧

The seventh spring of imprisonment arrived for Sanya.

As the difficult winter wore on, paradoxically it seemed easier for Sanya, simply because he had set himself a concrete goal that was very specific and important: to survive this winter, come what may. And he did indeed survive the winter, very well. He did not even have a serious head cold. He took only one day off for sick leave in December when, for some unknown reason, his temperature shot up, but nothing hurt. And so the winter passed, "and this immediate concrete goal was no more." And once again Sanya had to feel what he had not let himself feel during the winter, namely that, "as before, the end of the term seemed just as far away, and it was difficult to continue to live as I lived before."

❧

V.S., the assistant professor, quite often visited my department in connection with the affairs of the Riazan Mendeleyev Society. Or possibly that was a pretext.

Once he dropped in on me at the Institute just as I was getting ready to go home. He offered to escort me, and I invited him to come in and have lunch with us. Mother and he took a great liking to each other. When she suggested that he drop in on us, he started visiting from time to time, sometimes in my absence.

I had thought he was a childless widower, but he told my mother that he had two sons. Anxious about my uncertain future with Sanya, she was especially warm to our new friend.

When V.S. asked me to become his wife, I said that this was absolutely impossible, and after a while I explained why. V.S. persisted nevertheless.

Later, Aleksandr Isaevich was to consider this man "a scoundrel for tempting into marriage a wife whose husband was still among the living." Still later, however, he himself would not shrink from tempting another woman into marriage while his own wife was alive.

V.S. and I began to see each other more frequently. We had common interests at work, since we were both physical chemists. V.S. was ten years older than I. I received much useful counsel from him, and I began to feel in him, perhaps for the first time in my life, a real masculine support: I had, after all, grown up without a father, and Sanya and I were the same age.

In the summer of the same year, 1951, V.S. showed so much persistence in his courting that he went to see me while I was in Rostov. He tried to talk my mother into persuading me to marry him, and me into going with him to meet his family. Instead, I left for Kislovodsk, to visit my aunt Zhenya.

My cousin Nadya had just given birth to Marinochka, a

funny little bundle of wonderment, and Tanya's Galka was already six years old, wheeling around wildly on a bicycle. And how about myself—would I never have anyone, was that how it would always be? The future for Sanya and me seemed so remote. Sanya himself I could no longer perceive as a living person, in flesh and blood. He was an illusion. Soon it would be a year and a half since we had seen each other. The next letter would arrive only next fall or winter. The brief postcards addressed to Aunt Nina, acknowledging receipt of parcels, would begin to sound like faint echoes from another planet.

Sanya's past letters, suffused with love, admiration, and devotion, had been for me like bits of coal for a burning fire. And our meetings had been like dry firewood that would create a resplendent blaze. Now, suddenly, there was neither the coal nor the firewood, and the embers in the fireplace were slowly dying out. The distant, beloved image began to dissolve. It was like the condition of a person under anaesthesia—everything that is real begins to recede somewhere, dissolving, melting, until the moment of total oblivion supervenes. . . .

In Kislovodsk one day I received a letter from V.S. I felt that I had received a letter from a real person.

Meanwhile, Sanya sensed that something was amiss in my July letter to him, written from Kislovodsk. "It seems as though you had to force yourself to begin the letter," he wrote me later. "A kind of reticence fettered your tongue, and after a few lines you broke off."

Since the beginning of summer Sanya had been working in a "nonphysical" capacity. It was only many years later that I found out what this meant. Upon the publication of *Ivan Denisovich*, a former zek congratulated his "team-leader of the 104th team."

Sanya was managing to cope with his supervisory work. He

did not find it burdensome. He felt healthy and energetic. His team was international in composition. Apart from Russians, there were Ukrainians, Latvians, Estonians, even a Pole and a Hungarian. The Hungarian once introduced Sanya to a fellow countryman, Janos Rozsas, presenting him as "my team-leader —Sasha."

Sanya felt a great affinity for Janos and gradually learned his brief biography. When the Hungarian's sentence was read to him in Russian, which he did not understand then, he had been only eighteen years old—almost an adolescent, which was probably why he had so quickly learned to speak Russian fluently. Although he had been torn from his native country and interned for a long time, he harbored no bitterness. He regarded himself as "simply a victim of war."

Surrounded by Russians, Janos became increasingly attached to them. He grew to love and appreciate Russians, especially after, as he saw it, a Russian nurse saved his life. In the difficult years just after the war, Janos had been working in the forest, felling trees. When it looked as though he was beginning to reach his "breaking point," he was put in a hospital. Two nurses were in charge of the patients. Dusya, the more dedicated and selfless of the two, adopted a maternal attitude toward Janos. She even sold her ration coupon in the village to get milk for him. "It's a pity that she will never find out that I have never forgotten her," Janos Rozsas was to write me many years later.

He felt very close to the Russian people. Russian literature, poetry, and songs became ever dearer to him. He would memorize one Russian song after another, as well as verses by Russian poets. Lermontov became his favorite poet.

Janos was rehabilitated in 1953, and at the end of the same year he left for his native country, where he began to work as a bookkeeper. He married a year later. Now he has two sons and a daughter. It would seem that he has everything it takes for happiness, but not so. Janos misses his second homeland. He misses those distant friends with whom he once shared "the bitter fate of his younger years." He set up a little corner in his home which he named "Little Russia," and there he keeps albums of Russian songs and a collection of Russian books. His library contains a "full shelf" of Russian classics.

Janos wrote us that his work often involved driving out to villages. If the weather was good, he would go on foot from village to village, and he loved to sing songs as he walked: Hungarian, Russian or Ukrainian songs. "I am alone," he wrote, "no one can hear me, only the birds in the skies and the bushes on the edge of the road." Of Russian songs, he loved best of all to sing "*Vot mchitsia troika pochtovaya* . . ." ("Here comes the troika, tearing down the road, bringing in the mail . . ."). But when he began singing in Russian, he would grow sad at the thought that he would not be able to see his former Russian friends whom he had grown to love "for their kind hearts." He had lost track of everyone.

It would have given Janos great joy to be able to write an endless stream of letters to Solzhenitsyn, but Aleksandr Isaevich was prevented from replying; he had to place more and more value on time. To make Janos happy, I tried as best I could to take Sanya's place. We kept up a running correspondence and exchanged photographs.

Janos followed life in his second homeland with keen interest. He read Soviet newspapers and magazines. In 1966, when he read in *Pravda* about the proceedings of the Twenty-third Party Congress, he devoted special attention to the part in the report of D. A. Kunayev, First Secretary of the Central Committee of Kazakhstan, on the town of Ekibastuz. Janos

recalled "the rows of green tents on the roofs of which a re-
lentless rain drummed dismally. Later, houses were built. At
first, of wood; later, of stone. Smoke curled up from the factory chimneys; the first trains rolled out." Janos was proud that
he was "one of the first builders of the town mentioned from
the rostrum of the Party Congress."

Sanya's second letter permitted for 1951, which he wrote
in November, did not reach us. Thus it felt as though he had
not written us for a whole year, from March 1951 to March
1952.

Although his work allowed little free time, Sanya still
managed to do quite a bit of reading. When he drew up a
list after two years, it turned out that he had read "the poems
of Evgeny Baratynsky, Herzen's prose, Marich's *Northern
Lights*, Wilkie Collins' *The Moonstone*, Ivan Goncharov's
The Precipice and *Oblomov*, some Chekhov, five plays by
Ostrovsky, a little bit of Shchedrin." In addition, every day
he read his beloved Dahl.

Sanya's mood remained subdued, as can be seen from a
poem he wrote at that time, entitled "The Right of the
Prisoner."

> Of all of our rights
> Which we never had
> Let the least of them be
> The smoldering right
> Which we nurse in secret:
> The right to equal revenge.

The second Ekibastuz winter was not at all like the preceding one. Amazingly, it was "warm, snowless, some kind of
miracle." There had not been a single blizzard. The weather

continued like this until February, when he was "crushed by fifty-below weather."

In January a small swelling which had appeared earlier, but to which Sanya had paid no attention, began to grow very quickly, from day to day. There was nothing to do but to have it removed.

Everybody is nervous before an operation. Sanya, too, was uneasy. Moreover, he was not free. He could not choose his own doctor or hospital. What could he hope for? On what should he rely? On fate? He had believed in fate for some time now. But what was *fate?* His mother had always relied on God and had taught him to do the same in childhood. Why had he departed from this? Perhaps it was because in school he had become convinced that the existence of God could not be proved—nor could his nonexistence, for that matter.

Sanya was hospitalized toward the end of January. The operation was performed on February 12, under local anaesthesia. The doctors explained to him that "the tumor had not spread to the surrounding tissues. It had retained the mobility and insularity of the capsular variety up to the very moment of the operation. For this reason, it could not have metastasized." That was how Sanya described it to us. "That is why, as the physicians assured me, there are no grounds for further concern."

A parcel that had been sent to him arrived several days after the operation. It was very good timing. By then, he could eat everything, without restriction, and this was just what he needed to recover his strength.

Sanya was released from the hospital two weeks later.

He wrote us in March that he looked well, despite the operation he had gone through, and felt strong.

By this time he had received from Aunt Nina the textbooks

he had asked her to send him. He was getting ready to prepare himself for teaching. He had asked for books on arithmetic and geometry, and not just any kind of book, but one, "rather, that is not a standard textbook" (he disliked anything that was standard) and preferably an old edition, "where the text offers many problems for construction." He was sure that a person with a higher education in mathematics, who had worked at mathematics even in the *sharashka*, would certainly not have forgotten it and could easily teach it in a village school. But what Solzhenitsyn wanted was something for himself, for some sort of inner satisfaction, so that even in a village school he would be almost a reformer in the method of teaching mathematics. He would conduct his courses on the highest possible level.

What awaited Sanya in a year was a total unknown. The future remained enshrouded in fog.

There were some changes, here and there, in the camp. The regime was milder. The food situation had improved. Films were shown more frequently.

So many were leaving the camp that he could not keep count of them all. Dmitry Panin, Pavel Gai,* and others had left with another convict transport.

Sanya's work was different now. He was going to start learning the carpenter's trade. "It would be good to master this trade, too," he wrote. And he damned the education that had made him a "softie intellectual." How many vexations it had occasioned him in life! "A thirty-year-old blockhead grows up," he complained to us. "He has read thousands of books, but he can't sharpen an ax or set a handle on a hammer."

But fate decreed that Sanya was not to master the car-

---

* Gai appears under his own name in *Love-Girl*—Ed.

penter's trade. Soon thereafter he was assigned to work as a smelter in the foundry. He even kept a souvenir of this experience, an aluminum spoon. It was precious to him, because he had poured it himself into a sand mold, using melted aluminum wire.

It was Sanya's last year of camp. How onerous it had turned out to be! "It's impossible to express how slowly the weeks and months drag on." And the term that remained still seemed "very, very long."

When Mother and I returned to Riazan at the end of August 1951 we were met by V.S. A bouquet of flowers was on the seat of a waiting taxi.

V.S. and I saw each other at home and in the department. We started to conduct joint scientific work. But the whole winter was still marked by uncertainty. Another circumstance supervened to tilt the already wavering balance of the scales. One day the director of the Special Section of the Institute called me and told me that I was requested to fill out a form, which she thereupon handed to me. It was the same form that I had had to fill out in Moscow in the autumn of 1948.

Again I had to declare that my marriage was in the process of being dissolved. Now, as before, I entered the information about Sanya in the appropriate column—concerning "a former husband." This meant that the divorce action had to be renewed at once.

In those days it was necessary to announce an intention to divorce in the newspaper. As I did not want all this to become public knowledge in Riazan, I left for Moscow and, pretending to be a Muscovite, reinstituted divorce proceedings against Solzhenitsyn, A. I. I gave the Turkin residence as my address.

It was in the spring of 1952 that I made the decision to restructure my life in its entirety. There was no talk between V.S. and me about registering our relationship, because my marriage to Sanya had not yet been dissolved. Very simply, as of a certain time, V.S. and I became known to everyone as man and wife. And thus it remained, even though I later received an official divorce.

The letter Sanya had written in November 1951 had not reached me, and now both of us stopped writing. I could not bring myself to write a letter. I sent him only a birthday greeting, wishing him "happiness in life."

I lacked the courage to write Sanya about my hesitations while my mind was still not made up. But even after I made the decision I still procrastinated. Probably this was cowardice, but I tried to justify it. After all, there were no women in his camp, and therefore nothing could alter his life in that regard. If he were allowed at first only to suspect something untoward, then perhaps he would gradually find it easier to accept what had happened.

I continued to keep silent, although I knew and understood that this could not help but disturb Sanya. In the end, he repeatedly asked Aunt Nina to "clear up the uncertainty." In September 1952, at my request, Aunt Nina wrote to Sanya: "Natasha has asked me to tell you that you may arrange your life independently of her."

I shall neither justify nor blame myself. After all the years of trials, I could no longer sustain my "saintliness." I began to live a real life.

Aunt Nina's letter did not satisfy Sanya and he asked me to write him everything, just as it was. How was it possible that our marriage could terminate with "such an insignificant, enigmatic phrase"? He assured me that whatever the case, and whatever happened, he would not dare reproach me for anything, because it was really he who was guilty before me, because he had brought me "so little joy," and that he would forever remain my "debtor."

I wrote Sanya that I had a new family—and this was true enough.

Our correspondence was interrupted, for a while, on this note.

❧

Solzhenitsyn met Ivan Denisovich Shukhov not in 1950 but five years earlier, and they probably found little in common with each other though the resemblance was already there. The sly peasant Shukhov was quick-witted and self-possessed, and somewhere along the line he crossed swords with the quick-witted and self-possessed intellectual Solzhenitsyn. Both exhibited an economy of their spiritual and physical forces and, generally speaking, a rational attitude toward life: they were prudent and thrifty. Solzhenitsyn could very well apply the saying, "A thrifty man is better than a rich one," to himself.

But they differed sharply on one point: Shukhov, despite all his cunning and resourcefulness, was "a timid man," unable "to clamor for his rights and shake up the law," as was done so successfully by Solzhenitsyn in the *sharashka* and by Nerzhin in *First Circle*. Once he demanded and obtained five grams of sifted flour; another time it was Polish zlotys, his complaints having gone as far as the Supreme Soviet. On one occasion he blocked the authorities' attempt to confiscate Dahl's Dictionary, and on another he demanded and got back from the administration Esenin's small book of poems with my inscription in it: "And thus will it come to pass that everything lost shall be returned to thee." He knew his way around only too well when it came to his rights.

And now these two men even began to share a philosophy of life. What is to be will be. There was neither fear nor concern in the face of what fate had in store for them. A *Day in the Life* contained other simple people, too—team-leader Tiurin, assistant team-leader Pavlo—but it was Ivan Deniso-vich who was closest of all to Solzhenitsyn himself, and for this reason he was chosen to be the protagonist. By his spiritual attunement, his attitude to life, his evaluation of people and events, Shukhov was much closer to the intellectual Solzhenitsyn than Captain Buinovsky or the intellectual Caesar Markovich.

It would seem that the author conceived of Shukhov as the commonest of common men. At the front he was a rank-and-file soldier, in the collective farm he was a common laborer, and here, in the team, even though he was a good workman, he was nevertheless ordinary. The author stressed this all along. But if one stops to think about it, one can see that Shukhov is far from being an ordinary man, and it is exactly this quality that constitutes the resemblance between them.

7

The Village Schoolteacher

*A*fter serving his sentence, Sanya left Ekibastuz for Kok-Terek, a regional administrative center in Kazakhstan. On his way there he passed through Taldy-Kurgan, where Mother and I had been evacuated in 1942-44. Now it was the end of February 1953. I had not been there for a long time. But what did it matter. I was no longer his wife.

In early March, Solzhenitsyn received his deportee's certificate. Camp life had ended for him; now he was to begin the life of a deportee, living in so-called freedom but within an assigned area. How does one make a new start in life?

He was not permitted to take up teaching immediately. He

had first to work as an economist planner at the regional consumers union for a certain period of time. Nevertheless, Sanya became a teacher before the end of the school year.

He was at once saddled with an extremely heavy teaching load, including preparing students for their graduation examinations. Sanya appreciated the fact that his nerves had calmed down over the past years, that he had become good-natured and more easygoing. Now he was somewhat apprehensive that the turmoil of school life might bring a return to his former unquiet self.

He did not feel like settling down in the real sense. Perhaps he would not have to remain for very long in deportation? Stalin was dead, after all. Sanya felt as though he were at a railroad junction: "At any moment I might pick up my suitcase, put on my knapsack, and hop on the train."

Here Sanya made the acquaintance of the Zubovs, an elderly married couple, also deportees, and they quickly became friends. The Zubovs are vividly described in the novel *Cancer Ward*, where they are known as the Kadmins. But the Zubovs were richer in spirit than the novel could suggest. Nikolai Ivanovich was a gynecologist, and in general a man of great erudition. What didn't he know! Languages, history, architecture, and many other things. His wife, Elena Aleksandrovna, had a deep and subtle feeling for literature and poetry.

Moreover, the Zubovs possessed the supreme virtue of taking joy in little things. No whining or complaining was ever heard in their home.

The new school year was about to start. An opportunity arose to rent a little cottage. Well, why not? The job at the school was steady. One had to build a normal life in some way or other. And if he were to have a separate cottage for himself, he could start writing without fear of interference, as much as he wanted and about anything he wished.

A vegetable garden adjoined the cottage. Immediately beyond the "fence," a hedge of prickly briar, stretched the steppes, and the bluish silhouette of the Chu-Iliy mountain range rose on the horizon. There was no traffic at all; indeed, there was nothing whatsoever "except for a forsaken little path through the fields," and in consequence "the silence was something not of this world."

The cottage had one main room, plus a kitchen and a hallway. Although it had an earthen floor, it was freshly whitewashed and aglow with light. The main room had two windows, facing south and west; the one window in the kitchen looked out toward the south.

The furniture was squalid, but it would have to do for the moment. The "bed" consisted of three packing cases on which lay a mattress and a pillow stuffed with wood shavings. Sanya arranged his books on a trestle stand. A suitcase served temporarily as a table. With a few blows of the hammer, Sanya transformed a big packing case into a "china closet" with plywood shelves. Soon a real table was to supplant the suitcase, and he already had a stool for it, though not a chair.

He dreamed of acquiring a radio so that his new dwelling could be flooded with music. His salary would be sufficiently high so that he could permit himself even this luxury.

Only one thing was lacking: a mistress to manage this tiny household.

Here in Kok-Terek he was regarded as quite an eligible man. There were many sweet, attractive young women on the teaching staff, and there were others elsewhere.

❦

I knew from Aunt Nina that Sanya had been released and had left the camp. I also knew the place to which he had been exiled.

SANYA

Of course, my dream was that Sanya's personal life should be settled once and for all. Only then could I have complete peace of mind. But was it necessary that we completely forget each other, and would we be capable of this?

Toward the end of August I wrote Sanya a letter, really a request. This letter entered our family history under the rubric "Letters About Parallel Staircases." I asked Sanya to maintain a friendly correspondence with me, a kind of spiritual communion, and wrote about our ascent in life "along parallel staircases."

Upon receiving this letter, Sanya, as he wrote me, at first experienced a feeling of joyous astonishment. It seemed to confirm what he had once been told in camp by an inmate who was familiar with graphology and to whom Sanya had shown my last letter. I had written about the "psychic letdown" I was then experiencing, about my awareness that there would be "no extraordinary life together," nor even a revival of the love I had formerly felt for Sanya.

Sanya replied that he would take me back with his former love if I would return to him, abandoning "everything" that I had "committed over these past two years." Unless I did this, our correspondence would not survive for very long anyway. Did I realize that this would require me to live a "double life"? And if he were to marry, even if "only for practical considerations," then "our correspondence, in any event, would cease to exist."

He assured me that whatever decision I made, he would not be personally hurt or angry with me, just as he had not been hurt even in the past. "I know how weak I myself have been in life," he wrote. "I have seen how others have behaved and it is easy for me to understand and to justify your weakness. That Sanchik whom you once knew and whom you loved quite undeservedly—that fellow would not have forgiven you. But the present-day Sanya doesn't even know whether there is anything here to forgive. Probably I am even more guilty toward you. And, at all events, I did not save your life, but you have saved my life and more than my life."

If Sanya had not sent me such an ultimatum, a correspondence might have developed between us, and perhaps everything would have turned out quite, quite differently. As it was, our correspondence broke off after this letter.

Almost immediately thereafter Sanya was stricken with an illness. He felt intermittent pains in the abdominal area. He had no appetite and kept losing weight. It might be gastritis, or maybe an ulcer. Nikolai Ivanovich tried to treat him, but to no avail. Tests were needed; he required the attention of specialists.

He received permission to leave for Dzhambul, the administrative center of the region, for a consultation with physicians.

Sanya was in a depressed mood. He wrote a letter to one of my women friends, then single, with whom he had struck up a correspondence. In the event of his death, he begged her to come to the village of Berlik and dispose of his few belongings. (He had in mind his literary productions.)

In Dzhambul the doctors put Sanya through all the analyses for abdominal ailments. An X ray disclosed, not an ulcer, but a tumor the size of a big fist, which had grown from the back wall of the abdominal cavity. It was pressing on the abdomen and causing the pains. It was entirely possible that this tumor, alas, might be malignant.

Could the tumor be connected with the one that had been removed in Ekibastuz? But that tumor had retained mobility until the last moment, and the doctors had been sure it had not metastasized. But it might have, all the same.

SANYA

Some of the doctors considered the abdominal tumor a metastasis of the old one: both its growth period and the lymphatic routes for metastasis supported this theory. Others thought the new tumor was independent, slow-growing, even chronic, and not at all malignant. Whom was one to believe? At all events, one had to be prepared for the worst.

In Dzhambul he learned about a root known as *Issyk Kul*. He managed to obtain some extract from the root and decided to try it in small doses.

Sanya felt well during the first days after his return from Dzhambul at the beginning of December. His appetite was restored. But he did not indulge in any illusions. Death seemed almost inevitable to him. The only consolation he found was that he did not believe in the finality of death: "Some spiritual substance must remain."

In Dzhambul he had been told to go to the Tashkent Oncological Health Center. It looked as if he would have to take a trip there during the winter vacation. But what should he agree to—an operation, or X ray and radiotherapy? Or should he rely on the *Issyk Kul* root?

The exit permit for Tashkent was received. Sanya's condition was satisfactory. He was again drinking extract from the *Issyk Kul* root, and he took some along with him when he left for Tashkent in January 1954.

The day after he arrived in Tashkent he went to the Oncological Health Center. The woman physician believed that this was a metastasis. An operation was unlikely. X ray therapy was indicated. She directed him to the radiation department.

The next day, January 4, Sanya was hospitalized in Ward 13 of the Tashkent Medical Institute.

On January 5 they made a drawing on Sanya's stomach, dividing it into four squares, and began to irradiate each square in turn. At first the treatment was administered every other day, later it was every day. At the same time they began to give him tablets to swallow.

Lidiya Aleksandrovna Dunayeva, chief of the irradiation department, and Irina Emelyanovna Meike, the physician in charge of his treatment, assured Solzhenitsyn that the X ray would destroy his tumor while the tablets would help the X ray do its job.

Sanya spent a month and a half in the health center. He had fifty-five X ray sessions, receiving 12,000 Roentgens. The tumor was considerably reduced, although not totally destroyed. He was told to come back to the clinic by the first of June. That in itself was not a bad sign; others were ordered to return in a month, or even in two weeks. But there was still the lingering doubt: Was life being restored to him or were they just beguiling him with the promise of life? He celebrated his release from Ward 13 by going to the ballet, to see Riccardo Drigo's *Esmeralda*.

After a trip to the mountains to procure more *Issyk Kul* root from old man Krementsov, who gave him a handful of it, Sanya returned to Kok-Terek in an entirely different frame of mind from the one in which he had left. At that time he had felt little hope, but now he sensed a return to life. He had no pain at all. What happiness! But how long would this last? The root, in the meantime, was being brewed. Soon he would begin drinking it. Let the X ray and the root take their respective courses.

In one of his letters to my mother, Sanya asked her to send him a photograph of himself. He bemoaned the fact that he had no photographs of his parents. He wrote that "an attitude of concern for preserving the past has been engendered in me as in an old man. I don't want to lose a particle of it."

That was a long time ago, this concern for preservation. But what about today? Now Solzhenitsyn seems to have almost no past at all. "I have forgotten everything that I wrote to you!" At the end of 1970 I was told: "You were a figment of my imagination! Do you understand? I exaggerated in my letters!..."

When he passed the zenith of his life, Solzhenitsyn did not acquire that farsightedness which comes with old age and which helps us not to notice the lines and wrinkles on the faces of those who are aging along with us and even helps to smooth them out, that saving farsightedness which helps us to see retrospectively what was greatest and most important in the past, and which no longer allows us to ruminate over the petty, dismal facts of one's existence, over trivial shortcomings and trespasses, whether our own or those of others.

On the contrary, Solzhenitsyn, as the years go by, is becoming increasingly shortsighted. Rummaging in his past life, digging trivial facts out of his memory, he examines these through a magnifying glass. But when it comes to the important and principal events of the past, he looks at them through inverted binoculars.

The large is diminished, the small is magnified. The scales are reversed. The order of magnitude is inverted.

What I am saying refers to Solzhenitsyn's judgments about the actions of people once close to him, and about his own actions with respect to them. As to whether this now extends to larger issues or not, I cannot presume to judge.

❧

While Aleksandr Solzhenitsyn was undergoing successful treatment at the Tashkent Oncological Health Center, Nikolai Vitkevich, his one-time closest friend and "partner in crime," obtained his freedom and arrived in Rostov. The camp where he was completing his term had conducted a "review of records," and as a result he did not have to serve the full ten years of the original sentence, but was released after serving a little less than nine years. He was not granted a residence permit in Rostov, so he settled down in nearby Taganrog.

I received a letter from Nikolai at the end of March 1954. He wrote that his time was "totally taken up with looking for work." The initial difficulties he encountered upon returning home did not frighten him. After all, he had already gone through the mill, or as the saying goes, "through fire and brimstone." Moreover, he was compensated by the loving care bestowed on him by his mother and grandmother.

When I saw Nikolai in the summer of 1955 he was living in Rostov. He still was not a regular member of the university faculty, but our old friend Emil Mazin provided Nikolai with mathematics students whom he coached very successfully, even acquiring a degree of fame in this connection.

There was no resumption of the lively correspondence that Nikolai and I had enjoyed in the past, but we did write to each other from time to time. He was eager to offer comments on any chemistry reports or lectures I happened to be working on. "I'll reply first by giving my impression, then I shall pose two or three naïve questions and finally you can judge for yourself: Am I ruined for chemistry forever or is there still some hope for me?" he joked.

I did not risk his criticism of a lecture, but I did send him a popular "chemistry play" I had written, which was entitled *Real Champagne, or The Birthday of a Chemist* and had been successfully staged by the Institute's theatrical group. After praising me for finding a felicitous way of popularizing chemistry—because anything can be demonstrated in a play, whereas chemistry without demonstration gets nowhere—

Nikolai proceeded to give a devastating criticism of my "hero," whom he perceived as an "overeducated crank." In his opinion, what was required was a hero who could "demonstrate the power of chemistry, in simple but substantial terms, to the ignoramuses who surrounded him." In a word: "More chemistry and less champagne!"

Having begun his post-camp life as a mathematics tutor, Nikolai quipped that although he had not forgotten that he was a chemist, "the same cannot be said for chemistry itself," because it had forgotten him.

Two years after Nikolai's release, times changed for the better. He had accumulated fourteen years of productive service (four years at the front and ten years of credit for factory and construction work for the country, as his mishaps were now euphemistically referred to), and this fact played no small role in his being accepted, in the autumn of 1956, as a postgraduate doctoral candidate in the Department of Organic Chemistry at Rostov University. He passed the examinations brilliantly, and this was topped by the arrival of a photocopy of the prewar research work which Stepukhovich and he had conducted jointly and which the latter had forwarded from Saratov University.

❧

In early 1954, Sanya finally bought a house for himself in Kok-Terek. It had an earthen-walled cellar for cold storage. It was agreed that although the former owner would take care of the vegetable plot while he betook himself once more to Tashkent, the produce from it would go to him. Where else could he find such quietude? The moonlit nights were particularly splendid. The soul would simply evanesce in the face of the steppes, the sky, and the boundless emptiness. And when the weather got warmer, he could walk along the river Chu and sleep in the open air. And in Kok-Terek he still had the Zubovs, who treated Sanya as their own son.

Sanya felt fine now. He had a sense of immense well-being. But there was nothing to be done—he had to go to Tashkent.

He was back again in Ward 13 on June 21. The staff of the Oncological center received Solzhenitsyn very warmly and affectionately. Everyone found that he had changed beyond recognition. Even before giving him a thorough examination, the doctors told him that he would be there for a month, but as it turned out, he had to spend almost two months in the health center. The X ray treatment was curtailed when his white blood count dropped markedly, and subsequently the treatment itself was stopped. Solzhenitsyn was to be here again ten years later, in the spring of 1964. That time, however, he was to come not for consultation, not for treatment, but to gather material for the novel he was planning about this "cancer ward."

After his discharge from the health center, Sanya roamed the streets of Tashkent. He bought himself a macintosh and, in particular, a camera. The animals in the Tashkent Zoo were the targets of his Zorky.

Sanya greeted the New Year 1955 with a girl of whom he was quite fond. Still, he could not bring himself to marry her, although he was deathly tired of living a solitary life. What if he should become ill again? There would be no one to take care of him. It was bad to be single. And since he could not find a suitable marriage partner in Kok-Terek, a plan began to mature in his mind whereby marriage would ensue not through a direct face-to-face relationship, but through an exchange of letters.

His first post-camp life experiences were born of fantasy, of pure speculative constructs. A correspondence began. The desire to meet each other was expressed. He would go to her in the summer. . . .

The summer of 1955 was the first vacation Sanya had had since 1940—a full fifteen years. Insulating himself against the debilitating heat of Kazakhstan, he spent entire days sitting at home: writing, reading, listening to music. In the evening, when the heat subsided, he would go to the river and swim for hours. At night he would sleep under the open sky.

He was putting the finishing touches on a play, "The Republic of Labor" (the eventual title would be *The Love-Girl and the Innocent*), and little by little he began working on a novel. The novel was about the Marfino *sharashka*.

Just at that time a chance meeting occurred, when I ran into Evgeniya Ivanovna Panina at the entrance of TSUM, the Moscow Central Department Store.

Very animatedly, Evgeniya Ivanovna began to recount what she had gone through when, at long last, she had been able to join her husband in Kustanai, where he had been exiled. After she finally reached him, it turned out that he was— not alone! Nevertheless, she was still petitioning the authorities and worrying about how to get her husband back to Moscow.

Evgeniya Ivanovna bombarded me with questions about Sanya. It was then that we found out that our husbands had remained close friends in camp. Her Dmitry wanted to find Sanya, no matter where he was. Did I know his address? Yes, of course. Another camp crony of both men, Lev Kopelev, was living here in Moscow.

The two friends, having thus learned of Sanya's whereabouts, began writing to him. Letters flew back and forth. Even a pencil portrait, which Sergei Mikhailovich Ivashev-

Musatov had made of him, was forwarded. Kopelev and Panin tried to talk Sanya into petitioning the authorities for a cancellation of his residence restrictions. Evgeniya Ivanovna wrote to Sanya about this too. But Sanya was in no hurry.

This summer, Sanya was making a trip not to Tashkent but to Karaganda, to seek some diversion and perhaps to marry. But he did not bring back a good wife for his home in Kok-Terek.

The general amnesty announced in the autumn of 1955 aroused a spark of hope. Perhaps it had some bearing on his case? Might he be freed from exile?

For what locality should he apply? He did not want to live in a city, with its hustle and bustle, trolleys, neighbors, and their loud radios. If only he could settle down somewhere in a rural area in Central Russia, not near a railroad or a regional center, but somewhere in the backwoods, away from everything. In many respects, Sanya was so content in his Kok-Terek that he almost felt he wanted nothing else.

Most unexpectedly, I received a letter from Sanya in April 1956. He told me that he had been freed from deportation and that, in addition, his previous convictions had been expunged from the record. He wrote that he wanted to live in some remote but fairly comfortable place, and that with this in mind he had written to the Ivanov and the Vladimir Regional Departments of Public Education. He asked me to inquire whether the Riazan Region might need someone in the field of physics or mathematics, and he assured me that if he should take up residence in Riazan there would be "no shadow cast upon your life."

I was informed by the Riazan Regional Department of Public Education that there was a "surplus" of mathematicians and physicists. I passed this information on to Sanya, suggesting that he try to settle in a city.

The school year was coming to a close. For the fourth time Sanya was giving final examinations to graduating students. He had managed to sell the house. The simple, artless items of furniture were given away.

Solzhenitsyn bade farewell to the school and to Elena Aleksandrovna and Nikolai Ivanovich Zubov, and on June 20 he left Kok-Terek.

〰

Aleksandr had written that, wherever he might find himself, the wife of his friend Panin would always know his whereabouts, and he gave me her telephone number. One day, when I went to Moscow to visit Lida, I telephoned Evgeniya Ivanovna at work. I had told her by postcard that I would be arriving that day and would call her.

"Sanya is here and is waiting for you at our house."

In the evening I made my way the short distance to Deviatinsky Lane. I went on foot . . . to my day of reckoning. I found it hard to climb the stairs. Evgeniya Ivanovna met me and led me into the room. Sanya and Panin were sitting in a corner at a round table, drinking tea. Both stood up.

The Panins soon left us alone together. And suddenly, somehow, we were talking.

Sanya shared with me his plans about his future: most probably he would settle in Vladimir. I listened as he spoke about the possibility—indeed, almost a reality—of his full rehabilitation, and this seemed to promise a continuation of our lives, of the common misfortune that had befallen us.

Later Sanya escorted me back to Lida's house, his hand under my elbow. It started to rain. We took cover, as we used to do in our youth, in the main entrance of some building. He began to question me, trying to understand how all this had come about. I mumbled something or other in reply, feeling that I was living either in the past, into which I had plummeted from the present, or in a present which had somehow risen to the surface out of the distant past. I told him, "I was created to love you alone, but fate decreed otherwise."

When we parted he handed me a sheaf of poems that had been written to or about me over all these years.

Late that night, when everyone was fast asleep, I began to read:

> Now again, again all night
> In dreams appeared
> My dear, sweet wife.

And again:

> The evening snow, the evening snow
> Reminds me of the boulevard
> Your upturned collar
> Your bell-like laugh
> Sparkle of snowflakes
> Vaporescent breath of air . . .

And the lines that hurt most:

> But at road's end
> There stands my home
> Where in loving vigil waits
> My own, forever mine, my wife.

SANYA

When I woke up in the morning I tried to shake off the overwhelming impressions of the night before. I deliberately increased the pace of everything I did, although I did find an occasion to confide to Lida that my meeting with Sanya, and his poems, had opened up old scars in my soul.

That evening I left for Riazan. Having decided that I should suppress my confusion, come what may, I became so brave at home that I even told V.S. I had seen my former husband, and that nothing had changed as a result—everything would remain as it was.

I became more and more tormented by a guilty conscience. I tried to stifle it, not to give in to it, but I could do nothing any more to help myself. Withdrawing into solitude, I kept reading and rereading Sanya's poems.

V.S. was the first to sense that I was drawing away from him, that I was disappearing into the shell of my selfhood. He did everything he could not to let me slip away from him: he took me on a boat ride along the Oka (we had our own motor boat), he drove me to Solotcha (for some reason, we had never been there before), where he made reservations for August at a house of rest. But my thoughts were far away; nothing could distract me from them, nothing could amuse me. The forest on whose edge we were vacationing stretched to the Vladimir Region, the area where Sanya might be taking up residence. A narrow-gauge railway pointed in the same direction.

And from that direction came a letter: "... If you have the inclination and should you find it possible—you can write me. My address, as of August 21, is ... Vladimir Region."

After a month of torment, I was convinced that my feeling toward my first husband had not simply been resurrected, but, indeed, was increasingly and imperiously asserting itself. I decided to have a heart-to-heart talk with Lida, my closest friend, and I went to visit her in a rest home outside Moscow. Having become very fond of my new family, Lida was most upset, and she came up with many arguments against my impulses. In reply, I only wept. But the compounded feelings of guilt and newly inflamed love demanded a resolution. Reluctantly, Lida gave her blessing to my writing Sanya a letter.

As it turned out, when I wrote the letter Sanya was in Rostov. From there he went on to Georgievsk, Piatigorsk, and Kislovodsk to visit relatives. But before Rostov he had gone to the Urals, where Elena Zubov's sister was living with her daughter, Natasha. The Zubovs had decided that Natasha would be a suitable bride for him. He and Natasha had never seen each other before; they had merely exchanged a few letters. He spent two weeks with her and her family. He liked the girl and asked her to become engaged to him, but she was frightened by his impetuosity, and when he left he did not know just where he stood. Nothing was decided.

The school year began. What free time I had away from the Institute I spent at the piano. Only to the piano could I convey everything that was happening within my innermost being. I remembered the words of a person who had once told my fortune by reading my palm and by scrutinizing photographs, in that critically difficult period when my husband had disappeared without a trace, when his letters had stopped arriving from the front. The fortune teller told me the truth about the past and was vague about the present. But when I asked him whether my husband and I would ever be reunited, he replied, "This will depend upon you yourself." This had struck me as farfetched at the time, but now it was beginning to resemble the truth.

In one of his letters Sanya wrote that he was astonished by his great shift of feeling toward me during these two months. With increasing frequency he had started to reflect that perhaps a new happiness was indeed possible. He suggested that we meet so that we could sort out our feelings. Inasmuch as he was not the one responsible for our separation, the initiative was incumbent upon me, and I should come to him—for three days, he suggested.

V.S. had been invited to Odessa to attend a celebration in honor of a professor we knew. I told Mother that I was being summoned to Moscow in connection with Sanya's rehabilitation. She noticed my agitation but could not understand the reason for it. On October 19 I went to the station and bought a ticket to Torfprodukt, Vladimir Region.

That night the moon shone in through the train window, and although I still felt guilty, a presentiment of happiness stirred in the depths of my heart.

Sanya met me, wearing a brown overcoat and a gray hat.

From the station we walked along a lonely road, across the steppes, in the direction of the village of Miltsevo. There, in the hut owned by Matryona Vasilyevna Zakharova, lived "Isaich," as she called him (or "Ignatich," as he is called in the short story "Matryona's House"). Overhead the moon shone bright as ever. We stopped in the shadow of a neatly formed haystack and kissed each other passionately. My head was thrown back under the weight of his kisses and, as used to happen when we were younger, my pretty brown hat with the tiny feathers tumbled to the ground. Everything, everything came back at once. There was no need for words to feel this, to understand, to believe in this passionate resurrection of an old love.

"How did you manage, over these months, to lose so much weight, to look younger, to look more beautiful?" Sanya asked me.

And, indeed, that summer I had stopped wearing a chignon and had shortened and waved my hair so that now it fell down to my shoulders. I had lost weight because I had lost my appetite as a result of everything I was going through. And I arrived in an apricot-colored blouse of crêpe de Chine cut in a style that Sanya had once liked. But this was not the main point. If I had become more attractive, then it came from a glow within me.

The house, the room with tubs of fig plants, the landlady herself, are all described in detail in "Matryona's House." I shall only add that I was moved by Matryona Vasilyevna's tact and discretion. Not once did she question either "Isaich" or me about anything until I myself volunteered to tell her our story. In reply, she told me about her own life, which is described in the same story. More often than not, she left us alone together.

October 21 fell on a Sunday. Moreover, this had been the name day of Sanya's mother. On this day, which we named our reunion day and which for several years we considered a red-letter day for mutual celebration, Sanya and I were inseparable. We talked without letup, each grasping instantly the meaning of what the other was saying. We took many photographs of each other.

Sanya felt it his duty to keep warning me about what I was getting myself into. He was, after all, seriously and hopelessly ill. He was doomed to a short life. A year, maybe; well, two at most. But I was unshakable. "I need you in every way—alive or dying." For me it meant that he needed me now, he needed me especially to make the last years of his life beautiful, to ease the possible sufferings and, perhaps, even to help him conquer death. But was I capable of this now?

While Sanya was at his school I did a little housekeeping.

Most of the time, however, I read what he had been writing—written very concisely, in that microscopic hand, on tiny sheets of paper. The narrow margins too were often crammed with inserts.

But during that visit, my first, I read very little. We either talked or simply enjoyed being together.

As we discussed our joint plans, I was ready for everything. I was quite aware even then that I was causing enormous sorrow to good people, but only now, looking back, do I comprehend the enormity of it. Was there anything that could have stopped me? Probably not.

Even if, along the coordinates of time, I could have heard the words—"Well, how shall we divorce? Amicably, or through the courts?"—could I have believed that this could happen someday? And even if I had believed it, no, this would not have stopped me.

"I beg of you, my little girl, be firm to the end and do not stoop to a single compromise. Force me in this way to believe in your new character." Sanya was already treasuring what he had acquired and was afraid of losing me.

I tried to still my conscience by telling myself that I was more needed by the person before whom I was more guilty, by the one I loved more than anyone and anything in the world. To give him happiness, to revive in him a strong desire to live, was my goal, my one aspiration. Between *that* life, which I had just left, and *this*—there could be no comparison!

When a person is possessed by something, he or she does not stop at obstacles; in the process of overcoming them he or she becomes cruel. I myself, probably, was cruel. Among my friends and colleagues, as well as among friends of V.S., there were many, very many, who censured me.

After the November holidays V.S. and I finally divided our

modest possessions, and those of his things still remaining on Kasimovsky Lane were moved to his new place on Svoboda Street.

Aleksandr came to Riazan for the first time just before the New Year, on December 30, 1956. The next day we strolled together around the town, undeterred by the fiercely cold weather. But our aim was not simply to take a walk to the Kremlin of Riazan, to the cathedral and along the Trubezh River waterfront. On that day we were also going to register our marriage all over again, and with this purpose in mind we stopped at the Riazan Civil Registry. However, our wishes were frustrated because Sanya's passport contained no record of a divorce from me!

Not yet as lawfully wedded man and wife but as a very happy couple, we greeted the New Year with my mother. A few days later Sanya and I took a trip to Moscow together, to visit some of his friends and mine. We also went to the Moscow City Court, where the notification of divorce intended for him was dug up from the archives.

A tragic event occurred that winter: the sudden and senseless death of Matryona Vasilyevna. Sanya moved to the house of her sister-in-law. The house was better, cleaner, and he had a separate room, but he could not feel at all as he had felt when he lived in the house of his Matryona.

Finally, farewell to Torfprodukt. Farewell to Miltsevo! Farewell to Matryona Vasilyevna's mutilated hut!

We spent a week in Moscow during the winter, staying with my uncle, Valentin Turkin. During that visit we bought steamer tickets, planning soon to go on a small river cruise. We made several purchases for the trip, the most important of which was a typewriter, Moskova-4, in GUM. Really, the time had come to start thinking about typing up the finished manuscripts. Sanya had to learn how to type himself. I already had some typing skill which I had picked up during my Moscow University days.

Now began the "quiet existence," as my husband called this segment of our life together.

8

The "Quiet Existence"

O ur "quiet existence" opened with a burst of activity. The arrival of Sanya's baggage, arranging and rearranging furniture, rewiring electrical circuits, salvaging packing cases from the baggage for use as building materials, making sundry small repairs which were unavoidable—all this we did ourselves in the house on Kasimovsky Lane.

Finally, our new arrangements were in order.

The square little room, ten feet across, that my husband and I were to share was a combination of two studies, a library, and a bedroom.

Two writing desks faced each other: my husband's was

large and impressive-looking, with a great number of drawers; mine was small, antique, resting on thin, finely carved legs. The walls were lined with bookshelves. Near the bed stood a small round table, also an antique, on which we placed the books we read before falling off to sleep.

Facing our windows, and in every other direction, high buildings towered over us, electric lampposts glowed in the evening, and innumerable windows lit up in the new apartment houses. The city was encroaching. But in our cozy room and little back yard we felt remote from all this. The garden adjoining the back yard was quiet and deserted. Our neighbors had no children as yet; the house across the street had not yet been converted into a noisy produce storehouse; and the newly asphalted yard of the neighboring Radio Institute had not yet turned into a testing ground for motorcyclists.

My husband set up a table and a bench in the far corner of the yard, near a fence where an overgrown apple tree formed a sort of natural pergola. In addition, there was space enough there for a convertible bed and an armchair. A whole green room!

"I don't remember ever having had such living conditions in all my life," wrote Alexandr Isaevich to Dr. Zubov and his wife, his friends in distant Kok-Terek. The sound of city noises was muffled. The sun did not beat down and the heat was lessened. The air was completely cleansed by the trees, so that the dust could not penetrate. And overhead hung the apples— one had simply to reach out a hand and start munching.

The invisible thread of his ties to the Zubovs, who were the first and almost the only people at the time who had read his post-camp literary productions, was to unfold with a seamless continuity until the moment Aleksandr Isaevich became famous, when he would find himself inundated by a flood of other letters, different events, new acquaintances.

The "Quiet Existence"

For the time being the Zubovs, as it were, substituted for the rest of mankind, and the correspondence with them remained a sort of mutually observed religious rite. Traveling along with the letters across thousands of miles were newspaper clippings, interesting letters from other correspondents, and, in particular and frequently, photographs.

My husband was in no rush to meet my friends. Moreover, I had to be prepared to slacken my ties with them. After all, not a single person in town was to know anything about, nor even to suspect, my husband's *real life*, his creative work. Thus we were gradually turning into recluses.

An exception could be made only for tried-and-true friends from whom there was no need to hide anything. Nikolai Andreyevich Potapov was the first such guest to appear under our roof. Mother and I had met "Andreich" in our home in July, and we liked him very much. He was congenial and had a gentle humor. He regaled us with tales about his past misadventures and talked with great enthusiasm about his present work, building the Kuibyshev Hydroelectric Station.

Andreich was gradually appraised of my husband's literary activities. He learned that the *Sharashka* was a work in progress and he was given a chapter, entitled "The Buddha's Smile," to read.

Our next guest, another of my husband's camp friends, visited us some six months later. This was Dmitry Mikhailovich Panin.

Whenever any business required my husband to go to Moscow, he would always arrange to meet with his camp friends there: Kopelev, Panin, Ivashev-Musatov. At that time Aleksandr greatly valued his friendship with them.

One compensation for our secluded life was gradually getting to know the Riazan Region. We went about it leisurely, one step at a time.

SANYA

That summer I was invited to deliver a lecture in Spassk, on the Oka River, and my husband accompanied me on the steamer trip. I could not help noticing that he was amazed, even somewhat annoyed, at the well-dressed merrymakers. Over the many years, he had become unused to this. Besides, he never did appreciate leisure-time activities.

In September, my husband started to work as a teacher again. Aleksandr had met the director of Riazan's Public School No. 2 in the office of the supervisor of the City Department of Public Education. My husband's assertiveness—he presented incontrovertible arguments why he should be the first on the list to receive employment—impressed the director and he began to question Solzhenitsyn in depth. It developed that during the war both of them had fought almost side by side somewhere or other, and this coincidence turned out to be more important than the university diploma with honors, or the excellent character references, or the right of the rehabilitated to receive priority treatment in employment.

Gradually we both conquered the typewriter. I learned the keyboard, guided by a textbook on the touch method. When I had memorized the arrangement of letters I started to pick up speed. Aleksandr Isaevich typed with two fingers only (the forefinger of the right and the middle finger of the left), but I had to give him credit: he typed faster than I.

The first work Aleksandr typed was an article on future artificial earth satellites which he had been asked to write for the *Notebook of an Agitator*, published by the Regional Committee of the Communist Party.* This article was not fated to see the light. In October our first Sputnik went up. One of the

---

* *Notebook of an Agitator* is a periodical, pocket-sized, which contains articles on current political and cultural themes. While having a common title for the whole country, it is published separately in dozens of larger towns—Ed.

October issues of *Prioskaya Pravda* carried an item about lecturers who had spoken in connection with this event. Among others appeared the name of "a teacher of physics at a secondary school, Comrade Solzhenitsky."

The anniversary of our reunion went by quietly. We celebrated it alone (my mother was away) with a glass of light wine, resuming our normal activities right after the festive repast.

I made a note of this occasion in my diary, adding, "Am even frightened sometimes for our happiness, it's so complete!"

In point of fact, although it was happening later than we had once expected, and although life had been more complicated, more dramatic—still, it seemed that everything we once dreamed about had indeed come to pass.

And we possessed still another essential element of a happy family life. In 1950, when Mother came to live with me in Riazan, she received a letter from Aleksandr in which he said that in his view there could be no home without a "guardian angel of the hearth," a woman who was not working anywhere, who was always at home, who knew everything, and who somehow, "in herself and through herself," welded the inhabitants of the house and the things which filled it into one indivisible whole, creating an organic unity that was "unique and dear to the heart." He concluded, "I hope to see you this way for many, many years to come, living with you under the same roof."

My husband, too, was conscious of the happiness in our lives. "Natushka and I live bound indissolubly to one another," he wrote the Zubovs, adding that we meant so much to each other especially because we had no children, which made us aware that with our deaths we also would end. But he had absolutely no regrets about the lack of children.

We lived by a set of strict rules on going to movies, concerts, and theaters. We permitted ourselves movies only twice a month; as for concerts and theaters, these were limited to once every two months. All this was recorded. If in any one month we exceeded the quota, we had to "fast" during the following month.

I was complaisant (probably too much so) and obediently accepted all these restrictions. After all, I loved my husband, I believed in him as a significant and extraordinary personality, and I wanted everything to be as he thought necessary. Totally aware of what I was doing, and acting completely of my own free will, I let myself dissolve in his personality. It was with utmost sincerity that I promised him to be "a little darling."

Thus imperceptibly, little by little, an impoverishment of my life set in. And I was becoming impoverished in those areas that were accessible to anyone. In these first years, however, I was quite unaware of this. We had few outside amusements, but in return, a great deal of joy at home.

Two, three years later I was to become largely indifferent about going or not going to the movies; about buying or not buying books; about winning or not winning a bond on a lottery ticket (winning would not have mattered anyway, because it would not have been marked by an occasion; my husband did not like to receive or give presents).

The light teaching load at school, and maximum economy in carrying out his duties there, gave Aleksandr Isaevich the opportunity to work many hours on the novel. But rightly or wrongly, he viewed this work as a dangerous, forbidden, and punishable occupation. Attitudes similar to his had been openly expressed ever since the Twentieth Party Congress, in 1956. By now Vladimir Zorin's *Guests* had appeared, as well as Dudintsev's *Not by Bread Alone,* and many other works in this vein. But Solzhenitsyn was as remote as he could make himself, and not only from the literary circles where these new productions were being passionately debated. His deliberate self-isolation had proceeded so far that it was almost as though he did not notice the enormous changes that were taking place around him and were felt by everyone else. In accordance with all the rules of secrecy, he hid himself from people, whether this was when he was a deportee, or in Torfprodukt, or in Riazan. All his creative work in the years of our "quiet existence" was accomplished under conditions of strictest seclusion, as though he had consigned himself voluntarily to the underground.

If someone dropped in on us, which happened very rarely, the door to our room would be firmly shut, so that not a sound could be heard from it. Aleksandr Isaevich would not put his name on the typed copies of the manuscripts, and he would immediately burn his handwritten copy once it was typed. Since our stove was in the shared kitchen, the burning had to be done late at night, when our neighbors were asleep.

Understandably, given such a secretive life, we could not possibly have friends in Riazan, or even casual acquaintances. At work, Aleksandr did not become close to anyone. Almost all my own comradely ties with others had for all practical purposes been broken off. Much later, a fellow worker at our Institute told me that everyone had the impression that Aleksandr had stolen me from them, had taken me away from life, from everyone, and kept me in hiding.

That whole year, beginning with the summer of 1957 and ending with the spring of 1958, passed for us under the banner of work on the *Sharashka*. At first, up to mid-January, we worked on the second draft, rewriting the entire novel from beginning to end. Then, from January through April, there was one more careful and critical reading, followed at last by the final typing.

I also read *The First Circle* in all its stages of revision, and I read the first drafts of certain chapters. These were, for example, "The Buddha's Smile" and those chapters in which Nadya, the wife of Sergei Kerzhin (the name initially given to Gleb Nerzhin), figured.

In many ways these chapters were born of my diaries. Now we discussed them together.

Today I can distinctly see that I had an all too uncritical attitude toward everything my husband wrote, especially the Stromynka chapters. If the author transformed my Stromynka girl friends into fictional characters of such small and superficial interest, it is quite possible that the blame lies with the meagerness of my diary entries and my inability to convey in narrative form the atmosphere of our lives, the complexity and drama in the fates of the young postgraduate women I lived with.

I knew that Solzhenitsyn could understand, feel, imagine how one ought to write far better than I. But it is clear to me that Aleksandr Isaevich, with his tendency to recognize only the zeks, and in part their wives, as interesting human beings, may simply have turned a deaf ear and a blind eye to my experiences outside the range of his interests.

I have saved a letter from one of my friends who read *The First Circle* in manuscript, in 1964, and who expressed her opinion of it without mincing words. She had the right to do so, because in that first draft she was one of the lively and moving personages of the Stromynka chapters. "The way it comes out," she wrote me and my husband, "is that life in 'freedom' is depicted very one-sidedly and prejudicially, especially in regard to the women portrayed in the novel."

She went on to recall other women, Olga Chaikovskaya in particular, who had received news of two deaths on the same day, those of her husband and of her brother. She still had a son to look after and bring up. Awareness of this and her sense of responsibility had given her the strength to overcome everything.

"Why, then, is this novel so out of focus? Why is it that only the wives of zeks are portrayed as suffering and noble beings, whereas the rest of the women come off so unattractively? Each one had her own burden of sorrow, her own suffering that was not always displayed to everybody. For what reason, then, are these women treated so shabbily? One cannot look at the world only through the prism of one's own sufferings (and in the chapters on the Stromynka everything is shown through the prism of Nadya's sufferings). One ought to try to understand that others, too, are in pain."

In the same letter she recalled the poetic images of Russian women in Pushkin and Tolstoy. How could Solzhenitsyn allow women with such a difficult lot in life to be portrayed so flatly and vulgarly?

My husband found a simple solution. He excluded the letter-writer from the list of active personages in the novel. The Olenka into whom the formerly described Sanechka was transformed had even less in common with the intelligent and talented young woman, capable of deep suffering, whom I had known, and the descriptions of "Room 418" suffered from the deletion.

Whenever I see my former Stromynka roommates, we talk a lot about the old days. We remember how stimulating it was for us to gather together in the evening after having studied our heads off separately during the day. Among us were philologists, a historian, a political economist, an archaeologist, chemists. In the evenings our room used to turn into a second university. No subject left us indifferent or was beyond the sphere of our interests. We argued about the goings-on in the Biology Department. Just what was genetics? Was it a science or a pseudoscience? We talked about how my Professor Kobozev was being criticized and ridiculed for his experiments on insects, whereas these experiments had proved to be one of the avenues of approach to cybernetics, which in those days was also regarded as a pseudoscience. We were rather restrained in our appraisals of everything that went on—such were the dues paid to the epoch we were living through—but we were so knowledgeable of each other's interests that during a trolley ride our political economist would argue fiercely with the chemists who were then attacking the theory of ensembles introduced by my *maître*.

Each one of us had her own griefs and worries. And if to a certain degree I lived for Sanya, others, too, had someone to care about. For Zina, the political economist, the object of constant concern was her charming young sister, Mashenka, and later her little nephew, Zhorik. Knarik, the doctoral candidate in philology, so in love with her Turgenev, was caring for and supporting her aged parents. Zhenya, the archaeologist, saved every penny she could from her expenditures on food and clothes, to send what money she had to her talented brother, an artist studying at the Leningrad Academy of Arts. Only Shura Popova had no one to worry about, and this was the greatest sorrow of all. In the course of one year of war she had lost her father, her mother, and her only brother. Studying, for her, was the purpose of living.

And even Nadya Nerzhina, who was pieced together from my diaries and Solzhenitsyn's memories of what I was like at our meetings, is quite far removed from the real Natasha

Reshetovskaya. The ordeals of the dissertation by no means led her to despair, as described in the novel. Nadya was a whiner. Natasha Reshetovskaya, when action was possible, never fell into a mood of despondency, even when things looked bleakest. She did everything she could to complete the dissertation as quickly as possible, knowing that sooner or later there would be an end to all the ordeals, and she even faced some of them with a sense of humor.

Furthermore, the girls were also richer in spirit, to say nothing of their intellect, than the description of them in the *Circle* suggests. Even if they disapproved of something about me (for example, my excessive infatuation with music or chess), this never was, nor could it have been, a subject of malicious gossip behind my back. To be sure, there was talk about it, but only in the open. Even if they had begun to guess that my husband was alive and that all was not well with him, they would not have gossiped maliciously but instead would have sympathized with me.

The New Year 1958 approached. Again there were the three of us, as the year before. For this occasion my husband brought a special piece of lighting equipment from the school, where he had already set up a well-equipped photographic laboratory, and we took a lot of photographs. Among them is a very good picture of my mother sorting out the New Year's mail.

In bidding farewell to the Old Year, my husband liked to review it and to make plans for the new one. Plans for our summer were also ripening. As top priority, my husband dreamed of a trip to Leningrad, where he had been longing to go all his life.

We borrowed a rather old guidebook from the library; on

the basis of the information it contained, Aleksandr set up an elaborate card-index file on the city's history and art. I had become very much interested in Leningrad's architecture back in 1949, during my trip there with the Moscow University Amateur Arts Group. Thus it was decided that I too should set up a card-index file, on architecture.

Dmitry Panin was the first guest of the New Year. By this time he had separated from his wife and son and had moved in with his sister. Such was the epilogue that befell a beautiful, dedicated woman after having waited so many years for her husband.

A sinful man had returned to a sinless wife. But he made up for it by becoming a believer. Now both she and her son were supposed to become believers too. There followed persuasions, attempts to convince, demands, ultimatums. Officially their marriage was never renewed. To what purpose? What if suddenly the same story repeated itself? Would she again have to put up with it?

At that time Dmitry Mikhailovich was of the Russian Orthodox faith. Then he became a Catholic. Later he married a Jewish woman in order to leave for Israel, but he turned up in Paris instead. To his true wife, who had dreamed of sharing old age with him and with whom he had spent the summer months in their country cottage, he left a "letter of consolation" in which he declared that he loved her more than all the other women who had been his in the past and that he wanted to spend the rest of his life in a monastery.

Dmitry Mikhailovich read the *Sharashka*. Basically, he accepted it without reservations. My husband consulted him especially in connection with the disputations between Sologdin and Rubin (then called Levin). Together they invented themes for these disputations. Then they discussed what he had written.

In the spring I went to Moscow to attend a scientific conference on catalysis that had been convened by the "Kobozevites" at Moscow University. The reports produced very lively debates, with both sides taking pot shots at each other. Kobozev himself gave one of the reports. As always (though he rarely spoke in public), it was logical, to the point, at times sharp and witty, and amazingly resourceful in finding *le mot juste*.

The conference lasted several days. All through it I sat next to Tamara Pospelova. We had been almost inseparable in those days when we were the only women in Professor Kobozev's laboratory.

To my amazement I realized that I had not been forgotten in this scientific world. References to my works, in particular to my discovery of the so-called "secondary ensembles," were made in the reports. Kobozev himself referred to them. Later, when I visited the new, spacious premises of the Kobozev Laboratory, in its own building in Lenin Hills, I saw on a display stand, among others like it, the title page of my own dissertation.

Perhaps everything could have been different? But then what would my personal life have been like? Did I have any right to be displeased about anything? I had a home, I had the means to support a family. Aleksandr did not need to work full time at school. He could even quit teaching altogether if he chose.

❦

Aleksandr's illness was not causing pain, but it required continuous attention. That spring he had to be hospitalized for almost two weeks to undergo chemotherapy. It was expected that he might have to stay longer, but he insisted on release, although he continued to receive treatment as an outpatient. He felt all right throughout the treatment, so he continued working almost without letup.

The typing of *Sharashka* was proceeding at full speed.

During the treatment my husband gained about six and a half pounds, which horrified him. However, the tumor seemed to have subsided. After completing the chemotherapy treatment, Sanya was filled with optimism and decided to regard himself as a healthy person. To get rid of the excess weight and tone himself up, he finally agreed with me that we should buy ourselves bicycles.

With great delight I made up for lost time in my life. I had dreamed of having a bicycle ever since my schooldays, but we could not afford one then. Now I became the owner of a lovely green woman's bicycle from the Lvov Plant! My husband got himself a road bicycle that was rather heavy on the pull. But I stood to gain from this. When I got in training, I would not be lagging behind him unless we were traveling against a head wind or on steep uphill grades. It wasn't like walking, where I was not up to my "trotter."

Now our first bicycle excursions "to commune with nature" began: at first to the Oka, then up to Polyany, and then even to beautiful Solotcha, which was more than thirty miles away and which my husband considered "a marvelous place."

The big card-index file on the streets and sights of Leningrad was already completed and the cards were sorted out according to certain routes. With his typed card index in hand, Aleksandr Isaevich could easily have qualified as a guide around Leningrad. We subscribed to *Leningradskaya Pravda*, which for us was tantamount to entering the stream of the city's life.

Finally, after packing the writing and photographic equipment, the essential clothing, the travel aids and other things, all itemized on a detailed list drawn up long before, that happy moment arrived, early in the morning of June 29, when we were on our way.

We arrived in Leningrad on a blindingly sunlit morning. Spring had come late to Leningrad. The streaming lilac bushes were in full bloom along the streets and in the squares, whereas back home they had faded long ago.

In the evening we went out for a stroll, festively dressed for the occasion. Walking along the Nevsky Prospekt in the direction away from the Palace Square, we turned left and found ourselves in front of the building of the former Assembly of the Nobility, the present-day Philharmonic. "You wouldn't have an extra ticket, would you?" someone asked us. It turned out that this was the final concert being given under the direc-tion of the American conductor Leopold Stokowski. We, in turn, began to ask the same question of passers-by, and we finally got ourselves into the top tier. Here, although the seats were not exactly the best in the world, we could also walk around freely without looking at the stage, surrendering our-selves exclusively to the amazing unity of the orchestral sound.

After the concert we went out into the streets. It was light, and the street lamps were unlit. Although it was after eleven, it seemed as if the evening were just beginning. Lilies of the valley, ice cream, soda water were being sold everywhere.

We strolled along the banks of the Neva until four in the morning, taking photographs and simply admiring the pano-rama unfolding before our eyes.

But, of course, Leningrad first and foremost means theater. We saw Bulgakov's *The Flight* in the Aleksandrinka Theater, *The Flying Dutchman*, *Giselle*.

Curiously, what impressed us most was a little French play by Jarry, *The Sixth Storey*, staged by a touring troupe from Riga. "The subject is elementary," Sanya wrote the Zubovs.

" 'He' deceived 'her' and did not marry; but here, precisely, one becomes convinced that in art the most important thing is not what is said, but how."

In the course of his life, Aleksandr Isaevich would naturally return more than once to this thought. And yet he could not conclusively persuade himself of its rightness.

"But listen! In art it's not the *what,* but the *how* that counts," said Caesar Markovich, the script writer, in *One Day in the Life of Ivan Denisovich.*

"No! To hell with your *how* if it doesn't awaken good feelings in me!" Prisoner X-123 replied.

The author offers no continuation to this argument, thereby tacitly expressing agreement, in this instance, with X-123, who had the last word.

Perhaps the whole point is that *both* the what and the how are important. After all, the "elementary" subject of *The Sixth Storey* is eternal. And that this subject is also eternal in life Aleksandr Isaevich was to confirm by himself serving as an example.

Brimming over with travel impressions and memories of friendly gatherings, weighed down with new acquisitions and innumerable rolls of film, we arrived in Riazan on August 11, exactly on time according to our planned schedule.

"It's nice to travel, but there's no place like home!" my husband murmured as he unpacked and prepared for a return to his regular routine.

During our period of "quiet existence," time was marked off, not by the calendar, but by academic years. In the fall, winter, and spring my husband had the school and I had the Institute. Although by now teaching was not of paramount importance, even for me, nevertheless the school and the Institute, our teaching schedules, the preparation for courses, lent a certain rhythm to our life.

Every year Solzhenitsyn taught a course in astronomy for the tenth- and eleventh-year students. In physics he accepted an eighth-year class and taught it through the rest of the grades. As for mathematics, Aleksandr Isaevich rejected it outright. Correcting papers would take up too much time. He declined an offer to become head teacher of the school for the same reason.

Aleksandr Isaevich's teaching load varied from semester to semester, but it never exceeded eighteen hours a week. The school did take up a certain amount of his time, but it was beneficial to him in every respect. It introduced both a mental and a physical relaxation into his central life. He spent no more time at school than was absolutely necessary; he was never late for classes, but he never stayed overtime. He would not allow himself to become overengrossed in his teaching.

Would the teaching experience be somehow depicted in Aleksandr Isaevich's creative work? Unfortunately, no. And yet he did have an idea once of writing about a school. I remember one night when my husband, seated in the corner we reserved for photography, was feverishly making notes, in the weak light emitting from the radio dial, for an outline of "One Day in the Life of a Teacher."

Instead, however, on May 18, 1959, he brought to life an old plot that had lain for a long time in his memory, maturing. He began to write a novel which his readers would later come to know as *One Day in the Life of Ivan Denisovich*.

The novel was written in less than three months, almost in one breath, so to speak, although the intervening summer vacation divided the work into two time periods. The first was from May 18 until the end of June; the second, all of September and part of October. The book was completed on October 11 of that year.

I read the novel as it was being rewritten for the second time. I must confess that the slowly developing action of *One Day*, presented as if by an objective onlooker, appeared a little dull to me at first.

Ivan Denisovich is by no means an accidental figure in Solzhenitsyn's works. If the novel had been centered on a Nerzhin or a Markovich or another counterpart of the author who was sent from the *sharashka* to Ekibastuz, a great deal of space would have to be devoted to ties and associations with the past, to attempts at analyzing what had happened to him alone as compared to what was happening to everyone else, and to reflections about the future.

The author of this novel was not burdened with the need to structure a thematic line, to lend form to the work, to enter into a hero's complex inner world, to deal with the "overlay" that every civilized man acquires and without which it is impossible to depict his life.

Solzhenitsyn probably realized that without portraying a common man, especially a man of the village, it is impossible to become recognized as a real writer in Russia. Such is our literary tradition going back to the time of Pushkin. And in Captain Solzhenitsyn's battery there was no lack of village lads, even though for the most part it was composed of "civilized men."

Although the image of Ivan Denisovich was a collective image, someone was still needed as a point of departure. Ivan Shukhov, the middle-aged cook in the battery, served Solzhenitsyn as just such an initial springboard. Since he had not found a living prototype in the Ekibastuz camp, he transported the real Ivan Shukhov into it.

The language of the novel gave rise to many arguments. Strictly speaking, the author's own language almost never intrudes in the novel. It is the language of the real Ivan Denisovich Shukhov.

Work on *Ivan Denisovich* was interrupted at the beginning of summer. We received our leave, moved our aunts from Rostov in with Mother, and then went off to the Crimea. On the Black Sea coast, where the Zubovs then lived, we spent the hottest part of the day, the interval between our morning and evening walks to the sea, at home, either in the little room we had rented or in its small, shady yard. It was here that Aleksandr Isaevich began the short story which he called "No Village Is Worth Its Name Without a Just Man," later renamed "Matryona's House."

I knew that Aleksandr was planning to write about Matryona Vasilyevna, his landlady in Vladimir, and I was eager to see the result. I had grown to appreciate and love Matryona Vasilyevna in the short time I knew her, and I was deeply grieved by her tragic death.

However, this story was not finished in the Crimea. My husband asked me whether I realized why he could not write further, and, unable to wait for an answer, explained that he had already exhausted Matryona's image and that there was nothing left for him to say about her, though the theme itself had not yet been fully developed. This story was not to be completed until the autumn of the following year, 1960.

The difference between the style of *Ivan Denisovich* and "Matryona's House" is obvious, but I did not appreciate the reasons for it then. Now I can venture to guess that, in contrast to the novel, the story of Matryona lay outside the scope of Solzhenitsyn's life in the camps. It is a narrative of events that transpired beyond the confines of the world behind barbed wire. Later, Aleksandr Tvardovsky was to tell my husband that this work seemed "less pithy" than *Ivan Denisovich*.

The desire to raise a series of ethical questions that, as Aleksandr Isaevich believed, should be the concern of any human being, any society, any state, prompted him the next year to begin a play entitled *Candle in the Wind, or The Light Within You*. The image of the little candle symbolized the image of the human soul, which man must not extinguish, and which the twentieth century was enjoined to pass on, solicitously, like a baton in a relay race, to the twenty-first.

However, a play with such lofty conceptions did not easily lend itself to dramatic treatment. Solzhenitsyn started working on the play at the end of 1960 and worked at it through 1964. After writing several drafts, he declared it a failure.

For my part, I liked the play. The only thing I found unconvincing and superfluous was the desire of Alex, the author's stand-in, to put a stop to the development of science. Now I understand that the fact that many of the characters in the play were based on living people very close to me was an important reason for my liking it.

Take Mavriky. For the most part this was my uncle, Valentin Turkin, the professor at the Film Institute. The role was replete with details of his life, his character traits, and the tragic separation from the daughter whom he had not set eyes upon for so many years. Mavriky's daughter, Alda, in many respects was my cousin Veronica.

Solzhenitsyn had Nikolai Vitkevich in mind when he created the character of Filipp. But the character was enormously exaggerated, endowed with an overweening ambition and credited with myriad successes in life. Indeed, Filipp is made to appear as a high priest of science at a time when Vitkevich, in real life, was no more than a newly hatched doctoral candidate in the chemical sciences.

And, finally, there was Alex, who was in many ways my husband.

The General, Terbolm, Sinbar, and all the other members of Filipp's learned scientific entourage were fictional.

Surnames and given names were selected to lend the action a vaguely foreign flavor, so that one is made to feel that it takes place in the middle of the twentieth century "somewhere on our planet." For the same reason the language in the play is deliberately "neutral," almost flat.

When Solzhenitsyn asked the Leningrad producer Nikolai Akimov to decide "whether this play is worthy of the stage, of publication, or of the stove," he replied, "I liked your play." But in the same breath he suggested that Solzhenitsyn take it instead to the Vakhtangovites. . . .

A friend of ours expressed himself with greater frankness than had the theater directors and producers: "I read it with interest, but I would not want to read it a second time. And this has nothing whatsoever to do with the treatment of female characters, but, rather, with the author's unusual dramatic concept."

Actually the play's conflict remains partly unresolved. The protagonists are so abstracted from real life that, probably for this very reason, all their fine talk leaves the reader cold, and by the same token would leave an audience cold. Alex, most of all, was programmed to act as a spokesman for the author's ideas. And if Filipp did have a life plan of sorts, albeit a misguided one, that of his antipode Alex—the "positive hero" —was wholly negative: I reject this, I don't want that! He required pure abstractions. When Alex takes up "cybernetic socialism" one can't help but expect that this, too, will soon be a source of disenchantment.

Here it is appropriate to add that the author himself came to view these abstract ideas about conscience and goodness as rather fragile in the test of time and of life. The time would come when he would allow that conscience was a "facultative feeling" on the basis of which one could "both break a vow and harmfully misuse someone's trust."

※

To write, to write everything down as conceived, and maybe even more, one had, above all and at whatever price, to enjoy good health. One had to feel fit. A healthy body makes for a healthy spirit.

Regular morning exercises, gymnastics, and other such ordinary measures would not suit Aleksandr. His overdeveloped individualism found such routines unacceptable. Even here he demanded something distinctive, something different from what most other people were doing. And suddenly the answer came to him: yoga!

The infatuation with yoga came to us from Panin, with whom it was a real and total obsession. Solzhenitsyn duly took note of the fact that Panin was already taking nine hundred complete breaths in twenty-four hours, skiing for many hours "on only a few complete breaths," and standing on his head for a long time every day after work, counting the strokes of the metronome. As a result of this way of life, however, the physicians stated that he had a preinfarctal condition, adding that if he kept it up they could promise him a Group II invalid status.

No infarction developed, but one day, after a prolonged yoga fast, Panin did land in a hospital. What he feeds himself now in Paris, and whether or not he still stands on his head in the evenings, I don't know. But I would venture to guess that Aleksandr, although an enthusiast of lesser degree, probably continues to do his series of yoga exercises every morning.

❧

By 1959 the other family in our apartment had moved away. That summer we helped Aunt Nina and Aunt Manya to move in with us from Rostov. They were both in their seventies now, and it was getting more and more difficult for them to keep house and provide the basic necessities for themselves. And during his years in Ekibastuz and Kok-Terek, Aunt Nina had become a very dear and close relative for Sanya.

The trip we made to fetch the aunts was memorable for us, not only because of the problems of packing, the innumerable worries about details of moving, the difficulty of finding cartons and packing cases, and of handling the ancient pieces of furniture—which could not be squeezed through the doors and, instead, had to be lowered into the yard from the window and by way of a neighbor's balcony—but also because we had so many joyous and heartwarming reunions in Rostov. The most important one was with the Vitkeviches.

Nikolai was putting the finishing touches on his dissertation. Along with this he found time to engage in heated scholarly debates with the "authorities" in the field.

When we talked with Nikolai and his wife Egda, or with Emil Mazin, we felt young all over again, as though there had been no war, no separation, as though we were still students. This feeling was not diminished even by the presence of the

Mazins' daughter, Natasha, who was already a student herself. She was the little girl I had seen on the wharf in Baku when Mother and I were in flight from the Germans in 1942.

From then on our family had the whole apartment. My husband and I were now in the room that had previously belonged to the neighbors: it was twice as large as the one we had occupied before.

My mother continued, as always, to be the guardian of the family hearth, and the two aunts became her helpers. I had very little housework to do. But it was a must that every autumn I was assigned the task of pickling and marinating. The jars of cucumbers, tomatoes, even plums, stored in the cellar were more than enough to see us through the winter. The sideboard contained a supply of jams freshly made by Mother, a delicacy that my husband particularly relished. My husband was responsible for stocking potatoes and vegetables for the winter, and for assuring a sufficient supply of logs for the stove, which meant that he sawed and chopped wood. At first his partner in wood sawing was Pavel Alekseyevich, the yard keeper at my Institute, but later I took Pavel's place. Why hadn't I tried it earlier? I found it most pleasant and not at all difficult. My husband and I liked to count how many back-and-forward movements it took to cut through particularly thick logs.

In addition, my husband was our house doctor, as we liked to call him, half-jokingly, half-seriously. I once wrote to the Zubovs: "Pursuant to a remedy prescribed by Sanya (recognized by all of us as house doctor) both of us (Aunt Nina and I) are drinking gillyflower extract to strengthen our constitutions."

Once my husband treated me for a headache with a fashionable "stimulant" that had to be dribbled on the top of the head, drop by drop. And in the spring of 1960 Aleksandr Isaevich bought himself a medical manual, *The Reference Book of a Practicing Physician,* to acquire even greater self-assurance in this domain.

In this, as in so much else—indeed, as in everything else—Solzhenitsyn's desire for independence was clear. Efficiency! Self-reliance! I want to, and I must, do everything myself. Be tied to no one. Depend on nobody. Have no recourse to any kind of outside consultation. Finally, be absolutely sure of the correctness of the diagnosis. Once you make the diagnosis yourself, then you can be sure!

In all other matters as well, Aleksandr Isaevich preferred to depend on no one. What does one do, then, with a wife who does not always restrain herself when shopping? Frankly, the motto "Earn little and spend less" did not always sit well with her. Sometimes he had to admit defeat. "Natasha has 'perverted' me in the sense that she has dulled my vigilance with respect to kopeks and even rubles," my husband complained to the Zubovs.

And when the wife decided to celebrate her supplementary earnings, which came from giving lectures at a medical institute, with the purchase of a large carpet, Aleksandr literally became despondent and proclaimed that the acquisition of things "is an endless and insatiable process, conducive only to the crushing of the spirit."

But all this is really neither here nor there. My husband and I were living in a state of complete harmony. Congratulating the Zubovs on the advent of another anniversary of their marriage, Aleksandr wrote that only as we grow older do we begin to understand and savor this new taste of a well-aged nuptial drink—not the carefree champagne of youth, but the rich ambrosia matured from a warm heart and a clear mind.

There was an element of posing in this, to be sure. After all, we weren't feeling all that elderly yet, especially when we could hop on our bikes or take off on our skis.

In addition to maintaining our health we also had to continue expanding our knowledge of world literature. Aleksandr Isaevich procured an encyclopedia of literature and, going through volume after volume, carefully read biographies of writers and the analyses of their works. He inscribed everything that was most germane about a given author on a separate sheet of paper, usually torn out of an exercise book, and then placed it in a special file folder.

Back in the years of exile, Aleksandr had started a collection of musical data in a thick exercise book, and one of literary data in slim copy books. The notes on individual sheets, devoted to this or that writer, were filed in alphabetical order in folders marked "Russian Literature," "Soviet Literature," and "Western Literature." These folders began to bulge enormously. The project turned out to be excessively time- and labor-consuming. But even more time was required to read through all those works about which Aleksandr hoped to form at least a general impression.

Aleksandr Isaevich tried to read only those works regarded as models of literature. When he moved to Riazan, he made an appraisal of all the books of my very modest library, and as a result, a long-range plan was made for "Operation Library Scoop-up." In the first phase of the "scoop-up," for example, the following books got caught: Herzen's *From the Other Shore* and *Memoirs* (read for the second time), Dostoevsky's *House of the Dead*, books by Mikhail Prishvin, Graham Greene, Hemingway, Richard Aldington. In the second phase: *Anna Karenina* (also read for the second time), Konstantin Paustovsky, Dostoevsky's *The Idiot*. In the third phase:

The "Quiet Existence"

Tolstoy in the Memoirs of Contemporaries, Montesquieu, Voltaire, Swift, Rousseau, and others.

As he read individual short stories and, in particular, poems, Aleksandr Isaevich liked to rate them, beginning with a dot. Then came a plus sign, and finally exclamation marks, up to three of them, which were conferred, for example, on a poem by Tyutchev, entitled "Silentium."

As for foreign literature, Aleksandr Isaevich infinitely regretted that he was unable fully to appraise what to him was of paramount importance, the writer's language. It is no wonder, then, that the only foreign writer he envied, so he told me one day, was a Russian. This was Vladimir Nabokov, who was cut off from the country of his birth. Solzhenitsyn used to say that he liked Nabokov's resourcefulness in finding the right metaphors, his linguistic virtuosity.

The moment Aleksandr moved to Riazan, a ban was imposed on my purchasing books. To like a book or simply to want to read it was not sufficient reason to buy it. What for? Such a book could be taken out of the library. And, indeed, my husband registered with three libraries, the City Library, the Regional Library, and the Library of the Officers' House. At home one should have only books that were essential, that would be needed today, tomorrow, a month from now, and even years later. Accordingly, the first thing to be done was to replenish the collection of classical writers. We either bought outright whole series of editions of classical writers, or subscribed for their purchase. Among them were the collected works of Chekhov, Aleksandr Kuprin, Paustovsky, Prishvin, Anatole France. (Incidentally, Aleksandr Isaevich was soon disenchanted with Anatole France.)

It took a long time for my husband to read a book. The lion's share of his free time was devoted to creative work, and

he considered it absolutely imperative to study Dahl regularly
—ideally, every day. He used to say that he needed to create
within himself an internal ambience of the Russian language,
to become suffused with its spirit.

But it seems to me that in his search for *le mot juste,*
Aleksandr Isaevich owed much to the mathematician in him.
Mathematical precision, to the point of pedantry—this was
the crucial element of his creative work. He would make note
of "new words" and sayings in the margins, but would not permit himself to exceed a certain preset quota of them per page.
Even in the selection of given names and surnames, complete
order reigned. No chaos whatsoever. Everything was thoroughly thought out and organized, everything was registered
so that the same name would not be repeated too often.

Many of the family names he used were those I brought
back from the Institute. My husband would jot them down
and later they would crop up in his writings. This is what
happened, for example, with the surname Shkuropatenko,
which was given to one of the zeks in *Ivan Denisovich.* Several
years later I learned of the distress this had unwittingly caused
to the family of a former student of mine. His grandfather had
suffered a similar fate in his time.

Once a woman colleague of mine lent me an exceedingly
rare book, published in 1904 to commemorate the centennial
of the Riazan Secondary School for Boys. Aleksandr Isaevich
made note of the surnames that interested him from a long list
of the graduating class. The surnames of other former students
of the Riazan Secondary School for Boys may well figure in
the pages of Solzhenitsyn's future novels. Varsonofiev and
Obodovsky are already living characters in *August 1914,*
whereas in *Cancer Ward* Dr. Vera Kornilyevna Vega has received the German surname of Gangart.

The "Quiet Existence"

After Aleksandr Isaevich came to Riazan he acquired an addition to Dahl's Dictionary, a dictionary of proverbs compiled by the selfsame Dahl. This led to intense activity—reading, making cross-references, excerpting and reclassifying. We did part of this work together. After he marked the pages I would retype the proverbs. My husband's dream was someday to have a big vase filled with cards inscribed with all the best proverbs, so that he could pick them out at random and sift through them.

As for Aleksandr Isaevich's literary tastes and appraisals, these were subject to continuous and radical change. As a student, Solzhenitsyn was smitten with Jack London. As a frontline fighter, he esteemed Gorky above all others. Much later, and for a long time, it would be Tolstoy. But in general, authors could disappoint him overnight and, just as suddenly, others could beguile and captivate him totally.

It occurs to me that a parallel exists between this impetuosity and Aleksandr Isaevich's tendency to form an opinion about a person at the very first meeting. First impressions have always played a major role in his life. It is as though he strove to draw a conclusion as soon as possible, to harness all his mental energy, all his powers of observation for this purpose—and the conclusion had to be arrived at forthwith! Perhaps his passion for saving time was also a factor in this drawing of quick conclusions? In life (in everything except his writing), speed was the order of the day. And often, on the basis of a single fact, he was ready to make a vast generalization. If one approaches this from the point of view of dialectics, then what he often seemed to do was miss the link in the cognitive process that should follow the "discrete"—the "particular." In theory, one passes from the discrete through the particular to the general, but with Solzhenitsyn the process appeared to be shortened by skipping from the discrete straight to the general. In consequence he was ready to accept what might be misinformation as information, perhaps because then he would not have to waste time verifying it. We had much of this sort of thing in our conflict.

On the other hand, if time was expended, he felt it must be justified. A letter that is written has to be sent. Time should never be spent for nothing. As for the possible consequences of this attitude, that was a matter of tertiary importance.

Solzhenitsyn stopped liking France, Kuprin, Paustovsky. He suddenly viewed Kuprin as a writer whose themes were "weak and shallow." Anticipating rebuttals, he even tried to explain literary events in mathematical terms: *The Garnet Bracelet, Sulamith*, and in part *The Duel* were the exceptions that "proved the theory of probability whereby some successes are bound to occur given the number of attempts." In his polemical fervor it never occurred to Aleksandr Isaevich that, pursuant to this theory, any graphomaniac ought to produce masterpieces. My husband's appraisal of Paustovsky, of whom he had been very fond, cooled more gradually, but he began to accuse this writer of "not having found his theme—this in an epoch in which one could not but find one's theme." He reacted disapprovingly to the fact that Paustovsky had "gotten bogged own into an autobiographical narrative which threatens to become two volumes out of the seven volumes of his collected works."

More oil was poured on the fire when *Novy Mir* began to publish the memoirs of Ilya Ehrenburg, which Aleksandr Isaevich initially disliked. In general, he felt that an "autobiographical narrative" was on the one hand "a product of narcissism on the part of the author," and on the other a consequence of his helplessness, of "the inability to elevate himself to an artistic generalization of what has been observed."

Solzhenitsyn was not against memoirs in general; he was against only memoirs by writers. And he was against those in principle.

It is usually considered that Solzhenitsyn's first published work was *One Day in the Life of Ivan Denisovich*, which appeared in *Novy Mir*. Not so, really.

In March 1959, three and a half years before publication of *One Day in the Life of Ivan Denisovich*, *Priokskaya Pravda* carried an article, entitled "Post Office Curiosities," whose author was Solzhenitsyn. It was a commentary on the delay in mail deliveries.

A year later Solzhenitsyn wrote another composition in the same genre, complaining about the sale of two railroad tickets for the same seat. It was sent to the newspaper *Gudok* ("The Train Whistle"),* but for some reason the newspaper never published it.

In November 1960, Aleksandr Isaevich sent the *Literary Gazette* an article called "The Epidemic of Autobiographies." After adducing what seemed to him rather weighty arguments against this "epidemic," Solzhenitsyn asked: "Why does a writer who is capable of *creating* need to write a simple autobiography? Those who prove to be worthy will be written about by their contemporaries, or by 'literary scholars.'" So "isn't it time that magazine publishers, at least, put a stop to this epidemic of literary autobiographies?" challenged Aleksandr Isaevich.

The signature at the bottom of the typescript read:

---

* *Gudok* is published by the Union of Railroad Workers—Ed.

A. Solzhenitsyn, Teacher. And a little lower down was a post-script: "I should like not to receive a courteous apology to the effect that 'Unfortunately, the editors do not have the space for publishing this.' If I am right, I request that this article be published. If I am wrong, I request a rebuttal."

The reply from the *Literary Gazette* arrived eleven days later. The editors thought it was ". . . pale, devoid of talent."

Thus Solzhenitsyn was not understood by the *Literary Gazette*. Nor was he understood by Paustovsky, to whom he sent a copy of his article, "The Epidemic of Autobiographies." There was no answer at all from him. Aleksandr was per-plexed. After all, Solzhenitsyn had highly praised the first part of Paustovsky's autobiographical novel, which was constructed in the form of "a chain of free-flowing novellas."

Aleksandr Isaevich's comments about Ehrenburg's memoirs were very cutting at first: he thought Ehrenburg was arguing with dead men and trying to prove to the living that he was honest, that he was something of a genius and also very clever. But the second part of the memoirs pleased my husband, and he wrote friends that Ehrenburg was reminiscing "in a busi-nesslike manner" along with an attempt to gain a deep under-standing of the civil war. "There are profound thoughts which I have never encountered elsewhere. Many of the portrayals are also interesting."

Thus wrath was supplanted by mercy, and even respect. Perhaps one reason for this was that the civil war theme had always intrigued Solzhenitsyn. It probably would have been far more interesting for our painter friend Ivashev-Musatov to read Ehrenburg's writings "about pictures he hadn't seen," which interested Solzhenitsyn as little as Ehrenburg's opinion of them. Any literary work was naturally evaluated in terms of his interests, his particular mood, the direction of his own work. And when one is rigidly focused, impatience comes easily. The need to assert the primacy of one's own interests often compels criticism of those who differ. Thus are literary and worldly tastes born.

Much later, after Solzhenitsyn had achieved fame, when other writers were no longer indifferent to his opinion, Georgy Vladimov sent him his novel, *Three Minutes of Silence,* which had just been published. Aleksandr Isaevich began to read it with interest. He liked the basic situation: the hero, a seaman, was bidding farewell to the sea. But he put the book aside as soon as the seaman decided to return to his trawler. It was as if all writers had to orient themselves to Solzhenitsyn's criteria and tastes:

> Nerzhin never read a book simply for entertainment's sake. In books he sought either allies or enemies and on every book he read he would mete out a precisely worded verdict, which he liked to foist upon others.*

Aleksandr was to have this attitude for a long time to come. He would return to the theme even in the short story "For the Good of the Cause," written in the spring of 1963. It hardly seems plausible that the given problem should agitate the students of a technical school to such a degree, but this did not disturb the author. In the story, a boy "wearing eyeglasses and with a funny-looking crew cut" launches an attack on the writing of memoirs. "Anyone who has lived fifty years feels the compulsion to publish his memoirs—how he was born, how he got married—but any fool can write such stuff."

And what about Aleksandr Isaevich himself? I am not

---

* From *The First Circle*

speaking of *Archipelago* now, but of his purely literary works. Doesn't he, like most writers, throw out segments of his auto-biographical self, merging them now with one and now with another of his literary heroes, who are not simply himself but an alloy of himself and someone else, sometimes someone who is a purely imaginary personage? Is this so different from writing memoirs?

Most of all, Solzhenitsyn is amalgamated with Nerzhin (*The First Circle*). But we find him also in Nemov (*The Love-Girl and the Innocent*), in Shukhov (*One Day in the Life of Ivan Denisovich*), in Zotov ("An Incident at Krechetovka Station"), in Alex (*Candle in the Wind*), and in Kostoglotov (*Cancer Ward*), in whom there is also much that was taken from Ilya Solomin; there are also hints of him in Vorotyntsev (*August 1914*). In the latter, Solzhenitsyn projects himself into an entirely different epoch and adapts himself to entirely different circumstances. He describes himself as he would have been then, or, quite often, as he would like to have been.

I remember another extreme judgment, one of Aleksandr Isaevich's thoughts in favor of the classics. In his opinion the fundamental problems of the contemporary world are essentially the same eternal problems ever besetting mankind, which "only change their apparel every decade." "That is why one can draw much more from Pushkin's 'The Prophet,' 'Anchar,' or 'As Down the Noisy Streets I Wander' than, for example, from an Aleksei Surkov or an Yevgeny Yevtushenko."

Once we saw Part II, *The Boyars' Plot*, of Eisenstein's film *Ivan the Terrible*. It did not elicit Aleksandr Isaevich's approval. "Such a conglomeration of eccentricities, tricks, devices, novelties—so much art that it is no longer art, but God knows what," he wrote the Zubovs.

In the same year, 1960, that he attacked writers for occupying themselves with writing autobiographies, Solzhenitsyn also took up arms against the movies. No articles on the film as such were written and nothing was sent to the journal *Cinema Art* or to any newspaper. Only the Zubovs got to read these gloomy prognoses for the future of the film: ". . . one gets the impression that the quality of cinematography all over the world is constantly on the decline. . . . There is more pleasure to be derived from an average book than from an average film."

From this appraisal one might have gathered the impression that Solzhenitsyn had just returned, at least, from a world film festival. But in the context of the letter this sounded less convincing, inasmuch as he had started with the admission that we had missed seeing *Krotkaya* (*The Meek One*), that *Tamango*, it was rumored, was stuff and nonsense, and that although *The Judge* was "all right, one could afford not to see it."

Even later Solzhenitsyn could not shake off his misgivings about the fate of the film. "I'm afraid that the future of the film, as foreseen by L. Tolstoy, is either already a thing of the past, having exhausted itself, or simply never was," he wrote.

❧❧

Alas, the Institute increasingly became for me merely a means of earning a living. I had always approached everything I did with enthusiasm and dedication, but I could no longer call up these emotional reserves. It was as though I had burned myself out. I felt I had reached my limits in teaching; I could go no further. And as for real scientific research work of the kind I used to do in Moscow, I could not arrange for this in Riazan.

It gave me far more pleasure to help my husband, to occupy myself with music, the English language, and photography than to give lectures. I had learned how to live not for myself but for my husband.

I sorely missed guidance in my music studies. Following the advice of my husband, who offered himself as an example, I tried to move forward by studying Heinrich Neuhaus' *The Art of Piano Playing*. I made an attempt to join the Riazan Philharmonic Society, but without guidance I had lost form.

My husband teased me about my diverse infatuations and fits of enthusiasm and said that I still had not found my fulcrum in life. In fact, my individuality was still begging for some sort of expression. But the fulcrum was there. It was my love for my husband. Our relationship was such that my life was completely, or almost completely, subordinated to his interests, to his work. It was no accident that our friends, the Zubovs, making gentle fun of me, would call me "the Chekhovian darling."

Yet "a darling" was precisely my husband's ideal. At that time he used to tell me (later, he recalled this in a letter to the Zubovs) that while he was in Kok-Terek he had made photostats of Tolstoy's afterword to Chekhov's story, "The Darling," and either gave or sent these to be read by his "numerous prospective brides." And "only Natasha, in 1956, in Torfprodukt, after having read the pages, agreed at once and in full." This was by no means a sacrifice. It was my natural bent. How difficult a future separation was to be, for exactly this reason! Only then, too late, did I understand that in our century one cannot become a "Chekhovian darling" for anyone, not even the most outstanding human being.

Variety was injected into our measured life, with its strictly set routine, by the arrival of guests, though they were now very rare.

Nikolai Andreyevich Potapov came to see us again. By that time he and his wife had moved to the hydroelectric construction works on the Kama River, where he was executive director of electrical installations. Dmitry Panin came to see us a few times, and there were visits from other friends.

Of my many friends, only Shura Popova came to visit me, and once on her way to some other place, Irochka Arsenyeva of Rostov, a childhood friend of mine, came to see us. When Shura visited, we could not do without making music together. Once we even made a tape recording of our small concert: Schumann, Schubert, Rimsky-Korsakov, Weckerlin.

None of our guests arrived unexpectedly. They were, so to speak, planned guests. But one visitor fell in on us like a bolt from the blue. Although my husband had not seen the unexpected arrival for fifteen years, and had seen him then only once, during a train ride, he recognized him instantly. The countenance and the general appearance of Leonid Vlasov were too striking to escape instant recognition. Having once been able to make friends so quickly and so successfully before, Aleksandr and Leonid kept up an animated conversation throughout the evening.

Vlasov often had to go to Moscow (he lived in Riga) and he indicated that he would be glad to come to see us again. But by the time of his second visit he had sensed Aleksandr's extreme reserve and understood that it wouldn't do to drop in on us like this. Thereafter the relationship was confined to an occasional exchange of letters.

Our encounter with Vlasov was memorable to be sure, but a fleeting one nonetheless. Whereas when it developed that Nikolai Vitkevich and his wife were preparing to move to Riazan, I was in seventh heaven. I was not aware of all the difficulties. As I saw it, he and Aleksandr had gone through a great deal together. My husband had met Nikolai ten years before he met me. They had always been side by side, at school, in the university, at MIFLI. They had been together at the front and in prison.

But Solzhenitsyn at once dampened my enthusiasm: "They'll start visiting us. We'll have to exchange presents."

Of the relatives, Aunt Zhenya, my mother's sister in Kislovodsk, visited us occasionally. And my husband's aunt came in the second half of January 1961. Irina Ivanovna Shcherbak was the wife of his uncle Roman, his mother's brother.

Aunt Ira, who "adjusted herself very well to all our little old ladies," as my husband put it, was happy and at ease in our home.

We showed her Riazan, we drove her to our beloved Solotcha. This trip had another, practical aspect to it. We were toying with the idea that Irina Ivanovna might consent to move closer to us. A house with a garden was for sale in the village of Davydovo, adjoining Solotcha. We could buy the house and settle her there. And we ourselves could visit her constantly, provide her with all the basic necessities, help her with housekeeping, spend our days off there, and occasionally even stay for several weeks.

Aunt Ira liked it there very much. But still, she somehow panicked at the idea of moving from a spot to which she was so accustomed. And what would she do about her cats? After all, you can't put them all on a train. "No," she said. "It's better not to budge the aged from their well-worn grooves."

Irina Ivanovna never did decide to make such an abrupt change in her way of life. She preferred solitude in her tiny closet of a room, a solitude she shared with her pets.

After her departure, a lively correspondence ensued between Aunt Ira and my mother. At first it seemed natural that

Mother shared the burden of the correspondence, that she should take upon herself all the concerns about sending her money and parcels. But as the years wore on, Irina Ivanovna started taking offense because her nephew hardly ever wrote her himself. The sickly imagination of the aged led her to believe that Mother and I were to be blamed for this, that we were fending her off from Sanya. I lost my temper and answered her, reminding her how once, feeling sorry for the cats, she had preferred to remain with them rather than stay with Sanya.

Those who are interested in Solzhenitsyn and his books are familiar with Irina Shcherbak. Solzhenitsyn had written about her himself long before her name appeared in the November 1971 issue of the West German magazine *Stern*. Irina Shcherbak has been described as she was in her youth under her own name in *August 1914*. In her old age she appeared in *Candle in the Wind* as Aunt Christina. These works celebrated her piety.

But Irina Ivanovna was not simply a believer. She expounded her original views in innumerable letters to my mother, often dedicated entirely to the cats that were under her care. One such letter contains the following lines: "They, indeed, are the true followers of Christ. People, on the other hand, are far removed from the teachings of Christ."

Let us try to understand this old lady. She could not forgive the insults I had dealt to the "true followers of Christ." So one cannot be surprised at the misinformation she gave the *Stern* correspondent. He, Dieter Steiner, in fact turned out to be on the same level as the old lady. Normally, an interviewer would try, in the first minutes of conversation, to determine whether or not he could rely on the comments of a very old person. In this case, evidently, Aunt Ira's version of events was more convenient to the publishers than the truth. Irina Shcherbak transformed me, a Cossack woman, into a "daughter of a Jewish merchant" and made me, Solzhenitsyn's wife, into his "mistress." She did not do so out of a desire to distort facts, but simply because these were the most abusive words in our little aunt's lexicon.

If anyone surprised me, it was Aleksandr Isaevich. In a four-hour interview, this time without his customary concern for saving time, he commented in detail on the *Stern* article. But he did not find a word to say in my defense. True, a year later he was to promise me a "posthumous rehabilitation."

∽∾

Infrequent trips to Moscow lent another type of variety to our "quiet existence." Usually they were professional errands, scientific conferences for me, official visits to the Academy of Pedagogical Sciences for my husband. Very seldom did our trips to the capital coincide.

In May 1960 I had the opportunity in Moscow to visit an exhibit of English artists; to see the exhibit of the younger Svyatoslav Roerich; and to see Oscar Wilde's brilliant *Lady Windermere's Fan*. And on that same trip I happened to ride in a bus along Novoslobodsky Street and see how the brick wall of the Butyrki Prison, which had once filled the heart with terror, was now being torn down. It struck me then as a symbol of how the terrifying past was receding forever.

Whenever Aleksandr got to Moscow, he always made an effort to see Panin, Kopelev, and Ivashev-Musatov. Once all four of them gathered in the apartment of Dmitry Panin's sister. It was February 9, 1959, the fourteenth anniversary of my husband's arrest.

Each of them had had the opportunity to see the art show in the Manezh Exhibition Hall. Aleksandr was shocked at the "obscene prank of the Polish artists" who used the entire space allotted to them for their profoundly abstract, or else totally expressionistic, works of art. There was not a single work in the spirit of realism! Nevertheless, the hall was filled with people; there were outbursts of spontaneous arguments and, in general, a great animation reigned. Ivashev-Musatov replied that all great artists were "to a certain degree abstractionists. Even Rembrandt and Rublyov balanced one figure not by another but, for example, by a curve; and color was not counterbalanced by color but, for example, by a glance." And even if present-day abstractionists were "people without heart" who were "creating not a home but a skeleton of a home, and then suggesting that we live in it," a complete disregard of abstract art would lead to "the decline of ornamental and decorative art."

***

These were our pastimes throughout the academic year—in the fall, the winter, and the spring. But what happened in between, during the summer months? Something entirely different, something new—with fresh, new impressions—burst into our measured life. We broke out into the open spaces.

Our vacations were almost never sedentary. With the possible exception of those two weeks in 1959 on the Black Sea coast, where all we did was go swimming morning and evening, we were usually on the move. The itinerary was always prepared beforehand, and a strict schedule made provision for transfers and stopovers and, in addition, for reunions with old friends. This required preliminary study of the railroad or steamer schedules; then inquiries were sent out, maps and guidebooks acquired, and index cards compiled for the particular sights to see in the area.

The trains radiating from Moscow carried us in various directions: to Leningrad, and from there to Ostashkov or the Baltic; to the Crimea and the Caucasus; or to Vladimir and even to Irkutsk. And from these places we could make trips to points nearby or excursions according to prearranged routes.

Besides the Volga, the Oka, and the Moscow River, we also sailed along the Dnieper, the Kama, the Belaya, and the Yenisei. Of course the Yenisei, the great Siberian river, was to us the most amazing of all.

On the Dnieper we fell in love with the town of Kanev, where the poet Taras Shevchenko is buried. Kanev has a picturesque site of rolling hills blanketed with forest. The innumerable lights of the metallurgical foundries of Dneprodzerzhinsk, blazing all night, are imprinted on our memory. The ancient city of Kiev rose majestically, seen from the Dnieper, as it faced the river with its monument to St. Vladimir.

We made many a walking tour through the splendid city of Kiev. We even managed to get into St. Cyril's Church, where restoration had been in progress for many years, and we saw Vrubel's interesting frescoes.

On November 2, 1959, Lev Zinovyevich Kopelev came to Riazan to give a lecture on Schiller. He spent only one night with us. Leafing through the manuscript of *Ivan Denisovich*, he waved it away with a casual comment: "This is just a run-of-the-mill novel." And he had the nerve to say that it was overburdened with details.

However, three years later, with the help of the selfsame Kopelev, the novel was to be sent to *Novy Mir*.

9

~~~~~~

Crossroads

*I*n November 1962, a few days after the publication of *Ivan Denisovich*, crazy with happiness, I left for Moscow with two new short stories by my husband. In my previous trips I had always found it cozy to spend the three-hour trip reading, and even making notes, on our comfortable Riazan-Moscow electric train, with its soft reclining seats and pull-out tables. But this time the trip passed in lively conversation with a fellow passenger, an assistant professor at my Institute. At one point the conversation touched on *Novy Mir*.

"Generally speaking, I don't read it," he said. "But I must get hold of the eleventh issue. By the way, have you read Konstantin Simonov's article in *Izvestia?*"

"Not only have I read Simonov's article, but *Ivan Deniso-vich* itself," I replied. Then, unable to hold myself back, I confessed: "The author is my husband!"

I was to meet the same assistant professor late one December evening in 1970, at a taxi stand, after I alighted from the Moscow train in Riazan. Our second encounter took place soon after Solzhenitsyn had received the Nobel Prize and during the turmoil of the dramatic developments in our personal lives. The assistant professor and I recalled that train trip we had taken eight years before.

He must have forgotten about that meeting a few minutes later, but our conversation made me relive many of the events of that now remote time. Those years were a turning point in our life—when old hopes were coming true and new hopes arose, and when the world appeared sunny even on a cloudy day, and nothing seemed to portend the disaster that struck later.

Sequences from the film of my own life flicker before my eyes, making me happy and excited again.

But how important it is when you know the end of the film! Things that appeared significant at the time sometimes recede to the background, while other events that once seemed not so important acquire greater meaning. And you cannot help thinking: how could I not have seen what this was going to lead to?

Over and over I view the film of the years past, now stopping it at one frame and now at another, to get a better look, to understand better. . . .

. . . I am trudging along a wintry, snow-covered street to the Institute. My husband has left on an early-morning train for Moscow where he is to have his first meeting with his editor. He is going to meet with Aleksandr Trifonovich Tvardovsky at *Novy Mir*. As for me, most inopportunely, I have to deliver an open lecture on polymers. Somehow this brings me down to earth, and my mind returns to daily concerns. Doubts start to creep in. Will there really be a change in our fate? En route to the Institute, I tried to divine the future: If the first person to greet me is a man, then everything will be successful for Sanya!

The first to greet me was the yard keeper of our Institute, our dear Pavel Alekseyevich, or Uncle Pasha, as we called him. And he not only greeted me, but, as is seldom done nowadays, he took off his cap and bowed low.

Aleksander Isaevich came home that evening. He appeared to be in a somewhat distracted state of mind. Silently he took out of his suitcase a large sheet of heavy paper with the word AGREEMENT at the top, and showed it to Mother and me.

Months followed months. Spring passed, summer was coming to a close. The question of whether *Ivan Denisovich* would be published was still not resolved. A letter from *Novy Mir* gave rise to hopes: ". . . there may be news any day."

And exactly a week after that, a curious event occurred. We were resting after lunch, each of us reading, trying to relax. Suddenly my husband said to me, "What kind of clock is ticking?"

"The alarm clock."

"No, that's not it."

"Well, then, it must be my watch ticking away," and I gave him my wrist watch to listen to.

"No."

At that very moment an ear-splitting ring from an alarm clock shattered the silence. Our surprise was mingled with a little fear. Aleksandr Isaevich went to the night table and from its drawer he removed an old, broken alarm clock that had been lying there forgotten for at least a year and a half. The amazing sound rang out in our home at 5:41 P.M. on September 24. Some day, perhaps, we will find out that something of particular importance to us was happening at that moment. Maybe it was simply a signal that it was time to wake up and go to Moscow to learn the good news.

If so, it was opportune.

Another visit to Moscow followed a month later. At ten o'clock in the evening I stepped out of the house to meet my husband. He was already on the threshold: in a gray coat, carrying a small gray suitcase, his face radiant with joy.

"My star has risen!"

Time sped by faster and faster. Other events—different in character and coloration—occurred in our lives.

The freezing night of New Year's Eve. Moscow's Sovremennik Theater, on Mayakovsky Square. The play had ended. The actors were preparing to greet the New Year.

Little square tables had been set up in the foyer. Each table was adorned with a low candelabrum with tiny lighted candles; there was no other illumination. Overhead hung fir branches from which dangled flowing ribbons, glowing balls, and Bengal lights.

Aleksandr Isaevich and I sat at one of these tables. Midnight was approaching. Three minutes before midnight we were joined by Oleg Yefremov and his wife, the actress Alla Pokrovskaya. Oleg Nikolaevich had just returned from the filming of *War and Peace*, in which he played the part of Dolokhov.*

---

* Oleg Nikolaevich was then chief director of the Sovremennik Theater—Ed.

Midnight struck. Champagne glasses were raised. "Happy New Year!"

Music blared forth from the phonograph, the Bengal lights sparkled, firecrackers went off.

Couples rose from the table. Scarves, fur capes were flung over the backs of chairs. For the most part the women wore décolleté gowns, their arms bare.

They danced the twist.

It was our first New Year's eve in such crowded and brilliant company. If I had been told that it would also be the last, I would not have believed it!

What would the next twelve months bring us? They would bring many developments, worries and cares, and also much of what could have been easily foreseen, which contained nothing threatening, but which nevertheless made my life more complicated.

More and more often my husband and I were apart. I would be in Riazan, he in Solotcha or Moscow. I would have liked to travel with my husband, to be near him in Solotcha—to keep house, to retype what he had written, to help him in everything. Sometimes the thought flashed across my mind: perhaps I should leave the Institute? Some of our acquaintances were positive that that was the right thing for me to do.

But earnings in the literary field are unsteady. To outsiders they seem gigantic. What is not taken into account is that royalties are not received every two weeks, and not even every year. So far we were pretty well off financially. The book had seen three editions. But this was today. What about tomorrow? Tomorrow my salary as an assistant professor would be much needed again. And it would be needed for a long time to come. So thus far, there could be no question of my becoming a "housewife only." When I was not busy at the Institute, I sorted out his correspondence (and there was a great deal of it) and did other secretarial work. When the weather was nice, I took the folders out into the garden. I devoted some time to housekeeping and much to playing the piano.

The Institute began to mean less and less to me.

For the first time I feared that I might not be able to keep up with my husband in that swift current of events. There was no basis for this. But I had an intuitive feeling. Perhaps my mother was right when she often quoted my father, who used to say that women's intuition is above men's logic. Suddenly, it seemed to me that I might fail to keep up with my husband, might lag behind him in that swift current and go to the bottom. It followed that I had better not lose sight of the shore I must reach before feeling solid ground under my feet. Provided I would not be too weak by then to get to my feet.

For a long time now my work at the Institute had ceased to be this coveted shore. More likely, my music could become that shore for me. My husband supported my illusions by promising that when he became a published writer the circle of our acquaintances would be immeasurably widened and I would have the musical communion and companionship I had so sorely lacked.

The need for self-expression is peculiar to the human being. "To find oneself and to express oneself"—that was how my closest friend, Lida, and I had once formulated the goal of human life. To express oneself in thought, to express oneself in feelings . . . In music I expressed myself with greater frankness than in words. Verbally I was reserved to the extreme, even secretive, before I was dealt that terrible blow in the autumn of 1970.

And that is why it always seemed to me that whoever did not hear me play did not know me.

In those days I did not miss a single opportunity to play the piano. I never thought that in a little while my husband would make an unusual evaluation of that aspect of my life. "After all, you are not a great musician," he would say. It followed that only the great had the right to express themselves. All the others must remain faceless.

This was one of those cases when Aleksandr surprised me with an odd, new perspective on things. Not only in regard to me. Similar notes sounded in his conversations with his friends and were noticeable in his attitudes toward them.

We visited the painter Ivashev-Musatov. He took us to his studio. It was not the first time that Aleksandr Isaevich saw the pictures he had painted after his release. But Aleksandr still hoped that Ivashev-Musatov would, in his work, turn to what they had gone through together. However, the painter still considered his *Othello* his lifework. He had painted several versions of the picture.

Aleksandr Isaevich knew that the artist had begun working on *Othello* back in 1956. He definitely refused to understand it: after all, Shakespearean personages had already been depicted in thousands of paintings.

On that occasion and later, Solzhenitsyn tried to dissuade his friend and to rechannel his creative activity. He would argue with him for a long time, but then would realize they were going in different directions.

Sergei Mikhailovich Ivashev-Musatov was captivated with man's strong personal emotions. And in Shakespeare he found the creative power which afforded him maximum perception of Good and Evil.

After one such meeting, a letter arrived from Ivashev-

Musatov in which he said that it is very frightening when people who love and appreciate one another are scattered about by life in such a way that they cannot even see each other and exchange some intimate thoughts, or say something that could never be said to a simple acquaintance, but only to a friend. "And I would like to suggest to you, dear Aleksandr Isaevich: let's meet more rarely. But when we do, let's make it very real, so that later that bitter sensation of estrangement cannot arise. Agreed?"

Sergei Mikhailovich's letter was an attempt to save a friendship that had always seemed to be unbreakable, and which Aleksandr Isaevich himself had cherished so much before—to save it during the new period of life that had opened for Aleksandr Isaevich. He was being given advice! But it was already impossible to advise Solzhenitsyn. Circumstances proved to be stronger. How would one find time for everything? How could one combine everything without stealing time away from creative work? One had to make choices; some things and some people had to be preferred over others. Had Aleksandr Isaevich selected the right things? And the right people?

I had always tried, both outwardly and inwardly, to justify my husband. In my thoughts, and once even in a letter to Ivashev-Musatov, I tried to bring about an understanding:

> Dear Sergei Mikhailovich! Try to remember how once, when you yourself were on a 'creative bender,' you did not answer us for a long, long time. But in my husband's case this creative bender has never been interrupted.

But the cause of their estrangement was deeper than that. Somewhat later, I heard Sergei Mikhailovich say that a man whose vision was directed only into the past could not live a full creative life. He recalled that after his release from prison he felt as though he had "sprouted new wings" and "new vistas opened up for creative endeavor," for new works and new joyful feelings. Clearly, given such a polarity in their mental attitudes, the bond between the old friends was bound to wither.

There was a cooling of relations with his other friends from the prison camp. Steeped in the past, both in his thoughts and in his creative work, Solzhenitsyn could not understand why his friends were losing interest in that past, why other themes were gaining prominence in their lives.

He could not help but be happy about the work and successes of his old kind friend, engineer Potapov, who with youthful enthusiasm was moving from one construction site to another and giving himself wholly and pleasurably to work. Yet at the same time Potapov's "easy" departure from a past that was so important and valuable to Aleksandr gradually washed away the ties that had formerly existed between them. A few years later he would say, sadly: "He does not need us any more."

The late Yuri Vasilyevich Karbe, an engineer, was one of the people closest to Aleksandr in the Ekibastuz camp. After their release they were at first fast friends, even though they lived far apart from each other. In the summer of 1962 we visited the Karbes in Sverdlovsk, and later they visited us. Yuri Vasilyevich was the first to wire his congratulations on the publication of *Ivan Denisovich*. He took it very hard when he realized that Aleksandr Isaevich had no time for his old friends.

When Nikolai Vitkevich, who had been offered a position as assistant professor in chemistry at the Riazan Medical Institute, moved to Riazan in February 1962, my husband was only moderately happy.

SANYA

The Vitkeviches' move, a very joyful event to me, was viewed by my husband with mixed feelings. Nikolai and he were no longer "two trains traveling at the same speed, so that one could jump from one train to the other easily," as it had been during the war. Their stay together at the Marfino *sharashka* had shown that. "Will we have anything in common aside from reminiscences?" my husband asked me.

Indeed, the friendship among the four of us in Riazan proved rather flimsy, although at first it was backed up by my common "chemical" interests with Nikolai, and by cycling outings together.

Our friendship of many years' standing permitted us to trust the Vitkeviches. They could have become the first readers of my husband's writings, but they never did. Literature, art and politics usually were not among the subjects of our conversations. We would talk about work, vacationing plans, domestic affairs. Anyway, we could not imagine that the New Year's party—greeting 1965—would bring a complete break with the Vitkeviches.

Not long before that my husband let them read his *Sharashka*, for there was a bit of Nikolai's life in it. And in general, how was it possible for them not to read his main work at the time?

We greeted the New Year of 1965 with the Vitkeviches, who were our guests on Kasimovsky Lane. And here, at the New Year dinner table, the atmosphere suddenly grew tense and heated.

Nikolai announced that there was no frankness between us. When I objected, he replied that there was only an appearance of frankness between us. Aleksandr, very much on guard, declared that if no frankness developed between himself and another person, then he stopped seeing that person.

The conversation turned to the novel. Nikolai had had
time to read only a few chapters. Nevertheless, he said that
on every page he had discerned a lack of modesty and a pretentious peremptoriness. But immediately he displayed the
same peremptory attitude himself in passing judgment on great
Russian writers: in the heat of polemics he spoke disrespect-
fully of Tolstoy and Dostoevsky. But he was particularly annoyed by "those who regard themselves as their disciples."

Aleksandr asked who he had in mind specifically.

"You, for instance," Nikolai replied promptly.

The next day Aleksandr went over to the Vitkeviches', and
on some pretext retrieved his beloved creation which they had
failed to appreciate.

The same year the Vitkeviches had a baby boy. I suggested
that my husband rise above the quarrel we had had and con-
gratulate them.

"I don't see how the birth of a child is a greater event than
the birth of a novel," he replied. "After all, they rejected my
Sharashka.

Many years later Aleksandr was to understand what the
birth of a child can mean. This is not to say that then, in 1965,
he was less sensitive. It was just that at that time the "question of children" lay outside his sphere of interest. And everything that was not directly connected with that sphere seemed
not to exist for Solzhenitsyn—and never had since his younger
years.

It was thus that, to some degree, a one-sided perception of
life had been formed. A bright beam illumined only a portion
of the darkness, making things stand out in relief. But beyond
the circle of light everything was barely discernible.

Hence, his naive, sometimes phantasmic views on very ordinary aspects of day-to-day living. Hence, his "plans," such as

those connected with the crises in our life together, plans that simply astounded people by their lack of realism.

Hence, failures often attending Solzhenitsyn's creative writing, when he tried to write about something which he had not seen himself, but only imagined. And considering the fact that our self-appointed "recluse" had always had a rather narrow circle of acquaintances—people with whom he talked and through whom he confirmed a perception of the world around him—is it any wonder that he made attempts to force on life conclusions constructed in his own brain?

This was due to the scant interest he took in the bustle of life around him, to a lack of experience with life and with people. He lacked the insight born of observation, which alone can furnish a writer with necessary material. What he did know was a narrow, solitary corner of the world—prison camps.

Irrevocably, Solzhenitsyn was losing old friends. He had acquired new ones from among his fans.

But now there was not a single friendship where he was on equal terms with another. If these people in his new retinue derived something for themselves from association with their idol, he in turned looked upon them more or less as "useful acquaintances."

Whereas formerly Aleksandr used to be drawn to people who had seen something of life, who could reflect upon it and who liked doing so, to people from whom he could learn a lot, now he became interested in those who could help him with his work, in a very narrow sense—to compile material, to get hold of a book or article he needed, to retype something, to arrange a meeting with a man who could give him some interesting facts, and to record his conversations. In other words, they were people who made his literary task easier, who helped to save his time.

Perhaps they did help to save his time, but at what a price!

If with his old friends he used to have serious discussions, even debates, on creativity, literature, and his own writing, there was nothing of that kind now. Solzhenitsyn was now such an expert on all questions that he felt no need for association of the former sort. (Once he even set out to explain to me, a chemist, what was a total mystery to himself—the octane rating of gasoline.) Solzhenitsyn was not concerned with the problems and cares of his "new friends." Their inner world did not interest him.

Thus he had dozens of so-called friends but not a single real friend.

Among such "friends" were some who were actually a nuisance. For instance, Zhorez Medvedev was so eager to have the reputation of "Solzhenitsyn's friend" that he did not mind, at times, tucking away his dignity. He lived in Obninsk, and preferred going to Moscow not by rail but by hitching rides, which took him past our *dacha*. He never missed a chance to drop in. He could not but feel that his presence was far from always welcome. And yet, although we once literally sent him packing from our home, he came back again and again.

In 1965 Zhorez Medvedev spent some time moving heaven and earth to get me a position with a research institute in Obninsk, so that we would move there. He was very much distressed when all his efforts failed. He had failed to become our family's benefactor! To this day he has not abandoned attempts or missed a chance to "defend" Solzhenitsyn. Thus, having heard that I was writing a book, but not having the slightest idea what kind of book it was going to be, Medvedev hastened to make a statement to the effect that I had told him I would devote the rest of my life to "avenging myself upon Solzhenitsyn." This statement was so pathetic that I could not even become seriously angry with Zhorez.

Lida Korneyevna Chukovskaya let Aleksandr Isaevich use

a room in her Moscow apartment, and her daughter Lyusha spent all her free time typing out what he had written. She and many others carried on so over him that Solzhenitsyn may have begun to feel that whatever was being done for him was properly his due. Some of them seriously believed that Aleksandr Isaevich was a genius for whom one must make generous allowance.

How eminently right was one of these ladies, Nadezhda Alexandrovna Pavlovich, when she later wrote:

"We are guilty of having perverted you . . . with our glorification and our near adulation of you."

I once asked my husband why he had such an entourage. I expected him to get angry, but he replied almost distractedly: "I don't know. It somehow just happened by itself."

For the sake of fairness, perhaps I should mention Solzhenitsyn's most fervent admirer.

Once, in a public library in Leningrad, a woman who was no longer young studied my husband for forty minutes before approaching him (he had allowed her to come to the library to make his acquaintance). Later, sharing her impressions with me, she confided that she was amazed at the deftness with which Aleksandr Isaevich had tossed a pencil into the air and then, without looking up, caught it in flight after it had made several somersaults in space. (At this he was indeed a virtuoso.) She told me, further, that she had been afraid to approach Solzhenitsyn. Would he live up to the image she had created? She had eulogized him in such lines as these: "We—there are thousands of us! You—you are one. And no one, not one of us, can dare to claim your attention. One cannot be angry with the one to whom one prays. I await your telephone call with impatience . . ."

This rhapsodical worshiper was Elizaveta Denisovna

Voronyanskaya. Soon after we made her acquaintance she went off on pension. She learned how to type—to be useful to her idol. My husband could approach her with literally any request at any time, and she would do everything she could for him.

In the spring of 1973 she refused to forgive herself for the harm she thought she had caused to the object of her prayers, and she hanged herself in her room beside a portrait of Solzhenitsyn.

His relations with other people were reduced to a bare minimum. For instance, as an author who had gained recognition, Solzhenitsyn began receiving dozens of requests from young writers that he comment on their work. Soon enough, however, he found a form of defense from them, which he called Form No. 1. It read as follows:

Dear ———

You have sent me your manuscript and have asked me to comment on it (revision, advice, can it be published).

I regret that you did not ask my consent beforehand. It may appear natural to you that any writer can, and should, give you his opinion about the level and quality of your work, and that this does not present any difficulty for him.

However, this is very laborious work: to give a superficial evaluation, after barely leafing through the pages, would be irresponsible; you could either be groundlessly discouraged or just as groundlessly encouraged. To give a professional critique, however, requires a serious self-immersion in your manuscript and an evaluation not only of the writing but also of the goals you

SANYA

have set for yourself as a writer. (After all, your aims and those of your reviewer may not necessarily coincide.)

The condition of my health and my late arrival on the literary scene compel me to place an extreme value on my time and make it impossible for me to comply with your request.

Believe me that a nameless (to you) reviewer who is constantly occupied with work of this sort for a magazine, say, for *Novy Mir*, would be able to satisfy you better than I.

All the best!

(Signature)

In earlier days young Solzhenitsyn had found it natural to turn to Konstantin Fedin and Boris Lavrenev with his first works. The replies he received from them were a far cry from what he set forth in Form No. 1.

One of a few exceptions to the rule was an episode with Tatyana Kazanskaya, a Leningrad authoress.

In the summer of 1963, Aleksandr Isaevich and I visited Anna Andreyevna Akhmatova in Leningrad. As we left her place and were walking to a trolley stop, a frail, bespectacled woman with small, sharp features caught up with us. She appeared quite young to us. Very nervously, she extended a manuscript to Aleksandr Isaevich and asked him to read it.

"Why have you chosen me in particular to do so?"

"Because I like immensely what you are writing."

My husband could not resist the compliment and took the manuscript, warning her only that he could not read it in Leningrad.

After some delay Aleksandr Isaevich did write to her, grumbling the while about how much time she had taken away from him, but giving her an extended critique of the story.

"Your story is on the threshold of success," he summed up. "To cross this threshold it would be desirable if . . ."

In a word, Kazanskaya was lucky. But, pushing her luck too far, she sent him another short story, and of course never received a reply.

Many other people, not only budding writers, found themselves out of luck when they tried to approach Solzhenitsyn. He refused point blank to see any journalists, readers and visitors in general. The wall between the writer and life was growing higher.

Once two Moscow sculptors paid us a visit. They were going to do a bust of Solzhenitysn, and if they could not talk with him, might they not at least take a look at him? I was trying politely to persuade the sculptors to abandon their enterprise, and not succeeding too well, when my husband lost his temper, came out, and, pushing me aside, slammed the door in their faces. I joked, woefully, that now he would be depicted just like this, slamming the door in the face of visitors.

And once we were taught a lesson for that. Two young journalists gained access to our house by pretending to be city electricity supply controllers. They drew up an official paper forbidding us to use an electric light in our cellar. For nearly a year after that we would climb down into the cellar for pickles with a flashlight.

In those years Aleksandr Isaevich also had quite a number of interesting people among his acquaintances, many of whom were sincere and well disposed toward him. Then why did he not prefer them to others? I think this can be well illustrated by the example of his friendship with Aleksandr Trifonovich Tvardovsky, which ended in failure.

Aleksandr Isaevich had had a liking for Tvardovsky for some time. As early as 1944 my husband wrote to me from the front that he had got hold of the first "truthful (in a spirit I appreciate) book about the war." It was Tvardovsky's *Vasily Tyorkin.*

Solzhenitsyn decided to ask none other than Tvardovsky to pass judgment on his *One Day in the Life of Ivan Denisovich,* because he had a high opinion of Aleksandr Trifonovich as a writer. Besides, Solzhenitsyn hoped that Tvardovsky would understand the story with his heart. Being of peasant stock, Solzhenitsyn reasoned, Tvardovsky could not fail to appreciate his choice of the principal character.

Tvardovsky's response surpassed all his expectations.

Later on Tvardovsky also accepted Solzhenitsyn's subsequent stories "Matryona's Yard" and "Incident at Krechetovka Station."

Tvardovsky was touchingly attentive toward Aleksandr Isaevich. Having received his "Krechetovka" story, he took pains to set his mind at ease—just in case. "It happens that one story pans out well," he said, "and the next does not." He asked Solzhenitsyn not to lose heart if that one proved a failure.

Not long before *Ivan Denisovich* was published, Aleksandr Isaevich received a long letter from Tvardovsky, filled both with hope and apprehension for Solzhenitsyn, for his future.

"By right of age and literary experience," Tvardovsky warned Solzhenitsyn that he would still have to face up to a confrontation with "interest in your person aroused, at times, by other than literary impulses." Tvardovsky as much as told him that he hoped that Solzhenitsyn would keep his calm, would show equanimity and a high sense of dignity.

"You have gone through many trials, in the course of which your talent was formed and matured, and it is difficult to imagine that you would not be able to stand up to the test of fame."

Curiously, Tvardovsky's anxiety was echoed in a letter from Miss V. K., a reader from Moscow. We received that letter three months after the appearance of *Ivan Denisovich*. "Dear citizen Solzhenitsyn," it began. "I'm writing under compulsion . . ." The writer of the letter then went on to explain that she had been compelled "by life itself, by its sacred meaning." She wrote that his story had aroused mixed feelings in her. She was worried that he would soon become a fashionable writer. And that meant that "someone will try, against your own will, to use you for some ulterior end."

She predicted that life would confront Solzhenitsyn with a trial far more difficult than all the privations of his prison camp years.

On Sunday, November 18, 1962, the day *Ivan Denisovich* was published, Solzhenitsyn went to see Tvardovsky at the latter's invitation, to hear his remarks on the "Krechetovka" story.

It seemed that Tvardovsky, without any preliminaries, had placed on the table before him a copy of *Izvestia* and opened it to page five.

Aleksandr Isaevich looked at it cursorily, laid the paper aside, and suggested in a decisive manner, "Let's get down to business" (meaning analysis of "Krechetovka").

Tvardovsky shrugged his shoulders and went out into another room, closing the door behind him. Thus Solzhenitsyn was compelled to read Simonov's article (while the review was favorable, Solzhenitsyn complained that Simonov "wrote nothing about the language, about the penetration into the soul of an ordinary man").

The discussion about "Krechetovka" began with Tvardovsky's question as to how the short story was to be examined: with or without an anaesthetic. Of course, Aleksandr Isaevich rejected the anaesthetic. Aleksandr Trifonovich made quite a number of comments. The author countered each one with vigor. "Why don't you try to hold the whole line instead of fighting for every foxhole?" Tvardovsky suggested, attempting to restrain him.

Aleksandr Isaevich wanted very much to hear Tvardovsky's opinion of *The First Circle*.

At first he let Tvardovsky read a few chapters in which the Gleb and Nadya Nerzhin theme was developed. On the whole, Aleksandr Trifonovich seemed to like those chapters. However, he considered that starting the publication of the story before he saw the rest of it, broken off in mid-sentence as it were, "would be unwise and might ruin the whole project."

Aleksandr Isaevich decided to make another revision of *The First Circle* and show it to Tvardovsky once again. Perhaps this time he would accept it for publication?

On May 2, 1964, Aleksandr Trifonovich paid us a visit in Riazan.

We drove to the station in our car to meet him.

I saw Tvardovsky for the first time: a large man wearing a light blue raincoat and blue beret, which made his eyes seem a brilliant blue. He felt cramped in our little "Denis" (as we had dubbed our *Moskvitch* car). I was wishing I could make more room in it somehow.

We had set our round table in the study for dinner.

We offered Aleksandr Trifonovich the use of my husband's

study. A large stack of typewritten sheets—the manuscript of *The First Circle*—lay on the writing desk.

The next morning, right after breakfast, Tvardovsky began to read the manuscript without interruption.

We placed a thermos bottle with tea in front of him. He was fond of drinking tea with honey. He had even brought a jar of honey with him. So as not to be in the way, we went out into the garden. My husband began tinkering with the car, and I puttered around in the kitchen garden.

After lunch the men went out into the garden, and I sat down at the piano. When they came back, Aleksandr Trifonovich heard me play and asked me not to stop, to play more and more. He praised me highly: how nice to have a wife like me, who could sit down at the piano, just like that, and play one thing after another. . . . And where had Aleksandr Isaevich run off to? How could one stand not to be listening to this music? He even tried to drag Solzhenitsyn out of my room where he was listening to a BBC broadcast.

Tvardovsky won the heart of everyone at home. And that was not surprising. His blue eyes and the open quality of his face with its acquired sadness . . . he was exceedingly polite with everyone, and very considerate.

He read again the next day, and the day after. We heard him hum a little to himself once in a while.

Meanwhile Aleksandr Isaevich, true to his principle not to engage in creative work when we had visitors, was again tinkering with the car.

During dinner my husband told Tvardovsky about the circumstances of his arrest. I showed some photographs to Aleksandr Trifonovich. I remember that he particularly liked one in which my husband and I were sitting on the trunk of a fallen pine at the front, reading Gorky's *Matvey Kozhemyakin.*

Leaving for work the next day, I overheard Aleksandr Trifonovich say that he felt very sorry for Simochka. "And Nadya, too," he added with sadness.

After breakfast on May 6, we heard Tvardovsky's remarks on *The First Circle*, page after page. As far as I can remember, most of them concerned the "Stalin chapters." Laughingly, I remarked that I was present at last at a *Novy Mir* editorial discussion.

What a pity that the relationship between Solzhenitsyn and Tvardovsky did not grow into a real friendship. Right before the publication of *Ivan Denisovich* it seemed that a friendship was beginning to form. In those days this was Aleksandr Isaevich's supreme desire. But at the same time he decided that there was something about this friendship that would act as a fetter on his independence. Friendship should be a two-way street. Tvardovsky was older, Tvardovsky was more experienced. He would be giving advice. But Aleksandr Isaevich felt less and less in need of advice from anybody. He felt that he knew better than anyone else how he should act. No one could become an incontestable authority for him, not even Tvardovsky.

Later on my husband would be repeatedly drawn to seek Tvardovsky's counsel, but he would still do everything his own way. He would not allow Tvardovsky to protect him against the rash actions that so complicated his literary and personal fate!

The revised edition of *The First Circle* which Tvardovsky had read contained a number of essential alterations. One of them concerned a tape recording which the prisoner Rubin (called Levin in the previous version) deciphered in the laboratory of the Mavrino Institute.

A new draft of *The First Circle* was in the hands of the

Kopelevs. How would Lev receive it? The point was that in the old version the prisoner Yakov Levin was deciphering tapes of telephone conversations to help the state apprehend a person was was betraying the interests of his country to an intelligence agent of a foreign power. Lev Kopelev, who was the prototype, had raised no objection to this version, which so closely paralleled real life.

But in the new version Rubin helps to jeopardize a good, kindly person who warns a likeable elderly scientist against careless contacts with foreigners. He does this not to a traitor, not to a spy, but to a decent human being who has never committed a reprehensible act. Kopelev himself, of course, could never have been capable of such conduct.

I was very much upset when my husband told me that he had an extremely agitated conversation wtih Lev. Why should he try to please the prototypes of his characters? Wouldn't it be simpler to ignore them altogether?

Later, Kopelev wrote a letter. It was a very important letter, requiring much thought. Kopelev felt that, despite their falling out, it was absolutely essential that he set down in writing everything he thought about *The First Circle.* "Muster your patience—read it, and then, after that, may heaven guide you."

This letter was by no means devoted to the question that had bothered Kopelev: whether Rubin's action, which led to the ruin of a good man, was justified or not. The letter was a very serious critical analysis of the entire novel.

First of all, it discussed the imbalance between Solzhenitsyn's faculty for direct representation and his faculty for speculative imagination. Hence the qualitative difference between the two "layers" of the novel: the depicted and the imagined. Kopelev discerned that a "subjective preconception," reflected in a "vagueness of the zeks' perception of what was out there, beyond the walls," pervaded even the "basic artistic texture" of the novel. He concluded that its consequent "inner duality" made it weaker than Solzhenitsyn's novella and his short stories.

Kopelev further expressed alarm over the fact that the success of *One Day* and the short stories, the attendant admiration and praise, had imbued his friend with "a dangerous certainty" that he was already "holding all the truths in the hollow of your hand." However, this success and recognition were not only a right, but also and above all a great responsibility. He suggested that Solzhenitsyn try to understand his basic motivation and "to bring up the flanks and the rear" only after this understanding had been achieved. He himself hesitated to believe "in those homunculi who perforce are conceived in newspaper and archival test tubes." This comment also applied to the writings that were to become *August 1914*. Aleksandr Isaevich jotted the words "We'll see" in the margin of the letter.

A few days later Aleksandr had an answer ready in which he explained why he could not take Kopelev's remarks seriously and reproached him for his incorrect appraisals of *Ivan Denisovich* and "Matryona." "Wouldn't I be an oaf if I had listened to your advice on both occasions? Therefore you cannot demand that I should henceforth accept your tastes without convincing proof."

However, Solzhenitsyn's answers to the individual questions Lev Kopelev had touched upon were far less persuasive than the latter's arguments. Only one point was specifically taken into account: "As for what you say about the interrogation chapters (others have also said the same), I shall give it some thought. Meanwhile, I'll keep silent."

"It's not for me to judge," wrote Solzhenitsyn in connection with the asserted disproportion between memory and imagination. "But I would be a dead duck if I were to believe that I cannot write out of my imagination, for one cannot see everything for oneself."

In the matter of Rubin, Aleksandr promised to do everything possible within the limits imposed by the novel itself.

There may have been people who, having read the novel only in its revised form, began to have doubts as to whether they should shake hands with Kopelev after that. He doubtless seemed an utter scoundrel to some of them.

We tried to find a way out. Solzhenitsyn wrote Kopelev a "rehabilitation" letter which he could show to anyone who might think he did not deserve a handshake.

❧

My duties as "secretary" were steadily gaining scope. I sorted out the letters and put them in numbered folders. There were also folders for newspaper and magazine articles containing reviews of Solzhenitsyn's writings. There were many such folders already, and as more time passed, their titles became more varied.

The first reaction to *Ivan Denisovich* that came in was entirely favorable. Among other things, it noted the literary merits of the story. But the main stress was on the fact of its publication and on the need for works on prison camp life. The author's biography evoked sympathy as well. Sympathy ran very deep for the innocent victims of the period of the personality cult.

Aleksandr Isaevich realized that the subject of the story was largely responsible for its success. Typically, when two of his other stories were published—"Matryona's Yard" and "Incident at Krechetovka"—he said to me: "Well, let them judge now. Then it was the subject; now we have pure literature."

Magazine articles, unlike newspaper pieces, were more thorough, and they examined the literary merits of the story. Quite often diametrically opposite views were expressed. There was much that pleased and much that hurt. But Aleksandr Isaevich took it all in his stride. He accepted praises as a matter of course, and he attributed negative comments to a lack of understanding on the part of their authors, or to the great difference between his views on life and literature on the one hand and those of his critics on the other. I was much more vulnerable to the criticism leveled at my husband.

File Folder No. 28, labeled "Reactions from Abroad," contained various clippings from foreign newspapers, or translations of them, which had come to us through *Novy Mir* and *Mezhdunarodnaya Kniga,* or which had been forwarded by readers.

At that time the reactions were much more frank than was later the case. They were devoid of superlatives and comparisons with classic writers, as well as of naked flattery—in short, of everything that was soon to appear in such profusion. The authors of foreign reviews had only a marginal interest in Solzhenitsyn himself. Their aim was not to give a critique of the novel, to sift out its merits and its shortcomings, or to help the author understand better what it was that the reader wanted from him. They were much more interested in whether or not the novel accorded with their ideology, whether it jibed with their conception of Russian life and Russian literature. Reviewers in the West (including, by the way, quite a high percentage of political observers) belonged to different camps. But there was something in common about them that struck the eye.

The Yorkshire *Evening Post* of January 31, 1963, carried probably the frankest and most outspoken review of the novel at that time, saying it had political but no literary value. On August 2, 1963, the London *Evening Standard* stated that someone would try to make political hay out of the novel.

Discussions of the book by Western reviewers were marked by multiple overtones bearing upon a struggle between "liberals" and "conservatives" in the USSR. One could tell that some circles in the West wanted to make *Ivan Denisovich* an arena in which passions clashed, a focal point in which all the currents of Soviet cultural and political life converged.

After a time, much literature on Solzhenitsyn would accumulate in the West. As legends and rumors around his name snowballed, he would be regarded as "martyr," "leader of the Russian democrats," "champion of human rights." He would be compared to Tolstoy and Dostoevsky.

His arrival in Europe would somewhat dampen the ardor of his Western "friends." The "truly great democrat" would turn out to be a far cry from what the Western press had made him out to be. Comparisons to Tolstoy would become more rare. It was not a martyr who was needed now but a politician. Herzen's name would be conjured up.

But of course, the ideals of the two are so different, as are the ways in which they found themselves outside their native country; different is their attitude to the Russian people, to revolution and progress.

True, both of them have published magazines. Both were married twice, and all four of the women in their lives were named Natalya.

In Moscow, Aleksandr Isaevich liked most of all to do research in the Basic Library of Social Sciences and in the Central Military-Historical Archives, in the former Lefortovo

Palace. There he managed to unearth some documents about his father. One of them even specified the church in Bye-lorussia where his parents had married during the First World War.

When, in late January 1964 my husband telephoned me, just before leaving Moscow to go to Leningrad, he said that he was abandoning his research in the library and the archives. It seemed to me that he had reached the very height of the investigation, and that he was interrupting it at the most crucial and interesting point.

Why should the research be interrupted? Why, for that matter, should he have to go to Leningrad? Couldn't the materials available in Leningrad also be found in Moscow?

My husband did not telephone me from Leningrad, but I received letters from him regularly about how well the work was proceeding in the "Publichka," the Leningrad Public Library.

I was rather calm and, finally, mustered sufficient fortitude to withstand this separation.

On February 12 I performed Kabalevsky's Concerto with a student from a music school. We had rehearsed many times at home, and we received high praise for our performance. Now all my energies went into preparing for a concert of my own. It was to take place in March, just before a trip to Tashkent which my husband and I had planned. He needed to visit the Oncological Center there to research some material for his *Cancer Ward*, and I was to go with him. I was being granted a leave.

And suddenly, during this heady intoxication with music, a telegram arrived.

It came on February 13 and was from Elizaveta Voronyan-skaya: BEG PERMISSION REMAIN ONE WEEK LONGER.

At first I attributed no particular significance to the telegram. I thought that it was just Voronyanskaya's idiosyncratic way of saying that my husband had gone into seclusion to complete his work by February 26, and was not permitting social interruptions. (As it turned out, that was more or less the case.) But later I began to worry. I became really upset only when I received a letter from Aleksandr himself in which he made the same request. He couldn't finish his work, he wanted to stay longer, he was asking my permission to do so.

Sometime in 1957, Aleksandr had written to me from Miltsevo about the indivisibility of our happiness, about how it was meaningless to wish happiness to each of us separately. "This means we are to be together. From now on we must celebrate all our birthdays together!" This had become our tradition. In all the years since then, whether we were at home, or in Solotcha, or studying for something, or on skiing trips, we had spent each birthday together.

And now, what had become for us not merely a memorable day, not merely a celebration, but a symbol of commitment that henceforth we should always be together, had begun to lose its value and significance.

The thought of a woman never entered my head. I had been hypnotized, once and for all, by my husband's words: "My creative work is your only rival." Lately I had developed this idea further, thinking to myself: This means that creativity is no longer simply a rival, but a *successful* rival, who is taking him away from me more and more. What can one do?

But in my husband's letter I could not help sensing a certain barely perceptible self-distancing. It struck a note that wasn't quite right. I felt immediately that something serious was going on.

My first thought was: On my birthday, I'll go to Leningrad myself!

A snowstorm was raging outside. Nevertheless, I rushed

twice to the post office, where I sent off two letters and a telegram. This was on the fifteenth of February. Late that same evening I sent one more telegram, this time by telephone: MUST DECIDE YOU TO RIAZAN I TO LENINGRAD WE TO MOSCOW? TELEPHONE TELEGRAPH.

The next day passed. No telephone, no telegram.

No, Aleksandr did not know me. After all, I had been the wife of a zek! What could hold me back? Barbed wire, or what? Why wait for the twenty-sixth? I'll take off for Leningrad. But, alas, just then I came down with viral flu, accompanied by a high temperature.

The next day a telegram arrived from my husband. It was vague and brought me no peace of mind.

I had become so weakened from the flu that the trip to Leningrad was now out of the question. The untimely virus had weakened me in a way that even the barbed wire had not. And once I had thought that nothing could be more terrible than barbed wire!

But the flu passed, and after it something occurred that was a hundred times more terrible than barbed wire. I had never suspected it.

I telephoned my husband as soon as I felt well enough to talk. It didn't occur to me that there might be a telephone in the apartment where he was staying, so I called Voronyanskaya to ask her to get a message to him. To my surprise, she knew that Aleksandr Isaevich was planning to go to Moscow within the next few days. Her voice betrayed no sympathy for me. There was nothing further I could do.

On February 21 I received a telegram from my husband. We would meet in Moscow. I felt somewhat eased, but not really at ease. Yes, something had changed.

On February 25 my husband and I left to meet each other:

I from Riazan, he from Leningrad, both of us Moscow bound. I traveled to Moscow in a somewhat more peaceful frame of mind. But still, upon meeting my husband that evening of February 25, I found myself immediately saying to him, right there on the platform, that he had changed and was "no longer mine." He denied it. On his part, he had done everything as I wished. And he had even brought me a present for my birthday—a pretty beige purse to which, not surprisingly, I took an instant dislike.

My husband had also bought a new sweater for himself. I was surprised by the change in his taste: the sweater was black but with a flashy design. He said that Voronyanskaya had picked it out and talked him into buying it.

That evening my husband tried in every way he could to dispel my anxiety. We had been here together, in the very same place, only one month before. While everything seemed to be the same as it had been before his departure for Leningrad, still something was amiss.

A few days later my husband and I went to visit the Teushes. Susanna Lazarevna,* a very observant woman, sensed a new nuance in my husband's attitude to me. When we were alone together, she asked me whether I feared that Aleksandr Isaevich might become infatuated with one of the actresses from the Sovremennik Theater.

"That's out of the question. I have no doubts: creativity is my only rival."

That same day I left for Riazan. My husband also returned a few days later, on the first of March.

---

* Susanna Lazarevna is the wife of Venyamin Lvovich Teush, who once chaired the Department of Higher Mathematics in the Agricultural Institute in Riazan. The author had become their friend—Ed.

SANYA

My mother got the impression that this time her son-in-law came home an entirely different person. Somehow nothing in the house gave him joy, as it used to. On the contrary, many things irritated him. As though maliciously, the clock, whose chimes had been stopped because of his arrival, would now and then ring out arhythmically, as though protesting against the indignity that had been visited upon it.

I was very busy at the Institute during that period, involved in a session with nonresident and correspondence students. Once home I rushed straight to the piano, since I had never abandoned the thought of giving the concert. For this reason my husband and I seemed to have less contact than normal. Basically, Aleksandr Isaevich was occupied with his *First Circle*, reworking it and polishing individual chapters.

Everything would have been all right if only I could have shaken off the disturbing feeling that my husband had changed in some imperceptible way. Something unspoken remained between us.

Finally, I could restrain myself no longer and asked him about this.

"An act of betrayal has been committed in our home," he said.

"By whom?" I exclaimed, not believing my ears.

"By your mother."

"Mother?"

As long as we were here, in Riazan, he said, he would not reveal to me the nature of this betrayal. Later, perhaps, when we went to Tashkent . . .

My mother and . . . betrayal?

Mother's open-heartedness, her sincerity and selflessness, and betrayal?

I shrank inside myself. All peace of mind was lost. I tried to prepare for the concert, but nothing, nothing went right. I was too scattered, absent-minded.

Somehow or other we lived to see March 17, the day of our departure.

It was sub-zero weather. We called for a taxi so as not to freeze in our light clothes: I wore a white coat and a straw hat, my husband a macintosh.

The train was not full. We had a sleeping compartment to ourselves, just the two of us.

In the train I gradually began to relax. My husband started to leaf through his notes for *Cancer Ward*.

At 3:00 P.M. we were in the capital of Uzbekistan, at the Hotel Tashkent.

Perhaps he had come here to no purpose, said my husband. These doubts, expressed to me on the first evening, were not dispelled even on the next day, after he had visited the Oncological Center, where he walked around in a white coat and participated in the "rounds," all the while being treated as a "distinguished guest."

Once more he became convinced that it was both impossible and absurd to "collect material." Collecting material was possible only by dint of one's own sweat, and without letting anyone know that one was a writer at all. Otherwise, one became an outside observer in the most helpless sense, with everyone around either pretending or nervously on edge.

"One can only write about what one has experienced!"— such was Solzhenitsyn's firm conviction. Was Lev Kopelev right, then?

The bitter day for me came on March 23. Outside, it was raining, turning into a heavy downpour from time to time.

"Well, let's talk!" my husband finally said to me.

He sat me on one of the two beds that faced each other across a narrow space, and, gazing at me fixedly, began to explain what he meant by Mother's act of betrayal.

She had spoken all too frankly with one of our female visitors about the health, or, rather, about the illness, of her son-in-law.

I did not believe it.

"How can you be so sure of this?" I asked. "To whom did she say it?"

My husband named the person.

I was taken aback. I had been inclined to trust this woman, a professor from Leningrad, although I did not know her personally. But another thought gave me a start.

"How could this visitor repeat to you what Mother said? Is it possible that a woman, a casual acquaintance, would discuss such a subject with you?"

My husband was silent. He was probably waiting for me to guess.

"Are you intimate with her?'

"Yes."

"She . . . has fallen in love with you?"

"Yes."

For some reason, I smiled. A learned woman professor had fallen in love with my husband. But in the next instant an irresistible flood of tears poured from my eyes.

I heard him say: "You have helped me to create one novel. Permit me to allow her to help me create another!"

And he went on to say that I was a weakling, that a walking tour was beyond my strength. But he had to wander around through the villages. She was less pretentious than I and had greater physical stamina. He and I, on the other hand, would travel together by car . . . after all, he was a writer. No ordinary yardstick could be applied to him.

Our world, where he and I had been inseparable, came crashing down. Another woman occupied the place in the world that had hitherto belonged only to us.

A faith of many years' standing turned out to have been an illusion.

"I understand everything," I mumbled finally. "My stage in your life has ended. Just let me go away altogether, go away from life itself."

"You must live!" Aleksandr replied. "If you take your life by your own hand, you will not only ruin yourself. You will also ruin me and my creative work."

In the end he convinced me: nothing horrible had happened; he loved me. His attitude toward me and toward her—these were "two planes that could never intersect." For me he had one feeling. For her it was "entirely different."

I had so accustomed myself to believing my husband implicitly, to living with the consciousness that he was a high-minded and exceptional man, that even now no doubts could enter my mind. But how was I to meet him halfway? How was I to remake myself and my principles?

Aleksandr, it seemed, had figured everything out quite well in advance. If only I would agree, how good it would be for everyone concerned! At the same time, his own conscience would cease to bother him. After all, his wife had agreed to it.

Had anyone told Solzhenitsyn then that his proposal to me violated elementary morality and religion, as well as simple kindness, he would not have believed it and would have been genuinely surprised. He would have suffered from the realization that a plan which he had carefully conceived was not being crowned with success. As it was, he kept on adducing new arguments. He said that his feeling toward me would become even deeper, that, on his part, gratitude and admiration would be added to his original feelings for me if I would make this sacrifice.

And, perhaps, this is indeed the height of love—to suffer, to be aware that one is sacrificing oneself. Perhaps it was in this that I would find the highest joy. But even if this were the case, was I capable of such sacrifice?

It seemed as though I were ready to accept. And then once again I burst into tears. Again I was at a total loss.

Thus ended the day of March 23, 1964.

I did not draw any parallels then, nor did I have the strength to do so. But, after all, there had been another March 23 in our life. March 23, 1942, was the day my husband had driven in to see me in Morozovsk—a Red Army man on the way to Stalingrad. The difference between that day and this one! Was this the same man?

On the day that followed, long ago—March 24, 1942— dizzy with happiness, I had written my husband a letter which he would say was the finest I had ever written him.

And now again it was March 24, more than twenty years later.

At breakfast, I could not eat anything. My throat was tight. I simply could not swallow.

Should I enter into this? Should I continue to provide what I had first given him seven years before—all the best conditions for creative work? Should I now try to recreate these conditions on new terms? At that time he had needed the comfort which I tried to supply for him with music, with a well-ordered household, with the ability to anticipate and fulfill his slightest desire. What he needed now, in addition, was the comfort of an untroubled conscience. After all, "Conscience is given to you only once."

On the other hand, as my husband was fond of repeating to me, I was for him the best of all women, no matter how beautiful and attractive other women might appear to other men. In fact, I was so assured that I was the only one for him that I humbly submitted and obeyed him even when he objected to my getting a permanent wave, or using makeup, or dressing according to the current fashion. One must not follow the fashion, because each person has his own style, he told me. And I foolishly went along with everything he said.

I know that I was not being very original when, the following day I went down to the beauty parlor and had a haircut and a permanent wave. Upon his return from the health center, my husband found a suffering being, but withal a more beautiful one. He was openly appreciative.

At times his eloquence had a hypnotic effect on me. I was enraptured, at moments even swept off my feet. It seemed as though I were ready to succumb. And then again I would fall into despondency. I was incapable of conquering my inner protest.

Solzhenitsyn was not only torturing me. He was also observing me. No longer as a husband, but as a writer, he asked me to jot down notes in my diary about how I felt. Later, Aleksandr Isaevich was to take excerpts from this diary of mine. He still has them. Some day, perhaps, he will share that personal diary with his readers.

We strolled in the park adjoining the Oncological Health Center. Perhaps there are some women who would approve of Solzhenitsyn when, one arm embracing me and the other the imaginary waist of another woman, he declared, "At that time I didn't have a single person with me, but now—I have two."

Why did he tell me this? He, of course, would always find an answer: for example, because this was the truth, and truth had to be looked straight in the eye.

So she and I were "planes that could never intersect"—an image conjured up by mathematicians. But I felt something different. I felt that, perhaps unwittingly, he was making a comparison between us all the time.

It was not with my reason, but with my heart, that I could not yield to my husband, could not betray my principles, my convictions, my nature. It was not with my heart, but with my reason, that I made an incredible effort to surmount myself in order to yield to the writer. In the name of his creative work, I tried to overcome myself, to change and betray my convictions, to sacrifice them for him, and, together with them, to sacrifice myself.

I was no longer struggling with my rival. Within me the woman was struggling with the wife of the writer. Which one would have the upper hand? What would turn out to be stronger, the heart or the mind? The love of a woman or the self-sacrifice of the wife of a writer? At that time I felt that Solzhenitsyn had the right to demand such rare qualities from a wife.

On April 2 we found a cold reception in Riazan, which had not yet emerged from the grip of winter. It was bitterly cold. We felt chilled in our light overcoats.

Home. Mother was frightened and alarmed at my loss of weight and the despair she read in my eyes. She could not conceive that in the greatest men there still dwells the primordial male, perhaps even more so than in a simple peasant. Or equally, that in the most outstanding women there is often more of the primordial wanton than in the most bourgeois of women.

Now, when ten years have passed and numerous events have compelled me to evaluate people and their actions in a different light, it is difficult to believe that an adult, a mature person who had passed through the enormous school of life, could attribute such serious, even decisive significance to some careless word uttered by an elderly woman (my mother was then seventy-four) whose devotion had been tested by time and many misfortunes.

My husband did not talk it over with Mother, either then or later, but for a long time he let her feel his silent censure. He never understood that he had created a mountain out of a molehill and, quite aside from the pain that was mine alone, caused both Mother and me completely unnecessary suffering.

I still had a week of vacation time. I went to Moscow to distract myself.

From Moscow I wrote my husband a letter in which I told him that I had thought everything over carefully and had come to the realization that I was unable to share him with another woman. He would have to choose. If he could not decide at once, I asked him to leave forthwith. It was unbearable for me to live with him within the same walls and see him so divided and estranged. I was tied to my work. He was tied to nothing.

He wrote a tear-soaked reply. Aleksandr could not understand how he could be "chased out of the house for telling the truth." He had done enough traveling. Moscow. Leningrad. Now was just the time when he needed home and hearth. And he was being denied them!

My deep mortification got mixed up with sympathy for my confused, distressed husband. I offered him an alternative: I would remodel the apartment in Riazan to make a separate study for him. We would live together in separate rooms until he could make a decision.

"Well, do that," Aleksandr agreed.

I rushed to the assistant rector in charge of economic affairs. "If you don't fulfill my request, I'll do it my way anyway. Let them sue me later!"

After such tactics, my request to move doors and walls in the apartment suddenly seemed to him most reasonable.

Fragments of plaster crumbled to the floor, bricks were knocked out. I dragged all this debris out of the house. I hurried the technicians, the plasterers, the painters.

I bought material. I sewed new draperies for the windows, for the doors; a bedspread for the ottoman.

The upright piano and the concert grand which sounded so good together, in unison and standing so close to each other, now had to part company and move into different rooms, just as my husband and I were doing. I let him have the grand piano in his study. The upright was moved into my little boudoir.

A great struggle was going on within my husband's innermost being. He had to make a decision, after all. And how many torments these weeks cost me! My husband could not help but surmise what I was going through.

As in everything else, any dilemma that confronted Aleksandr was probably examined first of all from the point of view of the benefit it would have for or the harm it would do to his creative work. Everything was to be for literature, everything "for the good of the cause."

Everything was sanctioned by "high purpose," by noble goals, by "supermission."

A change in the way of life might be detrimental to creative work. So Aleksandr decided to suppress his longing for the other woman.

"She didn't suit me as a companion in life," he would admit to me six years later.

Of course I understood nothing of this at the time. I simply hoped for the return of my husband's love. I lived, I tried to conceal my hurt, my fear.

Finally, the verdict was pronounced: That woman would not be in his life. I could remove her letters from File No. 21 ("The World of Scholars") and destroy them.

Thus, instead of his traveling about villages with a "female scholar," Solzhenitsyn and I went that summer on our first auto trip. Thus sank into oblivion the woman scientist from Leningrad, whom I never got to know, the bitter days of our domestic discord, and my husband's fantastic plan of establishing polygamy in the service of creative writing.

Time went by, blotting out the bitter taste left by that whole business, by Solzhenitsyn's assumption that there must be no restraints on a man who is a writer of his caliber.

There was not a hint, at the time, that this assumption would return to him and again begin to motivate many of his actions.*

Before taking a trip south, at a later date, my husband would leave a sealed envelope for me with the inscription "Consuello," asking me to read the enclosed letter "if I felt particularly lonesome."

He would come back sooner than planned, not being able to tolerate it there even in the best season ("it's much better in Solotcha!"), but by then I would have read the letter.

Aleksandr had written that our crisis was past, and that it

---

* Solzhenitsyn finally left Reshetovskaya in 1970—Ed.

had convinced him more than ever before that there was no one who could be so devoted to him as was I. Nobody could live by his interests as much as I did. And never had he felt so good, so natural, so much at ease with anyone else as he did with me.

"If you consider it thoroughly, you will see that our ties are becoming stronger and more durable as the years go by. Everything will pass away as transitory and subject to decay—the confusion of feelings, the clashing of egos, fits of temper, unjustly hurt feelings. Remember, they never lasted long—they were always ousted by love and mutual compassion that knew no bounds. You were hurt—I felt the hurt at once, too."

He asked me to preserve in my heart the sense of our closeness which is eternal and not subject to decay.

"This is not pathos," he wrote, "but the way it really is. Nothing can separate us now—only death.

"But let it be a long time before it comes."

I still have that letter. When I feel particularly lonesome, I re-read it.

Riazan, Moscow, Rozhdestvo Village,
1969—1974

Index

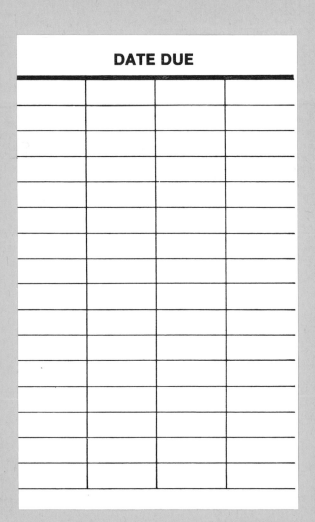

DATE DUE